ST. M... W9-BQL-402 ...LAND
ST. MARY'S CITY, MARYLAND

ST. MARY'S CITY, MARYLAND

THE SEVENTH DAY

(54134

THE SEVENTH DAY

Soldiers' Talk about the Six-Day War

Recorded and edited by a group of young kibbutz members

Principal editor: Avraham Shapira

CHARLES SCRIBNER'S SONS, NEW YORK

English version:
COPYRIGHT © 1970 BY HENRY NEAR

Hebrew version:
COPYRIGHT © 1967 BY SIACH LOCHAMIM

All rights reserved. No part of this book
may be reproduced in any form without the
permission of Charles Scribner's Sons.

B-6.71[C]

Printed in the United States of America
Library of Congress Catalog Card Number 77-134020

ACKNOWLEDGMENTS

Very many people helped in the making of this book. We should like to thank all those without whose encouragement, advice, and technical and financial assistance it would not have reached the stage of publication.

For the English edition, special thanks are due to Arieh Pincus, Mosheh Rivlin and the Jewish Agency, Jerusalem, who helped us at a particularly difficult time; and, above all, to Joyce Weiner of London, who has given without stint of her time, her professional expertise, and—most important of all—her faith, her enthusiasm, and her friendship.

Editorial Board

Amram Hayisra'eli
Amos Oz
Shlomit Teub
Rachel Halprin
Avraham Shapira
Giora Mossinson
Navah Benari
Bracha Dalmatzki
Yariv Ben-Aharon
David Alon
Aviezer Ya'ari
Abba Kovner
Muki Tsur
Bezalel Lev
Menachem Shelach
With the help and advice of Colonel Mordechai Bar-On

General editor of the English edition

Henry Near

Translators

Dvorah A. Sussman, Edna Berlyne, Charles Weiss,
Yael Feniger, George Ney

CONTENTS

THE SEVENTH DAY

INTRODUCTION

The Six-Day War began suddenly and ended quickly. What appeared
at first to be no more than bluster and verbal provocation turned
almost overnight into a threat to our existence. Ten days of tension,
uncertainty and apprehension were followed by a war which none of
us wanted, and a victory far greater than any expected. For all of us,
the experience was traumatic; but for none more so than those who
had never fought before. Those who bore the brunt of the fighting
returned dazed by the magnitude of their victory and, no less,
shocked by the revelation of what war really is: a revelation for
which they were not prepared, a reality they had been educated to
reject. Later, trying to distill his experience into literary form, one
of them wrote: "This mold of flesh which had always till now been
taboo for you (for so you had learnt: 'Thou shalt not kill') lies
around you now piled high, inanimate as the burnt out cars, the very
stones; and you cannot absorb such horror."

Many of these young men returned from the war in a state of
shock; and, as always, the effects of shock were varied and
unpredictable. Some became compulsive talkers, re-enacting for
themselves and their comrades the scenes of horror and triumph,
mulling over tactics, creating a legend, but never plumbing the
depths of their conflicting emotions; they were hidden behind the
screen of words and action. Others remained silent, withdrawn,

1

moody. "I think I was in a state of shock," said one of them later. "Nothing was clearly defined. I'm still trying to push it all away from me, I don't want to think about it . . . I want to forget . . . I get an awful feeling of disgust and nausea whenever the subject comes up."

These were the reactions of a whole generation of *sabras*, the native-born Israelis whose toughness has become a legend, but whose inner world is so hard to penetrate. The people who speak in *The Seventh Day* form only one segment of this generation: those known as the younger generation of the kibbutz. The bulk of this group are "children of the kibbuzim," born of a dedicated pioneering generation and educated to live by the principle "from each according to his ability; to each according to his needs." It is their character which, in no small measure, made *The Seventh Day* what it is.

In many respects, these young people are no different from the average *sabra:* in their pragmatism, their laconic mode of expression, their scepticism of rhetoric, of the "-isms," of the style of speech and thought of the older generation. They, like their contemporaries all over the world, came to maturity after "the end of ideology." So even those most devoted to the kibbutz way of life hesitate to formulate their ideals in terms of socialism, Zionism, or any other doctrinaire theory. Their values are expressed in actions and attitudes rather than in words.

Yet, however diffident he may be about the use of phraseology, the kibbutz child is in some way different from his town-bred contemporary. Physically, he has been used all his life to exercising his body to the utmost, whether in work or in play. Culturally, he grew up in a community which consciously strives to combine the best features of town and country. Socially, he belongs to a group almost universally recognized in Israel as an élite, dedicated to the furtherance of the country's national and social ideals. For him these ideals are expressed in the most concrete terms: in his intimate knowledge of his country and its history; and in his ability to live in a close-knit group, accepting its social and moral standards without forfeiting his own individuality. One of the speakers in *The Seventh*

Day refers to "the basic tenet of kibbutz life: that every man has his own world and the right to fashion it." Another finds the essence of kibbutz life in self-respect, conformity to a norm: "in one sentence: 'What will the others say?' " It is the combination of these two traits which characterizes the child of the kibbutz.

The standard biography of these young men and women is simple enough in its externals: school, combining a general liberal education with agricultural training, until the age of eighteen; army service of two and a half to three years (with reserve duty thereafter); return to the kibbutz and absorption into the adult community. At the time of the Six-Day War, those who made *The Seventh Day* were aged between eighteen and forty (though mostly between twenty-five and thirty-five), and served in all branches of the Army — as conscripts, regular soldiers and reservists — and in every rank from private to Lieutenant-Colonel.

Such people make up the bulk of the younger generation of the kibbutz. Within the same age range there are two other groups of kibbutz members, fewer in number, but no less characteristic of this generation: graduates of Israeli youth movements, and of Jewish youth movements in the Diaspora, who, after service in Nachal (the Army Corps which combines agriculture and military service) found a new kibbutz or join one already existing.

One of the editors of *The Seventh Day* wrote: "The public exaltation which followed the war did not make it easy to give expression to the private emotions, the revolution in sensibility which it caused in the individual. Our generation took off its uniform and buttressed itself in silence." Such silence was not uncharacteristic. It was the natural reaction of a generation used to discounting the speech-making and philosophizing of its elders. And, when it was first broken — in the discussions held by many kibbutzim to sum up what the war had meant to them as a community, in newspaper and radio interviews, in the exchange or reminiscences between friends — the subject was usually the externals of war, "what we did" rather than "what we felt." They looked for the reflection of their experiences in newspaper articles, in war albums and photographs. "It was hard to leave it all without anything to remember it by," said one of them later, "but all those pictures meant absolutely nothing to me." What they were looking for was, in the Hebrew phrase, "a spiritual reckoning." And it took some time until they were able to achieve it.

In the summer of 1967, a small group of young kibbutzniks met to discuss the possibility of recording in permanent form the effect of the Six-Day War on their generation. They were not strangers to each other, though they all belonged to different kibbutzim, and even to different kibbutz movements. They had previously co-operated in three separate ventures: a magazine for youth leaders within the kibbutzim, and in the youth movements connected with them; the establishment of clubs to promote social, cultural and intellectual contact between members of the younger generation in different kibbutzim; and a series of literary discussion groups within the kibbutz movement. In terms of achievement and ability they were an outstanding group. They included two writers of widely read novels; the editor of a magazine whose readership has spread far beyond the confines of the kibbutz movement for which it was primarily intended; the assistant editor of a national newspaper; several writers whose articles, stories and poems have been published in kibbutz journals and the national press; youth leaders and teachers. In another sense, they were a very ordinary group of young kibbutzniks. None was over thirty-five years of age. All came from the sort of background described above (either as children of the kibbutz or as graduates of an Israeli youth movement). All had been involved in the war: most in fighting units, some in the defense of their own kibbutzim on the borders of Israel. They knew what the war meant to the younger generation in the kibbutzim, because they were of that generation. As they said later: "We felt within ourselves the need to hear each other, to talk to each other, to open up a dialogue of heart and mind. We wanted to explain to ourselves and to our comrades what had happened to us in those six short days that lasted so long."

Realizing the magnitude of their task, and its tremendous responsibility, they asked two older people to join them: Abba Kovner, ex-partisan, veteran author and kibbutznik; and Colonel

Mordechai Bar-On, Chief Education Officer to the Israeli Armed Forces. They obtained minuscule grants from the kibbutz movement and the Histadrut, borrowed tape-recorders, persuaded their kibbutzim to release them from their work from time to time, and travelled from kibbutz to kibbutz organizing and recording informal discussions. Once the fact of their existence became known, little organization was needed. Groups sprang up almost spontaneously in every part of the kibbutz movement. "We were amazed," one of them wrote, "how open, how ready, how expectant these people were, how glad they were to give uninhibited expression to their hidden thoughts and emotions."

Throughout these discussions, the only motive was *self*-expression. This was a generation talking to itself, a true dialogue, with no thought for the outside world. As the themes became clear, so the interviewers attempted to explore them in depth, asking the same questions in different kibbutzim, bringing together participants from various places, confronting parents and children. There were, in all, some thirty discussions, involving about a hundred and forty participants. Some participated in several discussions, displaying different facets and layers of personality in different surroundings. Some failed to conquer their inhibitions. Some came and only listened. Many simply stayed away.

The method of discussion was, on the whole, free association, usually sparked off by some general question from the interviewer. Sometimes the interviewer had his own special interest, and even his own axe to grind. In these cases, the tables were often turned, and the interview became a many-sided discussion, a confrontation of several points of view. But, whatever the starting point, a number of themes returned again and again in virtually every discussion. "Dialogue opens that which cannot be opened in any other way," wrote Martin Buber. Such dialogue is the core of *The Seventh Day*.

The usual stuff of which war books are made — strategy, tactics, detailed descriptions of action — plays virtually no part in this book. The action forms a general framework from which the participants abstract their memories, their reactions and their hesitations. It also serves more than once as a retreat: when the emotions prove too powerful, the moral problems too intractable, it is easier to swap yarns or talk tactics. But in one sense the progress of the war had a decisive effect. For more than two weeks the army was mobilized, ready to move at a moment's notice, but inactive. During this period there was time for reflection, time for the relationships between the soldiers to crystallize, time to prepare oneself mentally for what lay ahead. Some emphasize the doubts and underlying fear of this period, some the extraordinary level of morale: "The response to the call-up was a hundred and twenty per cent — no one wanted to be left out." Others talk of political doubts and hesitations ("God damn it, why don't they make Dayan Minister of Defense?") and emphasize their contradictory emotions: the readiness for battle and the feeling of fear.

One question is scarcely discussed, for it is the assumption underlying all their thoughts, a prerequisite of their willingness to fight. This was a defensive war, forced on the people of Israel by an unprovoked threat to their existence. "Everybody knew that the crisis was created by Nasser putting his troops in. It was simply a matter of life or death for us." Had they had any doubts, they would have been dispelled by the evidence of their own eyes in the conquered territories: propaganda posters and schoolbooks designed to inculcate hatred, battle orders for the destruction of Jewish settlements. Some met the challenge more readily than others. The young pilot who says "I smelt the smell of war, and it was a sweet smell" is in a minority. Others simply say, "There was no alternative." Between them they sum up the mood of June 5, 1967.

"Suddenly this was history." It was also, for many, the valley of death, the time of supreme test and supreme achievement. And then, almost as suddenly, David became Goliath, and these same heroes were faced with "the tragedy of being victors." Little wonder, then, that they needed a long period of tranquillity to recollect their complex and concentrated emotions.

Some of these emotions are universal, to be found in the literature of any war. The sudden shock of contact with death paralyzed even the case-hardened doctor. "As well as the terrible anguish — your mind goes blank." And it often seems as if they had not yet recovered from the trauma; there is still an unwillingness to explore the implications of death, or to relate it to their personal faith in any more than the most general terms. As the parachutist remarks: "When I make it down safely, then I see things in a more balanced way."

With the presence of death comes fear. All were frightened, and none deny it. How, then, could they fight? "You're frightened until the first bullet," says one, and this seems to be the general feeling. In the heat of battle there is only time for action. The officers claim that the feeling of responsibility drives out fear; others take courage from their officers' example. All talk of their training, of technical competence, of acting automatically. None will admit to being a hero; even the young captain who asks "What is heroism?" will not stay for an answer. The truth, judged by the actions they describe, seems to be that the accepted norm was close to heroism; but they are reluctant to call it by its name.

How was this standard achieved? Part of the answer is clearly in the conviction that the war was both unavoidable and just; much, too, in the high morale and the "brotherhood of arms" found in any nation at moments of supreme danger and often described in these discussions, and in the high technical standard of training which characterizes the Israeli Army. But it resulted in no small measure from the special nature of that army.

It is, in the first place, an army of conscripts. The vast majority of its soldiers, both officers and men, were called from their peace-time occupations in the last days of May 1967; and it was no exaggeration to say, "This army is actually the nation, it belongs to the nation." The same notion is emphasized here in the discussions between the soldiers and their parents who stayed behind, whether in the words of the father who felt an almost mystic unity with his children at the front, or the officer who felt that the continuity of life in his kibbutz was a symbol for him throughout the war.

Its second special characteristic is summed up in the phrase "after me." The officer is taught to be first in the line of fire, to lead by his personal example. This theme recurs constantly in all the discussions of personal bravery: "Heroism has become almost a matter of technique," says one young officer. Of course, it is this and more. "How can you possibly force a soldier to go ahead of you?" asks another. "As I see it, it's just not ethical, not logical." This is not military technique. It is social morality.

A historical account of the development of the Israeli Army would stress the influence of the Palmach, the crack units of the Hagana largely recruited in the kibbutzim and imbued with their spirit. It would trace the principle of "after me" to the kibbutz principle known as "self labor": the belief that it is wrong to rely on others to do whatever job is needed, from physical labor to self-defense. It is easy to understand the comparison often made in *The Seventh Day* between the army and the kibbutz. The same relationship is expressed in other aspects of army life: particularly in the part played by women in the army; and in the informal relationships between officers and men. When one commanding officer said "I want to hear orders, not 'Come on, boys, let's do so and so'," he must have known that his protest would have little effect.

In this sort of army, the kibbutznik, physically tough, with his acute sense of social values, is at a premium. The number of officers who are members of kibbutzim is far beyond their proportion in the population as a whole; and they paid the price in the Six-Day War, with a similarly disproportionate number of dead and wounded. The interest in, and influence of *The Seventh Day* is not only a tribute to this sacrifice. It is the acknowledgment that, in a very real sense, these young men represent the spirit of the Israeli Army.

"The difference between the conscript and the professional soldier is the moral reckoning that the conscript makes with himself." In this too *The Seventh Day* typifies a whole army. There is none of the pacifism to which many Englishmen were brought by the First World War and many Americans by the Vietnam war; the feeling that Israel's case was just was too deep for that. But there is an overwhelming impression of waste, of protest at the reversal of all the values which they and their society hold dear. At the sight of an Egyptian convoy wrecked in the Sinai Desert, one says: "You mustn't show young people a thing like that. At any rate you mustn't show it to Israelis, because all our education is orientated towards construction. And this is a classic example of destruction."

But the destruction of property is the least part of the tragedy of war. More space in the book is devoted to the question of the soldier's attitude towards his enemy than to any other single problem. The same theme constantly recurs: fear of the brutalizing effects of war, and the danger of "losing the semblance of man." These soldiers are not superhuman; their dark instincts assert themselves under the pressure of war. In a passage reminiscent of Plato's *Republic*, several of them discuss the desire to feast their eyes on the sight of corpses, as a symbol of dehumanization. And there is almost an obsession with the question of hatred. "How can one fight without hating?" they ask. Indeed, should one do so? Not all of them think so. "I hate the Arabs, it's as simple as that," says the pilot whose comrades were lynched and tortured after capture. Others single out the Syrians: naturally: not only because of their part in bringing about the war, but because of their barbaric treatment of prisoners. Others again profess hatred for Nasser for his deception of his own people. But the majority by far profess to have no hatred in them. "I had no qualms of conscience about shooting [at an Arab soldier]" says one, "but I was glad when he got away." Perhaps a clue to this contradiction can be found in the words of one who had asked the same question about his German persecutors: "Real hatred has to have some definite focus — someone there's some sort of personal connection with. To say you hate Arabs — that's just talk." The same airman who hates the Arabs says later on: "Don't you understand the difference between you and me? From the air I just don't see people dying." Those who see the Arab wounded, defeated, surrendering, can see him as a man, suffering and deserving of mercy. So the agonizing problems of warfare are in the ambiguous situations. Will the man to whom you have given water in the Sinai Desert survive only to shoot you in the back? Can you risk not shooting a man who may be a civilian, if he may also be a soldier? Should you risk your own life to rescue Arab children trapped in the battle area? There can be no simple answer and no neat summing up.

On one thing, though, all are agreed: the war is with the Arab armies, not the Arab peoples; and, as a corollary, there is a revulsion from looting. There is no pretense that no acts of cruelty, looting or wanton destruction were committed by the Israeli Army; even though such acts were relatively few, they are here given a moral significance above and beyond their material effect. But, as one reads the account of the officer warning his troops against taking loot, backing his words with quotations from the Bible and rabbinical commentaries, or ending his injunction not to harm civilians with the biblical words "Their blood be on your heads," how can one fail to echo the question of one of these young men: "Is this a normal army? Is this a normal people?"

The Bible is an integral part of the education of every Israeli. But these were no mere literary references. The moral fervor of the war was widely seen to involve a return to the spiritual sources of Judaism; and its outcome gave this feeling a quite specific reference. Places familiar from the Bible and from Jewish history were suddenly physically accessible. "I feel as if a curtain has lifted, and the Eternal Book has sprung to life, familiar and immediate. The whole of the Promised Land is ours." This emotion reached its height with the conquest of Jerusalem, and particularly of the Western Wall, the symbol of ancient Jewish statehood and of Jewish yearnings throughout the ages. It was perhaps not surprising in religious Jews, who pray thrice daily for the return to the Holy City. To others it came as a revelation. "I had the feeling that I would like to bring all my ancestors, throughout all the generations, and say to them 'Look, I'm standing by the Western Wall'," said an airman, educated to atheism.

For him and many of his generation this was the culmination of a complete spiritual re-evaluation. The average *sabra*, in kibbutz or in town, feels himself to be a different sort of Jew from his brothers in the Diaspora. Few are able to understand how the Jews of Europe could be slaughtered almost without a fight. Most feel more kinship with their ancestors of the biblical period, who lived in the land of Israel, than with their more recent forebears in Europe and the Middle East. Suddenly threatened with annihilation, they identified themselves with the Jews of the Hitler era. "In those days before the war we came closest to that Jewish fate from which we have run like haunted beings all these years." And, after the victory, Jerusalem and the Western Wall were seen as symbols uniting them with the long generations of Diaspora Jewry. More than this. Under the stress of battle, they had discovered that the phraseology which they suspected in their fathers' mouths had a new meaning for them. "Before the war I always thought that all this talk about love of one's country was so much phraseology. But during the war I found that these were the things that gave you strength."

These emotions, and their implications, are explored in the discussions between parents and children. In some ways, they emphasize the gap between generations rather than close it: the ex-partisan cannot believe that these young heroes really thought that the State of Israel might be destroyed; the veteran Zionist cannot accept the way his sons express their patriotism in terms of their own physical attachment to the land. Within the generations too, there are varieties of opinion: in their attitudes to the Arabs, to the Diaspora, to Jewish history. But the dialogue shows the Zionist movement and its human outcome, the *sabra*, in historical perspective.

It also touches on a further aspect which is explored, at varying levels, throughout the book. When the doctor, treating an Arab prisoner, is greeted with cries of "long live Israel, ' he reacts with understanding, but also with disgust. How can they be so void of national pride? The victorious soldier finds himself emotionally identified with the Arab refugees. Schoolmaster and author discuss in intellectual terms the conflict of national and human rights involved in Zionist settlement: one even dissents from the general consensus, and sees Arab Jerusalem as a strange city. There is no neat solution, for there can be none; only an exploration, and a deep understanding, of "the tragedy of Zionism."

This tragedy is expressed in humanitarian terms: persecution and slaughter on the one hand, war and displacement on the other. A good deal of thought is also devoted to its political implications. With all their emotional attachment to the biblical land of Israel, few, if any, of these young men feel that it is theirs by inalienable right of conquest. They do not know what the price of peace will be; but they are willing to pay it, for that is what they want above all things. "Peace is the first thing to strive for. It's more important than love of country and all these other things that are so important in themselves."

But will it come? Here they are deeply divided. "They'll have to negotiate with us now," says one. Others see the future as a continuation of a past in which war has been a recurrent motif in their lives. "That's how we live, and that's how we've got to educate our children." And from here, again, to the moral problem with which the war confronted them. "How long can we, as ordinary flesh and blood, bear it? Will we always bear the sword in one hand only?" Can an individual or a nation live in a state of war without life becoming cheap or moral values eroded? And again the answer: what else can we do but try?

And so, with no exultation in their victory, these young men and women return to the problems of re-adjustment, to a normal life which now seems all the more precious in the perspective of danger and death. To them, this new perspective has further implications. After every great war there seems a chance of a new beginning: social frameworks have broken down, new horizons have been sighted. In this war, a whole generation came into its birthright. They were born of parents whose heroism they recognized ("There's no need to explain to you, who have done this all your lives, exactly what's meant by giving everything," wrote one to his father on the eve of battle), and which stands out even in this heroic book. Only now did they feel that they were their equals. In this process *The Seventh Day* played a vital role. Within the kibbutz movement, the very process of dialogue brought them increased self-awareness, the crystallization of new attitudes and new questions. Outside it, people suddenly became aware of the special character of a generation in the kibbutz of whose existence they had scarcely been aware. Through *The Seventh Day* this generation began to find itself.

The process continues. There has sprung up a network of discussion groups and inter-kibbutz activities, cutting across previous organizational and ideological barriers, which comprise a fresh, positive and idealistic force in the kibbutz movement and in the state of Israel. Another series of dialogues is being recorded, which will deal with the practical, moral and cultural problems of the kibbutz in the modern age. Above all, the dialogue begun in *The Seventh Day* continues in the heart and mind of every kibbutznik and every Israeli.

The interviewers became an editorial board. The tapes were transcribed and the themes which constantly reappeared throughout the discussions were isolated. They were pointed up by the addition of "set pieces" taken from kibbutz journals, extracts from diaries, and the like. An attempt was made throughout to reproduce the halting repetitive nature of the spoken word. It was decided to make a roughly chronological division of the material, and within this to divide the material under the major headings which form the sections of the book; but this division was not made rigidly, in order to retain something of the associative nature of the original discussions.

In October 1967 the first edition appeared, under the title *Soldiers' Talk*. Twenty thousand copies were produced — enough for each family in the kibbutz movement — and it was sold at production price. Within weeks, its fame had spread throughout Israel. Copies were passed from hand to hand. A further edition was demanded, and sold out within weeks. It became clear that the book touched on themes of universal import, and aroused interest far beyond the confines of the kibbutz. Reviews and extracts were printed in the national press, though the book had not, properly speaking, been published.

The editorial board was in a dilemma. The discussions had been private, even intimate. Would an edition for the general public not be a betrayal of trust? The participants, and their kibbutzim, were readily identifiable. Would they not resent publicity of this sort? And would publication not lead to irresistible demands from the mass media, which would distort the character of the original discussions? Already requests had been received for radio adaptations, even dramatic and televised versions. Even the most experienced and professional of the editors were frightened of the pressures of commercialization.

The dilemma was resolved by the Israeli public. It became obvious that the edition "for internal distribution only" had been circulated far beyond the kibbutz movement. A general edition was issued, and so far some seventy thousand copies have been sold in all — a runaway best seller in terms of the Israeli book market.

While preparing this edition, the editors were besieged with suggestions and counter-suggestions about what should be given the Israeli public: some thought that the protagonists appeared too

14

pacifistic, some too bloodthirsty; some that political questions were
too prominent, others that they were not put explicitly enough;
some complained of the participants' anonymity, others that they
were too easily recognizable. The editors resisted all these pressures,
and the general edition was, in all essential respects, a replica of the
original version. It is on this edition that the translation is based.

Part of the public's enthusiasm for *The Seventh Day* was the result
of the general interest in the Six-Day War; part, too, the unique
literary (or non-literary) form, unparalleled in Hebrew, and perhaps
any other, literature. Most important, however, was its content: the
direct and honest way it dealt with questions raised by the contact
with war, death and suffering; the concern with problems
fundamental to the State of Israel, and the frank way in which they
were discussed, without conformity to accepted views or the
accepted iconoclasms. It helped to crystallize conflicts and attitudes
that were—and are—relevant to every Israeli citizen.

THE TRANSLATION

The hesitations which beset the editorial board before the issue of
the general edition were repeated and intensified when a translation
was suggested. They were conquered by one consideration: the
belief that publication could add to the understanding abroad of the
nature of Israel and its youth, its moral achievements and its
problems.

Not all the text appears in the translation. Some is out of date,
some refers to quite specific problems of the kibbutz movement; and
the effort to reproduce the spoken word led to repetitiousness which
can add nothing for the foreign reader. But we believe that we have
reproduced both the spirit of the original and most of its essential
content.

THE INTERVIEWERS

The interviewers are all members of the Editorial Board. The
discussions they chaired are not reproduced in their entirety, and

different parts of the same discussion appear in different parts of the book in order to illustrate a particular theme.

Amram Hayisra'eli, thirty-one, father of three children, is a member of Kibbutz Giv'at Haim, Ichud, M.A. of Tel Aviv University, and a teacher in primary and secondary school. He was a leading member of a small group which founded clubs for younger members of kibbutzim in his area, and rapidly became a national movement. He has been active in educational circles in his kibbutz movement and has held a number of responsible positions. In the Six-Day War he served as an infantry officer.

Yariv Ben-Aharon, thirty-two, father of three children, is a member of Kibbutz Giv'at Haim, Me'uchad, and son of Yitzchak Ben-Aharon, formerly Minister of Transport and a prominent figure in the Labour movement. He served as a tank officer in the Sinai Campaign, and ten years later wrote a novel, *The Battle*, based on this experience, of which two editions have been published. He has been a member of the Central Committee of his kibbutz movement, and works in the canning factory in Giv'at Haim, writing in his spare time (he has edited two memorial pamphlets for members of his kibbutz who fell in the war). In the Six-Day War he served as commander of a tank company.

David Alon, forty-one, is father of three children, one of whom was killed on the southern front during the Six-Day War. He was one of the founders of his kibbutz, Mishmar Hanegev, where he founded the local history museum — he is a well-known amateur archaeologist as well as a secondary school teacher. He is a sergeant in the army, and during the Six-Day War he served in his kibbutz's defense force.

Shlomit Teub was born and educated in Kibbutz Mesilot, where she returned to work in child-care after her army service as a private, doing administrative work with an infantry unit. She writes in her spare time, and has had a number of articles published. At present she is engaged in further studies at Tel Aviv University.

Aviezer Ya'ari, thirty-seven and father of three children, is a member of Kibbutz Merhavia and son of one of the founders and leaders of Hashomer Hatzair and of the Mapam political party. He has worked in various agricultural occupations, in the printing press, and in cultural and administrative positions, including a period as secretary of his kibbutz. He has also worked for a number of years in the youth movement in Israel and England. He is a major in the reserves, and served in an armored division during the Six-Day War. He is now taking a course in Oriental Studies at Tel Aviv University.

Rachel Halprin, twenty-three, was born and educated in Kibbutz Yif'at. After her military service she studied music with the intention of teaching. Her course was interrupted by the Six-Day War, which she spent working at Yif'at.

Abba Kovner, forty-nine, was born in Poland and was active before the Second World War in the Zionist youth movement, Hashomer Hatzair. In 1944 he led the revolt of the Jews in the Vilna Ghetto, and he continued to fight the Nazis as a leader of Jewish partisans until the end of the war. After it he came to Palestine and joined Kibbutz Ein Hachoresh, fighting as an officer in the War of Liberation. He is the author of several novels, stories and historical works, and was awarded a literary prize for his poetry in 1968.

Avraham Shapira, thirty-one and father of one child, is a member of Kibbutz Yizre'el where he works in the orchards. He was born in Haifa, and as a member of the Noar Oved youth movement served in Nachal. He has been active in the youth movement in many capacities, and is founder and editor of *Shdemot*, a widely read magazine dealing with problems of the kibbutz and of Jewish thought and culture, which played an important part in attracting the group through whose initiative *The Seventh Day* was written. He studied Jewish philosophy and literature at the Hebrew University. During the Six-Day War he participated in the defense of Yizre'el, which is close to the Jordanian border. He is now engaged in further studies in Jerusalem, and in the production of educational material for the youth movement.

Muki Tsur, twenty-eight and father of one child, is a member of Kibbutz Ein Gev and son of Ya'akov Tsur, former Israeli Ambassador in Hungary, Argentina and France. He was educated in Jerusalem and on his travels with his father. As a member of the Noar Oved youth movement he served in the Nachal and joined Kibbutz Ein Gev, marrying a girl born on the kibbutz. He works as a landscape gardener in the kibbutz, and also teaches at the ideological seminar of his kibbutz movement. A graduate of the Hebrew University (in Philosophy and Kabbalah), and author of a number of articles on literary and historical subjects. During the Six-Day War he played an active part in the defense of Ein Gev, which is on the Jordanian border.

Giora Mossinson, twenty-seven, was born and educated in Kibbutz Na'an, where he works in field crops with a team which won the Kaplan Prize for productivity. He has also worked as a youth leader both in kibbutzim and in town. During the Six-Day War he was second-in-command of an advance tank company.

Amos Oz, father of two children. Born in Jerusalem, 1939. From the age of fifteen he was educated in Kibbutz Hulda, of which he is now a member. Taught literature in the kibbutz secondary school. Graduate of the Hebrew University in philosophy and literature. In the Six-Day War he served with the reserves in the Sinai front. In 1968 he was awarded a literary prize for his recent novel, *My Michael*. He is also the author of a novel on kibbutz life, a number of short stories and several articles. Currently he is a visiting fellow of St. Cross College, Oxford.

Menachem Shelach, thirty-three, with two children, was born in Yugoslavia, where he grew up in the rigors of the Second World War. On arrival in Israel he went to school at Mishmar Ha'emek, and later became a member. He is the author of short stories and poems, and writes for one of the newspapers of the kibbutz movement and for the army periodical, *Ma'arachot*. A sergeant in the reserves, he served during the Six-Day War with a commando unit. In the Sinai Campaign of 1956, he took part in the capture of Sharm el Sheikh.

PART 1
HOW IT BEGAN

ONE NIGHT BEFORE THE WAR

One night just before the Six-Day War, I was sitting on guard duty by the kibbutz fence, with nothing special to do. I cast a bored glance at the mountains round about. From time to time I would see if I could spot a sputnik or pick out some particularly bright star. The man on duty with me was considerably older than I, and preferred to sit in silence, perhaps because he still found Hebrew difficult. Suddenly he began to hum a Mozart aria. He's known as a lover of Viennese opera, an enthusiast for classical music, a European through and through. There he was, sitting by my side at the gate of Ein Gev, and yet the whole of his being was still steeped in the culture of the Austro-Hungarian empire. A delivery van belonging to a well-known biscuit factory drew up at the gate: it carried barbed wire for the kibbutz defences. How strange it looked, this van which normally, in peacetime, bore the sweet dreams of young children, and which now wore such a serious aspect. It was war it brought now to dispel our boredom. The other watchman began to speak — in a tired, emotionless tone of voice, as if he were throwing up his hands in despair: "Wherever I go — war follows me. I went through the First World War; later I even served as an officer in the Hungarian army, and that earned me 'special treatment' in a Nazi labor camp. In the end I was sent to a concentration camp." Then he began to tell me his life story, how after a peaceful childhood and a spell in a foreign army as a young Jew he had walked straight into the arms of death, and how he had later left the other-world of the concentration camps. I remembered the Mozart aria he had whistled, his European courtesy; but now I saw them differently — through the eyes of the wandering Jew, forever and everywhere seeking a home, and finding only Mozart, courtesy, and the threat to his existence.

We tend to forget those days before the war, and perhaps rightly so — yet those were the days in which we came closest to that Jewish fate from which we have run like haunted beings all these years. Suddenly everyone was talking about Munich, about the holocaust, about the Jewish people being left to its fate. A new holocaust did not seem as real a possibility to us as it did to the people of Europe; for us it was a concrete picture of an enemy victory, and we had decided that, come what might, we would prevent it. We know the meaning of genocide, both those of us who saw the holocaust and those who were born later. Perhaps this is why the world will never understand us, will never understand our courage, or comprehend the doubts and the qualms of conscience we knew during and after the war. Those who survived the holocaust, those who see pictures of a father and a mother, who hear the cries that disturb the dreams of those close to them, those who have listened to stories — know that no other people carries with it such haunting visions. And it is these visions which compel us to fight and yet make us ashamed of our fighting. The saying, "Pardon us for winning" is no irony — it is the truth. Of course, one may say that our doubts are only hypocrisy and nothing more; that we deck ourselves out in morality, perhaps even that our behavior is contradictory. But who says that war can be anything but contradictory?

When the fighting began, and the mountains around Ein Gev began to spit fire, a group of our reconnaissance troops on one of the hills next to the Syrian border was busy — putting out a fire in a little field belonging to an Arab peasant. "A field is a field," said one of the boys. Could anything be more paradoxical? And yet it seems to me that behavior like this really symbolizes the situation we are caught up in. Our feelings are mixed. We carry in our hearts an oath which binds us never to return to the Europe of the holocaust; but at the same time we do not wish to lose that Jewish sense of identity with the victims.

We, perhaps, are in a position exactly opposite to that of the ghetto Jew who saw the murder and felt his utter helplessness, heard the cries and yet could do nothing but rebel in his heart and dream of a time when he would have the strength to react, to hit back, to fight. We, it is true, do fight and do hit back, for we have no choice — but we dream of a time when we will be able to stop, when we will be able to live in peace.

This changed position perhaps explains the great difference between the reaction of the native-born *sabras*, and the reaction of those for whom the Diaspora was their formative experience. For the latter, the very fact of a Jewish victory is a miracle, a dream — for the *sabra*, it is a fact, and sometimes a distressing fact. The picture of an utterly helpless people living in a world indifferent to its suffering, a people that had no chance to rebel and react, is still before the eyes of those who came from the Diaspora; while the Israel-born sometimes raise their eyes to an abstract justice that will permit them to evade the destiny of war, the sacrifices it demands, and the refugees it leaves behind.

Muki Tzur (Kibbutz Ein Gev)

READY FOR ANYTHING

From a discussion at Giv'at Haim. Interviewer: Amram Hayisra'eli

Situated halfway between Haifa and Tel Aviv, close to the former border with Jordan, Giv'at Haim was founded in 1932 by immigrants from Germany. Today it has a population of over 800 and derives its livelihood from intensive agriculture and a canning factory.

Participants in this discussion:
Peter, forty, father of two children, who was born in Czechoslavakia and survived Theresianstadt concentration camp. He joined Giv'at Haim on his arrival in 1949. In the Six-Day War he fought as a Warrant Officer in a tank regiment. *Shimon*, twenty-nine, father of two children, who works in field crops and is studying agricultural economics. He was a lieutenant in a paratroop regiment. Others from Giv'at Haim who appear in *The Seventh Day*: *Gad*, eighteen, born and educated in Giv'at Haim, had been in the army only three months at the time of the Six-Day War, and served as a private in an armoured unit. *Ofer*, twenty-five. After his army service, as an infantry officer, Ofer returned to work in the kibbutz. Then he began to work with educationally subnormal children, and was to have started studying psychology in Tel Aviv University in the autumn of 1967. He was killed in the battle for

Jerusalem. He had been married for six months, and was an artist of some talent. A posthumous exhibition was held in Tel Aviv Museum, and a book of his drawings has been published.

Peter: I just couldn't believe it when I was called up. I was sure that I'd be back again the next day. I thought the Egyptians were putting up some big bluff, but since you can't rely on miracles happening all the time, I reckoned we must have decided to call up a certain number of reservists. It seemed just a straightforward call-up. . . .

Time dragged on and on without anything happening in the weeks just before the war, and morale was a problem. The unit officers were told to give the men talks explaining what was happening. That was a hell of a job for army men. The boys just don't see their army officers as speakers; they're fighters, not lecturers. But I must hand it to our CO — a member of Kibbutz Ginegar — he was brilliant at it, quite extraordinary. The boys really trust him and he's managed to get on personal terms with lots of them. First of all the men really know him, they've been together for about ten years now. He's never lied to them, he's never laid it on thick. And yet he's not a tough army man who just gives orders.

Amram: There's a feeling that they're prepared to follow him?

Peter: Yes, that's quite obvious. But at that stage, that wasn't the point at issue. There was another question: he had to explain to the men that all this waiting was for our own good, that it was essential, that it didn't spring from weakness or fear. It was a question of seeing that the men didn't lose faith in themselves or in the leadership of the country. I saw the danger at that point. And he succeeded in what he had to do.

Shimon: We were called up much later, and by that time everyone in the country knew that something serious was cooking. There was terrific tension, and it was quite clear that if anything happened they'd call us. I didn't worry about it. On the contrary, I kept saying to the others, "Ah well, if we're still at home, then it can't be serious. Nothing to worry about." Then, in the last few days, the tension built up even more. We pushed ahead of schedule on all sorts of jobs; we sowed the fields earlier, too, and worked a much longer day than usual so that we'd manage to get through in time, in case they did call us up. The last day, when you could just about smell war in the very air, we felt the call-up was due any minute, and we worked much later than usual. And that night they came to tell us we had to go. We were ordered to leave by six next morning, but by six we were already at the assembly point. We didn't have the patience to wait any longer — we went off with the first bus. . . . Just as we arrived, lots of other men started turning up, too, from all over the place, all of them a little ahead of time. I must say that things really got organized very, very quickly indeed.

Amram: How did all that sitting around and waiting affect your morale?

Shimon: It was just terrible. There was tremendous tension in the first few days. Then morale began to slacken off — and go down and down and down. When Eban came back, it picked up and we seemed to hit another high spot. . . . This is it, everyone thought, tonight — Eban's through with talking to them all. Then there was the historic Eshkol radio speech — the famous stuttering effort. And the next day — still no war, and then there began that awful, quite extraordinary fall off of morale. God, how well I remember it — I even remember carrying on about it in a letter home. Dayan's appointment as Minister of Defense did a lot to buck things up again. We were really waiting for that. The newspapers carried reports of all the negotiations about it. And all the time, whenever you talked to your friends, you kept on hearing, "God damn it, why don't they make him Minister of Defense?"

The first day we were called up, we all went round with big smiles, slapping each other on the back. I'd even go so far as to say that the men actually wanted a war at that point. I think lots of them saw it as an opportunity to prove themselves as soldiers, after they'd done everything for so many years on a sort of "as if" basis. They thought everyone would get a chance to prove himself now, to put into practice all the stuff they'd spent so much time over in training. Of course, they also shared the general feeling in the country, that the political aspect of the business was justified, and that it was a just war. You had the feeling, long before the call-up, that we were really going off to defend the country, to defend the Jewish people. That was the way we all felt.

Peter: You don't judge whether a war is a war of self-defense simply by the criterion of who fires the first shot. I mean, a war of self-defense can most certainly include attack, too. But if you can compare the two, then I would certainly say that this was more of a war of self-defense than the Sinai Campaign. I know I felt far more apprehensive this time, because it seemed clear that there was a whole military set-up ready and waiting for us — that they'd provoked us simply in order to push us into some move. But in both cases I saw that there was a limit, that nothing else was possible. A country that isn't a big power can't play around with things, it hasn't got any room to maneuver. I was very frightened about the possible outcome. For years we'd heard talk in the army about how much the Arab states had advanced, how much more powerful they'd become, all the equipment they had . . . it was crystal clear to us that they were ready and waiting.

Amram: I should imagine that in a unit like yours where most of the men are family men with kids and responsibilities, there'd be more concern about the price — perhaps not so much about what the final outcome would be, but about what each man might personally have to pay for it all. What did they say about that?

Peter: It didn't come up at all. I should think I was the only one in our unit to worry about it. Perhaps it did bother the others, too, but the subject never came up. Talking about it would have been taken as cowardice, or lack of guts. I can't explain it exactly. A young man certainly wouldn't dream of mentioning a thing like that — you need a certain sort of maturity, a knowledge of life and men, before you come out with something of that sort. . . .

I used to tell them, "You know, I'm afraid of what all this is going to cost us. I'm sure we'll win, we just haven't got any choice, we *must* win. . . . " But I was almost alone in this. The others used to say that at a time like this you leave personal problems out of it. But I'm sure that some of them at least weren't being a hundred per cent honest when they claimed that. They hadn't yet reached the stage of complete honesty. Later, after the war, each one of them had a shock to face. They'd all been through it. That's when they got more sincere about things.

Shimon: There were other aspects of this selflessness which made a tremendous impression on me. Lots of men from the *moshavim* had to abandon their dairy herds and their poultry; they left the crops before they'd been harvested, and the fruit in the orchards still had to be picked. It was real serious agricultural work, the sort of work you can't leave in the middle. I should think a lot of them really risked bankruptcy because of that fortnight they spent away from home, and none of them knew when they'd get back. I was terribly impressed by the fact that they never even mentioned it. No one tried to get any sympathy from the others for personal things that might be happening back home. I couldn't get over it. Generally speaking we're a very open crowd, we talk thirteen to the dozen — all of us. We talk about everything under the sun. Really, sometimes the most intimate of subjects get quite freely discussed, without any inhibitions at all. And yet, this was never mentioned. And it wasn't that they were afraid to talk about what was happening at home. I think it was just that it didn't interest them, it didn't concern them. We were all so up to our necks in what was going on, so ready for anything that might happen that everything else just got forgotten and pushed aside.

Amram: I remember getting a letter from you then. On the one hand, you wrote, you're living right in the thick of it, completely immersed in it, but on the other hand, there's just one thing that really interests you and that's what's happening in the fields. You said you couldn't write about it in case it gave the impression that you were still thinking about your work. . . .

Shimon: Yes, I remember quite clearly how I wrote you that letter. I think we'd been there about a week then. It was the first time I'd begun to worry about it seriously. When I wrote the letter, I tried to remember the last time I'd heard anyone mention what was going on at home, and I just couldn't recall when it had been. Yet the minute I wrote home, I started thinking about it: what the hell's happening to the maize? I wonder if they've finished sowing? Did it germinate okay? Because the night I left, I should have turned on the irrigation pipes at four that morning — to start the germination. I left Uri a note and asked him to go and do it for me. A minute before I left they told me that a bus had just gone past and the driver had asked where Uri lived. In other words, I knew that by morning Uri wouldn't be there either. There wasn't a single adult left to look after those fields. It was just that day that I started worrying about it, that I began to get scared about what was happening at home. So I wrote that we were sitting around and just wasting our time, and meanwhile the fields were going to hell back home. Perhaps I thought then that if we just went on sitting around like that without budging, then the boys would start talking about all their worries and that then they'd begin asking for leave.

Amram: And when it all started, when the war finally did begin, what sort of things did you think about in the rush of those first three days? Did it bring up memories of other times when you'd been in a war or a dangerous position? What about you, Peter?

Peter: No — you're caught up in the excitement. Everyone had a terrific feeling of enthusiasm: only let's get out there, get into it all — the unit mustn't miss its turn. Of course it changed a bit when the first casualties occurred, when the cost of it all began to be felt. Then it became something you had to do, a matter of duty. And that changed the atmosphere completely. The first casualty's a really big blow. I wouldn't say that it lowers morale or fighting ability, but it certainly does change the atmosphere. I'd even go so far as to say that it improves things as far as the unit's overall ability is concerned, because it makes people more balanced, there's less wild enthusiasm, less readiness to dash into danger, they take it all a bit more slowly, a bit more carefully, they try to make sure of every movement — and that's a good thing. I didn't like the way it all began, all that "three cheers for the fight" sort of thing that went on — it seemed out of place. Even if it's an enemy you're off to kill, it's not exactly something to be wildly happy about.

A PAIR OF DOVES

From a discussion in Gat. Interviewer: Shlomit Teub

Situated in the northern Negev, Gat was the first settlement in the Jewish area. In the War of Liberation it stood fast against Egyptian attack, and is today a flourishing community of almost 500.

Participants:
Dan and *Amnon*, both thirty-two, with two children, and both born and educated in Gat, where they work in field crops and where Dan is currently treasurer and Amnon is Farm Manager. They also both hold the rank of Major, second-in-command of a battalion. Dan was decorated for bravery in the Six-Day War.

Dan: Let's start with the waiting period. No one thought of himself. They just reported to their reserve unit without a thought for personal problems, which everyone had, or for their business or their money problems. They came ready to give up everything. And suddenly they see that nothing's going to happen for another month, two months. Some of the boys got fed up. "So that's the way it is," they said. And then everyone's problems became urgent — and the question of loyalty became important. I tried to explain the necessity of postponing any action, of not going straight to war then and there, in the light of the political considerations, as I understood

30

them at the time. I personally thought that this meant that we wouldn't go to war at all.

Amnon: In our unit, the boys were divided into two schools. One school had no use at all for the government. They said: "If we had Ben Gurion back . . . if we only had Dayan — we wouldn't have to put up with all this stalling around." I belonged to the other camp. I said: "We are soldiers under arms. We have to have complete confidence in our leaders. Though I don't belong to the party in power, I have no doubt that they have good reasons for what they're doing."

That same evening, I got into an argument with my second-in-command. He said: "Look here. You say you're a peace-lover. I want to go to war with a company commander who wants to fight." He said it as if he meant it. I was very hurt by it. Afterwards, he said he was kidding.

Anyway, the morning after our first battle, I asked him: "Well, what do you think about war and peace now?" (This was his first war, too.) He answered: "Amnon, I'm going to keep a pair of doves under my shirt for the rest of my life. I never want to hear about war again." That's the way it is after a war.

THERE WAS NO NEED TO EXPLAIN

Discussion at Hulda. Interviewer: Amos Oz

Hulda, a close-knit community of some five hundred inhabitants, situated in the Judaean hills, was founded in 1920, destroyed by Arab rioters in 1929 and resettled in 1932.

Participant:
Shai, twenty-eight, father of one child, who was born and educated at Hulda. During the Six-Day War he served as a lieutenant in an infantry regiment.

Shai: Leadership experience is what counts when it comes to your relations with your men. In many ways, the men are like pupils, especially in a unit like mine, where there are a lot of new immigrants, most of them older than I am, some of them thirty-seven, thirty-eight.

Amos: Did you have to explain what we were fighting for?

Shai: There was no need to before this war. There was a feeling that everyone would go all out. Of course there was no telling how they would behave once the bullets started flying. But, beforehand, I had the feeling that every single one was ready and willing for anything. Some of them had their troubles at home, lots of troubles, and came and reported for duty and did everything they were told to do. No one made a fuss over taking orders.

Amos: But didn't you have to give some kind of pep talk or say something to prepare them for the time when the "bullets start flying"?

Shai: I did a lot of talking. But all it was was a lot of slogans. My problem was how to turn the theoretical issue, the duty to defend home and country, into something you do on the battlefield. I tried as best I could to make it clear that during the fighting they'd have to empty their heads of everything but using their guns, following orders and passing orders on. I reckoned that if they were kept busy passing my orders on to the next man and in shooting, they wouldn't have time to get scared. This was all pretty theoretical since I'd never been under fire myself.

Amos: And they knew you'd never been under fire?

Shai: They knew.

Amos: And this didn't raise any problems of confidence? They didn't ask "How do *you* know?" — "What right have you to talk?"

Shai: For them, I was like God.

Amos: How do you explain that?

Shai: I think it comes simply from confidence in your commander, or at least a desire to rely on him. Because they were afraid. A kind of latent fear. I think this desire to rely on someone is only natural in soldiers who are also new immigrants. The figure of their officer symbolizes security — they have someone they can count on, be sure of. I've been working with this platoon for six years. You could tell they were afraid by the way they jumped to obey blindly every time I told them to get into position. And most of the time they knew it was just practice. I tried to stress teamwork. One of the things that bound them together was religion, praying. When it was prayer time, the whole platoon showed up. About half the men were observant Jews. Two of them organized the prayers, and the whole platoon would turn up and crowd round them, praying.

Amos: You, too?

Shai: Me, too. Mostly because I wanted them to see that I was with them.

Amos: And those moments of prayer meant something to you, personally?

Shai: Not the prayers so much, but the very fact of standing there with the whole platoon next to the Torah. That gave me something, I think.

Amos: Did you follow the service as well? Do you remember it?

Shai: Right now, no. But I remember that every morning we used to follow the reading of the day's portion over the radio and try and figure out whether it was a good day for war or not. I remember that the verse they read on the Wednesday before the war was very good.

Amos: What was Monday like? That was your first day of action, wasn't it?

Shai: We didn't do it on Monday, there was no time. But as soon as we got to Gaza and saw that we were winning and that we were going to become an occupation army, I sat the platoon down and told one of the boys — he's principal of a school in Ofakim — to read what the Book of Joshua has to say about Achan. If anything influenced the platoon in their behavior as an occupation army, it was that chapter.

Amos: How did your men take the pre-war period, the last long wait?

Shai: Some of them didn't want to work. We had tons of work, digging in. And in spite of the feeling of urgency, there was some slacking. People just disappeared. Some of them were fairly old, and a few weren't used to hard physical labor, so they tried to get out of it. With all the motiviation, after an hour or two of hard work you start forgetting the theory and begin thinking of the sweat and how hard it is and how tired you are.

And then there was the schoolmaster. Thirty-five, with a paunch, respectable, quiet, he worked till he fell off his feet. He did everything. He was limping during the fighting but wouldn't hear of being sent to the rear. A quiet Jew. If you saw him on the street, you'd see right away he was a teacher, with glasses, a *melamed*. And he was a real soldier who really knew how to operate a machine-gun. The way he dealt with blockages was a pleasure to watch.

Amos: How did you overcome your own fatigue?

Shai: I didn't have to. One of the things that solves all an officer's problems is simply the fact of being in command. The need to set an example, the very fact that you're responsible for men and their lives. It relieves you completely of the need to pretend. You don't even have to try.... After the battle, I spoke to an officer we'd captured. He was afraid he'd be shot. It took me a long time to quiet him down and convince him that we don't kill them. I think one of the soldiers in the platoon wanted to kill a prisoner. His reason was that his brother had been slaughtered in front of his eyes by Arabs. It was some job quieting him down. The prisoners were treated very well. One problem we had, after the war, was in dealing with the civilian population. I remember that the most outspoken in favor of humane treatment were kibbutzniks. But that wasn't the only criterion.

Amos: How did the schoolmaster from Ofakim behave, for instance?

Shai: He didn't even go and look at the prisoners. He carried out orders and that's all.

Amos: I imagine you felt that some of your men hated the enemy?

Shai: Definitely; in the main, those of them who'd suffered personally at the hand of Arabs.

Amos: Did you ever feel that you hated the enemy during the war? Can you remember a particular moment when you felt hatred?

Shai: Not hatred. In Gaza, we had to clear away road blocks. To get the job done, we got out their people. One of the men acted — I don't know quite how to describe it. It was a kind of cheekiness. He did what he was told, but with a leer. The way he looked at us, it was a mixture of contempt and insolence. And at that moment I felt that this character deserved to get something the others didn't. Today, when I try to think about it, I can't explain it.

Amos: And when you think about it now?

Shai: Now? Well, at least he had some self-respect as a person.

MY PEOPLE

... Again I behold my people. Not just my own kibbutz. There, with a hundred and twenty-five of our sons off to the front, their parents and their wives lived through the tension and the fear, and stood the test as expected. Now I have also seen the town.

Not the largest of towns, nor yet the most patriotic. A town in the Sharon — a medium-sized town — just a town. With its peddlers and its workers. Its tradesmen and its unemployed. It was a pleasant, clear morning. The sort of morning when a man gets up and wonders how it can be that on a morning such as this a war can break out! Until the voice from the radio broke through it all. The announcer's voice reading out the call-signs to mobilize the reserves.

Greater things than this are forgotten later. The voice was not like the hysterical tone of the announcer from the land of the Nile. Not like the arrogant tone of the announcer over Radio Warsaw in September 1939. It was not the tragic tone of the man from Prague. Nor was it the emotional tone of the immortal Yuri Levitan, speaking from a Moscow under seige. No, it was quite a different voice.

Like the sound of a mason's hammer on the stone, steadily and in measured tones, he read the meaningless words of the call-signs, then — without adding any slogans, any high-flown phraseology — finished and went off the air. And the town — the town itself — seemed to stop breathing.

I was leaning on a newspaper stall at the time. The newspaper seller was in the very act of stretching out his hand towards the paper I wanted when suddenly the voice caught his attention. His eyes widened, he looked through me rather than at me, and said, as if in surprise, "Oh! They've called me up too." He rolled up his papers and went. The salesgirl came out of the shop opposite, stopped jerkily at the door, adjusted her blouse, a little nervously, snapped her handbag shut, and walked off. The butcher took off his apron, pulled down his shutters, and left. A group of men stood huddled round a transistor in the middle of a patch of lawn. Whenever one of them heard his code word read out by the announcer, he detached himself from the group and left. Without a word, another left. Then a third. Silently the group broke up. Each went his own way. A girl came towards me, clicking along on high heels. She too was struck by the voice, and stopped. She listened, turned around, and left. A unique silence descended on the town.

I have seen cities on mobilization day. I have seen nations go to war. I have seen them marching off to the blare of raucous loudspeakers. I have seen them in the railway stations clasped in the arms of their weeping wives, their despairing mothers. I have watched them pass through the cheering crowds, receiving the embraces of foolish women. I have watched them go off, their bayonets wreathed in gay flowers, their hobnailed boots crashing out the rhythm of the marching songs that swell from their throats. I have seen them smiling, and proud. Always surrounded by crowds waving them on with shouts of "Hurrah!" "Viva!" "Hoch Hoch!" "Nych Dzhiah!" But never before have I seen a city rise so silently to answer the call of duty. This nation went to war filled with a sense of destiny, gravely and quietly prepared, in a way that cannot be surpassed. They went from Nathanya and Kiryat Shmonah, from Jerusalem, Tel Aviv and Beersheba. This, then, is my people. A people I did not know before.

Abba Kovner (Kibbutz Ein Hachoresh)

PART 2
INTO ACTION

THAT'S WHAT WE'RE HERE FOR

From a discussion between *Shoshanah*, at Giv'at Haim, and the friends of her son *Ofer*, who was killed in the battle for Jerusalem.

We often talked about the relationships that grow up between soldiers in the army, and afterwards on reserve duty. And he found it difficult to define them. Were they different from the relationships between the children within the group that he grew up in? It was difficult for him to find the right words for it. He said: "It's more than the link between brothers, more than the link between friends, greater than friendship." In fact he couldn't put a name to it. He only knew that the bond was such that he was prepared to give his all for any of the boys with him. Of course, Ofer never imagined for a moment that this might mean someone dying. That's not the way a young man thinks; even older people don't think that way. But he did say: "I know that if I go out on some mission, or if anything happens to me, then my friends will be ready to do as much for me as I would for them." I think this is the thing that's most likely to give a soldier a feeling of confidence, this knowing that there are people fighting beside him who are ready to lay down their lives for one another. And when it came to evacuating Ofer when he was wounded, I saw that these same soldiers were ready to die for him if need be. It was only luck that it didn't come to that, but it could have happened, under the circumstances. I was quite certain that these boys never for a moment thought of themselves, or of anything else that might have

41

delayed getting the wounded to safety. And I think that every parent (and you yourselves are all some parent's children) is somewhat involved in what happens to his child. It's not only encouraging, it's consoling for a parent to know that when his son goes off to war, he has this safeguard. I don't know how to express myself exactly here, but if you are sure that each one of you is prepared to lay down his life for the others, then the same feeling is shared by your parents when you go off to fight. And because of the circumstances you live in, no parent will turn round and say, "Don't put yourself in danger." That's what we're here for: it's our duty, and it's our sons' duty.

WHAT WILL THE OTHERS SAY?

From a discussion at Giv'at Hashlosha. Interviewer: Yariv Ben Aharon

Giv'at Hashlosha, established in 1925 a few miles north-east of Tel Aviv, is now a community of some 1,500, deriving its livelihood from both agriculture and industry.

Participants:
Zvi, twenty-five, unmarried, in charge of work assignment in the kibbutz. Fought in the battle for Jerusalem. *Ehud S.*, twenty-five, married with two children; fought in the Gaza Strip. *Hillel*, twenty-five, unmarried; fought in Sinai. *Yig'al*, twenty-three, unmarried; fought in Sinai. Others from Giv'at Hashlosha who appear in *The Seventh Day: Ehud R.* twenty-five, married with two children; fought on the West Bank and the Syrian Heights.

Yariv: One of the things the Chief-of-Staff pointed out in discussing the war was that there was no task that wasn't carried out, no unit which failed in its assignment. The question I ask myself is where did we get the strength from? What was it that gave men the strength to move forward under fire — and not just on an individual level. I saw it time and time again. How can you explain the fact that not just individuals, but the whole army, yes, the whole army acted in this way?

43

Hillel: I don't think I can explain it, and yet the fact is that it really was just like that. I saw it with my own eyes, and not just in my own unit, but in others too. There wasn't a single unit that would agree to retreat. Sometimes, from a tactical point of view, they ought to have withdrawn, so that they could attack from another direction or call up reinforcements. In my opinion, one of the really great things about this war was that they never pulled back. Sometimes some of them did show fear: there were times when a tank had to be refuelled under bombardment and the drivers of the refuelling half-tracks jumped out and ran off. Sometimes when a supply convoy came under fire you had to run after the drivers who'd gone off in a panic and haul them back to their vehicles. There were a few cases like that. But there was always *someone* who'd come back, even if it wasn't always the same driver or the same vehicle crew, and the one who came back would always carry on.

Yig'al: How do you explain it? I think it's rooted in a situation which we in this country have been up against for years now — it springs from something that's already a tradition, from earlier victories, from a feeling of just not having any alternative. And yet, on the other hand: when it actually comes to fighting — or so it seems to me at any rate — these very same troops don't think about patriotism and all that sort of thing. That just doesn't come into it. When a soldier is fighting, he isn't concerned with the renaissance of the Jewish people, or whether or not they want to wipe us out, or anything like that. That's all a long way away from him. . . . And it's not simply a matter of instinct. It's a way of thinking that comes from training. In the course of actual fighting everyone wants to go on living, to come through it all; they all want to survive, to remain alive. Nothing to do with Zionism.

Then there's also the point about the soldiers' feelings for one another; that's something else that distinguishes the Israeli army from others. It's not a question of everyone saying, "How do I get out of this mess and stay alive?" but rather of saying, "How can I and my friends pull through together?" "How will we manage as a unit?" "What do I look like now, in my friend's eyes, while I'm fighting?" or "What do I look like, to him, when he's wounded and I have to rescue him: what's the best way of doing it?" And that's just the point: without any question of ideology or Zionism, that's the important point: the issue of comradeship. It's simply a question of teamwork. When a tank crew goes into battle, every single member has a specific job to do, and at the same time they work as a team. The tank commander can duck his head out of the way and perhaps manage to avoid being seriously wounded. Yet one of the most typical things about this war was the number of tank commanders who were wounded on the upper half of their bodies. Lots of them were killed just because they stuck half of their bodies out of the tank. And why did they do it? Simply because pulling themselves back inside would have meant a betrayal of faith, letting down the rest of the crew. . . . That's one of the most important factors in this business: people worry about whether they're thought of as being alright. It isn't patriotism, or anything like that. When you fight, you're concerned with how you're going to win through, and how you'll look in other people's eyes.

Ehud S.: This business of the officers going on ahead of their men and shouting "Follow me!" — that seems to me to be *the* reason for victory.

Zvi: But there's also the question of relationships between people, of comradeship. It's not a professional army. You meet the same people every year, family men, parents of youngsters, men whose chief preoccupation and conversation is generally their home and family interests. It makes the whole business of soldiering much more human. It also makes for much deeper relationships between people, because you strike up personal friendships which aren't simply based on a military background.

Ehud S.: This business of knowing people and knowing their families is really very important. I hardly know any of the families of the boys in my unit, but I've seen photos of them. One of the boys went home on leave and asked his wife to call my family and give regards from me. When he was wounded, I immediately thought of his wife and what would happen to her. In other words, you have a bond with the boys' families, even if you don't actually know them. And then there's another point: heroism in the Israeli army has become almost a matter of technique.

Yig'al: Now we're back to this question of the officers going on ahead of their men. I think this really has become a matter of technique by now as far as we're concerned. Right through the whole period of national service we got used to going ahead and looking back over our shoulders at the others. That way you know exactly where everyone is and you're in control. It's simply a matter of technique, and it's become a habit which I find difficult to explain today.

Zvi: Everything we've discussed so far seems to me to have been made up of a number of interlocking pieces — what it was that made our men advance at a run: a sense of history, a feeling of having no alternative, a matter of education, a question of knowing one another. I think it can all be summed up in one sentence: "What will the others say?" In other words, everyone in the country feels like a member of a kibbutz, if I can put it that way. . . .

Yariv: Well, well, well — that's the best thing that's been said about this country for quite a few years. . . .

Zvi: Okay, perhaps I'm exaggerating a bit, but seriously: the size of the country and the relationships within it make it seem as if everyone knows everyone else. Or, if you like, everyone has the feeling that he's not a small cog in some huge machine, but rather that he's part of the overall effort, part of the whole business, a really active partner. He's recognized, he's known, he's part of the complete picture. Now, when it comes to a war, a man's place in society is already determined and he's just got to live up to it; he just doesn't have any other choice. And it isn't a question of a man acting in a certain way knowing that if he doesn't then the Jewish people will be annihilated, or our history will come to a stop, or that his wife and kids will be killed, or his home will be wiped out. . . . No, it seems to me that when it comes to the moment of truth, when he has to stand up and advance, then all that motivates him is quite simply this issue of self-respect. You just can't do things any differently than the norm dictates. I think this is also the reason why kibbutzniks are so prominent in the army, because in their case this whole question of social opinion is just that much sharper and clearer. They're even better known, their own position in the scale of things is even more defined and determined.

Then there's another point: every officer feels he's got to prove himself all the time in accordance with the norms that guide him. Otherwise he hasn't any right to be an officer. I know that there are men in my unit who are far superior to me as regards their general education — professors and university graduates. I would say that generally speaking we belong — as far as present-day standards are concerned — to different classes. As far as their army service is concerned, some of them fought in the War of Liberation and in the Sinai Campaign. But as their officer, it would be unthinkable for me to behave in any other way than the accepted one.

Let me tell you about just one incident in which there wasn't any justification for behaving as we did, if it hadn't been for these norms. After the fall of Abu Ageila, a reconnaissance squad and a tank unit were sent towards Ismailia after the enemy. The unit commander said enviously, "Lucky boys, I wish I were going along too." We got so far and then were ordered to halt, and pulled in for the night. In the early hours of the morning we were attacked by the famous Egyptian Fourth Division, their élite corps, equipped with the most modern tanks. They didn't know we were there, they just moved forward and rolled over us. The reconnaissance vehicles were completely wiped out. And you know what happened then? Eighty per cent of the men had no reason whatsoever to remain where they were. They should have spread out in the hills above in order to re-group and survive as a unit. There just wasn't anything they could have done, armed as they were with light personal weapons against sixty T 55 tanks. And yet most of them stayed where they were, and took cover; the whole business went on for an hour and a half. The tanks were forced to put up a heavy barrage of fire against our AMX guns — which were so light that they couldn't even penetrate the Egyptian tanks. I think this is a supreme example of those norms which state that there just isn't any justification for running away. And it showed up there with both officers and men. And another thing: it was dark and no one could have seen anyone else. I think this is a supreme example of the point I'm making.

YOU'RE AMAZED THAT YOU'RE STILL ALIVE

From a discussion at Mishmar Hanegev. Interviewer: David Alon

Mishmar Hanegev is one of a dozen settlements established in the northern Negev in 1946, when large-scale reclamation of this desert region was begun. In the War of Liberation it was the scene of a famous and decisive battle. Today it has some 600 inhabitants.

Participants:
Asher, thirty-two, married, with three children, an immigrant from Argentina and a doctor. In 1964 he was called up to the army as a doctor, and after his national service he stayed on in the regular army. He served in this capacity in the Six-Day War, and continued to do so until March 1968. At this time, he was wounded while helping to rescue soldiers trapped in one of the tanks destroyed during the action against the El Fatah base at Karaneh in Jordan and lost his left hand. He was decorated for his bravery in this action. *David.*

David: Were there times when you were afraid?
Asher: During my National Service I was in a battalion that took part in lots of operations. I knew what it felt like, this waiting period before going into action, the fear, the uncertainty, the expectancy. It's not just fear, it's a complex feeling with all these

48

factors in it. Yet the moment you go into action all these feelings disappear and you just function automatically. I can tell you when I was frightened, though — when four Migs strafed us. This time I felt that I had had it. We had heard planes approaching occasionally but hadn't even looked up. They got nearer. "Our boys are doing a good job, three cheers for our air force," we thought. The planes get nearer, they seem to be diving towards us. For some reason we're over-confident. We feel sure that today, the third day of the war, there just can't be a single Egyptian plane left intact. Anyway, this plane opens fire and an officer yells, "Migs! spread out quickly!" We run like mad among the sand dunes. The plane circles over us and fires. It was just like it is in the films — you hear *pap, pap, pap*. We look up and see more of their planes, three more Migs getting into formation ready for the strike. We run like mad and throw ourselves down on the sand about sixty meters off the road. The plane that just shot at us joins the other three who are waiting for him and then they all begin to strafe us.

When you're lying in the sand and there's no cover, no place to hide, no shelter, you just wait for the planes to come at you and they come, and you see this monster getting nearer and bigger, a terrific noise. They begin to fire when they're still some distance away, and there's nothing you can do about it. You just lie there. That's when you feel this is really the end. And you just wait, because perhaps it isn't. But it's all a question of luck.

Anyway, the first plane comes over, fires. The second plane, the third, the fourth — the minutes seem like hours — and then they've all passed. You lift your head up, completely dazed, and look to see if you're still alive. Really: you look to see if your hands and legs are still there and that you're not wounded. Is it possible you're still alive? Anyway, as soon as the minutes — or the seconds — are over (it's impossible to say how long the whole thing took) you suddenly remember that you must look around to see if anyone's wounded or not. It was then that I got up and looked around to see if anyone needed help. The boys shouted: "Get down, get down, they're coming back." But at that moment I felt completely indifferent to the whole business, for one reason only: I knew it didn't make much difference whether I was flat on my face or standing up. When I saw the four planes getting ready for another run, all sorts of thoughts passed through my mind. How stupid of me to have written home, I thought (I had written just a short while ago). The letter would arrive at a moment when I no longer existed . . . what stupidity, what possessed me to do it, couldn't I have waited until the war was over?

The first plane passes over. It fires. The shots ricochet between me and one of the first-aid men who's with me. I feel as if death had brushed past me. The second plane comes up. A deafening noise. It doesn't fire, it doesn't do anything. The third one drops a napalm bomb and a terrific pillar of smoke shoots up. We can hardly see anything at all. The fourth plane shoots again. And the whole thing is over in a matter of minutes. You look around and you're amazed to discover you're still alive. Then you notice that they're preparing for a third round; this really shakes you. You look around and you try to do something — perhaps you can find better cover, some little hole to crawl into. What wouldn't I have given for some little hole — and there's nothing. Just the sand, and that's all. And you notice that the others are also gazing around. Desperation — there's nothing. And they're getting ready for a third round.

Suddenly, our planes show up. At first, we didn't even dare to believe that they were ours, that we could have such terrific luck. It was as if the Messiah had arrived. We stood still, and high above us an air battle developed. Our stomachs turned over. It was difficult to see how things were going. Everything was happening at once, but I managed to look around and see whether any of the boys had been wounded. Some were still flat on their faces and didn't want to get up, they didn't know what was going to happen. Suddenly one of the Egyptian planes exploded in the air and all the others turned tail, with ours in hot pursuit. I began to call out, "Okay, you can get up, there's nothing up there any more." We looked around and took stock: not so much as a half-track hit. No one calling out for help, nothing wrong at all. But we were all completely dazed. The feeling of overwhelming fear was still with us. It still seemed strange that I was alive. It didn't seem possible. Everybody moved off very, very slowly through the sand towards our own vehicles. Suddenly news came in that one of our planes had crashed and we should get ready as the wounded pilot would be brought to us soon.

There was a tremendous upsurge of love for this unknown pilot. What wouldn't we have done for him at that moment! Everything, even the impossible! In fact, everything was ready for him. But nevertheless, we immediately started checking to see if the transfusions were really ready, if every little detail had been checked. You felt that you wanted to go beyond the absolute limit. That you were bursting to help the pilot. He was brought in and, luckily for all concerned, he was only slightly wounded. But he was completely broken up. He kept on repeating, "What an idiot I was, what a stupid thing to do. I got the wrong angle." You know that for them the wrong angle can mean the difference between life and death. He was very upset. When I had examined him and seen that there wasn't anything really serious to bother about, we tried to quiet him down and all the orderlies began to make a fuss of him. I don't think even a baby would have been fussed over like that. They calmed him down, and brought him a bottle of lemonade and God knows what else. All sorts of cigarettes, bottles of fruit juice which they'd already managed to swipe from somewhere, drinks and pills. They would have done anything for him. If they had been ordered to jump into fire for him they would have done so. The only thing that mattered was to help him with everything they could. So he lay there and they fussed over him. He asked for a cigarette and they showered them on him. You know these pilots have got an enormous number of pockets in their uniforms. Well, they shoved packets of cigarettes into every pocket. Then he began to get over it and grin. "Hey, boys, take it easy, it's okay, I only asked for one cigarette." Then everyone burst out laughing, and we suggested that it wasn't worth being a pilot, that he'd better volunteer for a spell in the Armored Corps. At least you get a chance of grabbing Egyptian cigarettes. And that's how it all ended.

But those were moments of real fear, moments when you felt that the end had come. Every time I passed that place again, without wanting to, I found myself having to look up at the ridge where we'd been pinned down on those dunes. That really was an experience! The only really definite feeling of being close to death that we had right through the war.

I'M NO HERO

From a discussion in Gat. Interviewer: Shlomit Teub

Shlomit: Didn't you personally ever feel any fear during the fighting, something that stemmed from the tremendous responsibility you had? Didn't you ever ask yourselves how you would stand up to things?

Dan: It's quite obvious and logical that a man should be afraid. I'd never been in a heavy battle before. In the Tawafik reprisal raid I was platoon commander. I think everyone — well, let me speak for myself: I know *I* was very apprehensive. I didn't know how good a company commander I'd be. It's a more responsible job, and the problems are more difficult — both from a military point of view and as regards actual command. . . . You've got to have the guts to do the right thing in the best possible way. For example, once we were travelling across open country towards the enemy positions at el-Kuba. I was in the first command car, an open one, when suddenly they began firing at us. It was heavy fire. There were bullets flying all over the place and my command car was hit too. It was like standing naked in the middle of Dizengoff Circus in Tel Aviv. Quite exposed, with no cover at all. You wished you could disappear inside your steel helmet. Everything was so open, and the only protection was the glass windscreen of the car. Yes, that was frightening — but of course, I didn't let it show. I got over it immediately. I had to, because I was leading men who trusted me. I don't know if they were more frightened than I was, but they had to see that I was less frightened, or at least that I'd got over it. If I couldn't control my fear, what would happen to them? Another time we were behind some building and I had to lead a dash across open terrain knowing full well that there was no cover and it was probably mined. They were firing with everything they had, a real inferno. Perhaps that sounds a bit too literary. But honestly it was very, very heavy fire. Running ahead, being the first man out, is a little less pleasant than following on after someone else. Maybe it's psychological, but even so. . . . We got to the objective with less than a platoon of men, and when the fight for it started there was less than half that number left. A bit later, when we had to attack, all we had were three command cars. That's what I fought with.

You should have seen how they all behaved. There were vehicles that took direct hits and had to stop; and that's where all those boys were — privates, section leaders, officers — without a company commander, without a second-in-command, without anyone to organize them as a force. Organization has to be a matter of initiative at a moment like that; initiative on the part of the platoon leader, the section leader, the ordinary soldier. There were lots of wounded and they had to get them out. There was tremendously heavy fire over the whole area and if you wanted to go and help someone who was wounded, it meant standing up and running a good chance of being hit. Yet a large percentage of the boys were wounded just because they took that risk and did go out and help those who'd been wounded in the first attack, or else help bring back those who'd been killed. There's a sergeant in my lot — to this day he can't get over it. He can't forgive himself that one of the section leaders who came over to help him when he was wounded took a direct hit and got killed. Most of them were just marvelous, even the simplest souls among them, they really behaved outstandingly. It was a pleasant surprise.

They kept on firing all the time. I think it all finished around dusk; anyway it went on quite a long time. It's difficult for me to try to reconstruct things. Other people have managed to. They say the fight went on for about fifty minutes. When my force got through we had only seven men left. Half of them were wounded, me included. At one stage I thought we weren't going to make it. We kept on cleaning up pockets, more and more cleaning up, more and more men falling, fewer and fewer left to carry on. There was a feeling that we weren't going to get out of it. But we never considered pulling out. I didn't have any doubts about what we were doing. It's not that I'm a brave character. I'm no hero, not one of these very confident people. But as I see it, if something has got to be done then you've just got to go ahead and do it.

Amnon: I think he *is* a hero.

Dan: No. I don't think that's heroism. Everyone was like that. Perhaps that's what's so special about the Israeli army, each unit did exactly what it was ordered to do under all sorts of circumstances, without a lot of thinking about it, or any unnecessary speculation.

Shlomit: Did you see things in a purely military light when you were fighting, or did you also remember the overall meaning of the war, your homes, that sort of thing? What went through your mind?

Dan: I can't say that I thought about Eshkol for one minute during the fighting! You have to think about doing things as well as you can and with the least possible number of casualties. There was perhaps a certain stage when I felt I was a bit cut off from life, from the family, my wife, the kids. But nothing more than that. There wasn't a single moment when I thought about things from a national standpoint. I wasn't thinking of my war memoirs.

Amnon: I think the kibbutznik fights the way he does simply because for him, the folks at home mean rather more than an ordinary family. Somehow that seems to rub off on you, even if it's only unconsciously. I can't say whether I think it's a positive or negative thing, but as far as I'm concerned, it's a fact. In the middle of it all, just for a minute, you do feel cut off. It's so big out there, and the night seems vast. The hellish firing, they keep shooting the whole time, and the fighting, and so on. But, nevertheless, being aware of the people you belong to, knowing that they'll value the way you behaved — it adds something. What influences you is that somewhere deep inside you, you know that your behavior will be examined by people whose good opinion you value. I didn't think about it during the actual fighting. But it did occur to me before it. And afterwards, the first question I asked myself was what they'd think. I didn't go into it in detail, but I thought about it. One of the boys from near here, a boy from Gal-On, was wounded and I knew they'd come to visit him. That would be about the first they'd hear of the fighting. Somewhere along the line, I asked myself what he'd tell them, and what would they hear about me at home from him? For me, it was a very important question.

Dan: I don't know — I never thought about that sort of internal pressure. The one clear thing that guided me all the way through was how to do the best thing, the most correct thing, the thing that would contribute most to the best possible result with the least possible casualties. All the thoughts that were buzzing round my mind at the time were along those lines. I don't remember thinking about whether people would look at what I'd done later, not even from the point of view of what the others in the unit would say.

YOU'RE SCARED UNTIL THE FIRST SHOT

From a discussion at Afikim

Afikim, founded in 1932, is the third biggest kibbutz in the country, with a population of over 2,000.

Participants:
Shai, twenty-seven, father of one child, was born in Afikim. During the Six-Day War he was a lieutenant, the second-in-command of a paratroop company which was dropped by helicopter behind the enemy lines at Um Katef in the Sinai peninsula, and which destroyed the Egyptian gun-battery there. *Hagar.*

Shai: The boys knew exactly what it was all about; they knew that there was no alternative, and they were ready for it. I think the whole population felt that way, not just the soldiers. It was never quite like that before, with everybody involved.

Let me give some examples: during the period of tension just before the war, some of the officers went to a village of Kurdish immigrants — and with the best will in the world I don't think you can say that they've got very clear ideas about Zionism, security problems, and so on. But when we came and asked them to let us use their citrus groves — and this isn't a simple thing to ask because the whole area gets mucked up and the groves are damaged because of the coming and going — well, when we came to one of the villages

56

with our request, he not only agreed but fell on our necks, kissed and hugged us, wanted us to take the whole grove, his house, everything he possessed. This is a really wonderful example of what I mean. Afterwards, all the time we were there, they kept showering food and presents on us, inviting us to their homes for food, showers, anything we needed. They wanted to give us everything they had. . . .

The attack on Um Katef needed simply immense endurance. It was particularly tough on the way back because we were very few and there were a lot of casualties. We only had enough men to make up two teams of stretcher-bearers, working alternately. Yet for all that, they stuck it out. I remember thinking as we started back that we'd really proved just how strong these links that had been forged between us, before the war, really were. I remember that when we first came up against the Egyptians the boys took off immediately and went straight into it at the first sight of the Egyptian gun-batteries. I don't know exactly how they felt then. I think they were very frightened, in fact I could see they were. I know I was afraid as well. Generally speaking it's like the old saying, "You're scared until the first shot." And then you're too much in the thick of it all. As an officer there were a lot of things I had to see to. I was responsible for the men, and that plus the worry forces you to be more level-headed about things, to control your fear and to get on with what you've got to do. But the men themselves don't have this responsibility for someone under them. That's to say, they have a responsibility to their friends — if they are hurt, for instance — but they've no direct responsibility for someone else. If they don't go straight into the attack with the first shots, then they're not letting down the men behind them — they're not leading anyone.

And yet, despite the fact that they were afraid — and I could see they were — they went straight into it. And these weren't men on national service, youngsters still unmarried, without kids and responsibilities; they were older men and they were really frightened.

I think it's a big mistake, to surround ourselves with an aura of heroism, as if we were all perfect, as if we all rushed into battle quite fearlessly.

The fear goes right through you, especially in the hours just before the fighting starts, from the very minute you know you've got to fight, right down to the second the attack begins. That's when you're most afraid. You don't know exactly what's in store for you but you know it's going to be dangerous. I remember looking around me and wondering which of us wouldn't return. Which of us would be wounded. And I'm sure they all felt the same way.

Nobody thinks he's going to be the one to get hit. Everyone thinks it can't happen to him. But that doesn't mean to say that you're not very frightened, especially just before the fighting starts. When you're actually in it, events themselves force you to fight. Of course, it can happen that you lose all capacity fo function, and that you're frozen by the first shot, utterly bewildered. What makes a good fighter? The ability to overcome fear. And what does that mean? It means being level-headed, avoiding hysteria, not panicking. Knowing how to think calmly even under fire. . . .

How do you measure heroism, anyway? What is a hero? I read newspaper reports of cases where soldiers were wounded and still carried on fighting, refusing to abandon their tanks. Of course that's really something. In our case we had soldiers who got a bullet in the leg, but made their own way back — the whole retreat — under their own steam. Another one, a sergeant, stopped a bullet in his shoulder and another in the hand, and he also managed without any help.

Hagar: And wouldn't you call that heroism?

Shai: That's just it, I don't know. The boys themselves wouldn't have considered it anything special. They certainly didn't think they'd done anything out of the ordinary.

Hagar: But you still remember it?

Shai: When I look at newspaper reports of bravery, then I really begin to see that we had a lot of heroes too, and when I think back to that attack, I see that at the time we didn't think that we'd done anything remarkable. There were two boys in our lot who each had a leg shot off. One of them told the doctor, quite simply, "Look, doctor, my leg's gone." It was a classic example of the calm way the wounded behaved. Then there was Gadi, one of the officers, who also lost a leg. They carried him along, he was in a very bad way, and they carried him all the way back on a stretcher. He never made a murmur of complaint. He just never said anything at all. He was hit at about one in the morning and it wasn't until seven o'clock that they managed to get his stretcher to a helicopter and get him out of there. They carried him all the way on a stretcher, and when you have to go up and down hill and through deep sand dunes, it's not easy. And he didn't say a word. I think he's as much of a hero as all the others who were mentioned in dispatches for what they'd done during the fighting. . . .

We had a quick victory, purely and simply because the officers went on ahead. Otherwise it wouldn't have been over so soon. How can you possibly force a soldier to go on ahead of you? How can you possibly say: "You go first?" As I see, it's just not ethical, not logical. You can't say to a soldier, "You go through the mine-field first." How can you do a thing like that just because he's a private and you're an officer?

Right through all the years of training, I kept asking myself: "Okay, so you've done your training, and it's all gone well, and you've been promoted. Nice work. But the question is, what happens when you're under fire? What will you feel then? Will you be able to prove yourself in front of your men?" It was a point which worried me all the way through the war: proving myself in front of the men under me. They trusted me to lead them as best I could, keeping casualties as low as possible, and I couldn't let them down. This tremendous responsibility, the demands you make on yourself as an officer, create terrific tension in you. It's really very difficult to explain.

On the one hand you're forced to get over all the fear. You just haven't got time to be afraid. You know there are more important things to worry about. But on the other hand you can't get rid of the tension. Even now, it still bothers me: could I possibly have managed, somehow, at some point, to have worked it so that there were fewer casualties? I keep going over and over in my mind the circumstances in which the people under me were wounded, and wondering if I could possibly have done things differently.

Because we were so close to each other before the war, the number of casualties hit us harder. We weren't specially excited or happy about killing lots of Arabs or knowing that we'd won. We just felt that we'd done what we had to do. But there's a big difference between that and feeling happy. I remember that after the battle our most immediate concern was how many dead we had and what state the wounded were in. I can still see the faces of the boys after the attack on Um Katef, as we waited for a helicopter to come and evacuate the wounded, and they weren't happy faces. They didn't exactly look depressed but you could see that everyone was upset about the casualties.

I remember that S. told us: "Pack it in, smile a bit, we've taken a vast amount of territory." And it was true. It was a great victory. But what was special and strange was that we weren't happy or excited, our only concern was the casualties. Of course it all comes from the fact that we knew one another in civilian life; we knew each other's families, and the sense of loss, when it's someone you know, is much stronger.

The experiences that I went through during this war have left their mark on me. I've got the answers to a lot of questions I used to ask myself before the war: how I see myself personally, how I would behave towards my men during a war, how they would stand up to a war. I think all of us have plenty of food for thought for the next few years.

TWO LETTERS

El Arish: among the deserted tents, the pictures of Nasser and the Egyptian propaganda pamphlets, a letter was lying around. It was an affectionate letter, written by a wife to her husband serving with the Egyptian frontline troops.

Wednesday, May 26

In the name of God, the merciful and all-compassionate!
To my dearest husband, whom I love and treasure in my heart, and whom I shall never forget: I am well and we are short of nothing except the sight of your dear face which we would wish to see with us now and forever. My dear husband, I send you my warmest greetings. I long for your dear presence as a sick man longs for health, as a student craves success, as the plants long for water, as a baby desires its mother's tender embrace. If one could send greetings on the waves of the sea, I would send a greeting on every wave, thousands and thousands of greetings — and if I could send you peace with doves, I would send you millions of greetings with every feather of their plumage. My husband and my eternally beloved, beloved of my heart, when will I see you, my darling, light of my eyes and breath of my soul?
May God preserve you, my darling husband, faithful and true,
Greetings to you.

61

Please answer quickly and let me know how you are so that our minds may be set at rest here. And may peace come soon.

Saida Ahmed Salah

A Letter from Bracha to Shimon:

. . . And I've started worrying again, because I have a feeling that tonight they're moving into Syria. Shimon, dear, you can't imagine how full of wonder, amazement, and almost disbelief I am at what the army has managed to achieve in such an incredibly short time. It's quite fantastic, unbelievable.

From your letter, received today and written before you went into action, I've begun to understand just why we are winning: the tremendous confidence you have in yourself, in the platoon and in the whole army.

You're marvelous! There's a tremendous feeling of love for all of you, wherever you are; a feeling of unity. There was a group of boys here who'd been in Jenin. We gave them dinner, everybody grinning broadly, shaking their hands and congratulating them excitedly. Yesterday we drank a toast to the Old City of Jerusalem, there was joy in our hearts and tears in our eyes.

PART 3
ORDEAL BY FIRE

I NEVER WANT TO GO BACK

This interview, one of the most immediate documents of
the war, was printed in the journal of the kibbutz youth
movement a few weeks after the war, and before the idea of
The Seventh Day was even mooted. Both the speaker and
the interviewer wish to remain anonymous.

I got my call-up papers while I was studying, in Jerusalem. That's
where my unit was based, too. We were angry because we wanted to
be on the Sinai or the Syrian front — we didn't believe that anything
was going to happen in Jerusalem. On the Sunday, they released us
all — sent us home. We cursed and cursed. I remember I got back to
my digs and there was nobody there except one or two that had
been sent on leave together with me and we sat there and swore.
Next morning we heard that the Egyptians had attacked. We just got
up and went to the base. We put our uniforms on and got ready. By
that time, the codewords were beginning to come over the radio
recalling us, but we were all set to go already. At 9:30 or so, the
Jordanian artillery opened up. But we still thought that they were
simply putting on a show. Then we heard that they had taken over
the UN headquarters and we knew that it was for real. After all, it
meant that they were just a few meters away from us.

They sent us to get it back. It wasn't much of a fight: we literally
chucked them out. Sure, there were a few shots fired, but it wasn't
much. We just got them out, one, two.

The next thing was that we had to take some dug-out positions.

65

Fantastic positions: thick concrete, sandbags, the lot. There weren't many aircraft — they didn't have any left and we couldn't spare them from the south. They sent us Fugas, trainers, you know. I saw two of them shot down. One just exploded in mid-air and the other one crashed straight into one of the enemy's dug-outs. I reckon the pilot must have been wounded and just did what he could before he died. We lay there and they threw everything at us. We could see the guns flicker from the embrasures. But it's a funny thing: when you first go into battle, you don't believe that you can die. You just can't imagine ending, *bom*, just like that. You think, well, who would ever take over my life. Later it's different, I'll come to that. And another thing: they don't send new troops straight into battle. They wouldn't be able to do a thing. It's the enemy who gives you your courage, you see. You don't just pick courage up from nowhere: the enemy gives it to you. You see your own boys dying around you, your friends, and you get mad. And all the time you hear the bullets and shells screaming and whining around you. Then there was one long scream that sounded as if it would never stop, it just kept coming straight at me. The shell landed about a meter away. It killed the boy next to me and I felt a stinging on my cheek. Just for a tiny moment. I put my hand up and felt the blood, running down, cool, on my face. They told me to put my bandage on it. It didn't hurt; it just burned for a while, but it made me so mad. That's when I got my courage.

They told us to charge — we had a few tanks supporting us, but they couldn't touch those deep dug-outs. In a charge it's every man for himself. You see people falling all round you, but you still don't believe it can happen to you. The second time, though, you know it can and your body is rigid the whole time, just waiting for the bullets to go thudding into you. You just go on, running like hell. And a few meters in front is the officer. However fast you run, you can never catch up with him. That's why so many of them were killed.

You find you've reached a dug-out and you throw in hand grenades and hose it out with your Uzzi. And that's it, till the next one. All the time you begin to get more and more scared and more and more angry. They gave us a rest when we'd finished that and then we were sent into the Old City. I remember when we rested I began to think what I'd done and I remember at one point — I think it must have been then — hearing that my kibbutz had been shelled. So all at the same time, I was scared but I wanted to get at the bastards all the more.

We went into the Old City and from then on it was hand-to-hand and house-to-house. That's the worst thing in the world. In the desert, you know, it's different. There are tanks and planes and the whole thing is at a longer range. Hand-to-hand fighting is different, it's terrible. I killed my first man there. Well, I suppose I must have killed before, but as far as I'm concerned that was the first, because the others I didn't see. All of a sudden I saw this man coming out of a doorway, this gigantic Negro. We looked at each other for half a second and I knew that it was up to me, personally, to kill him, there was no one else there. The whole thing must have lasted less than a second, but it's printed in my mind like a slow-motion movie. I fired from the hip and I can still see how the bullets splashed against the wall about a meter to his left. I moved my Uzzi, slowly, slowly, it seemed, until I hit him in the body. He slipped to his knees, then he raised his head, with his face terrible, twisted in pain and hate, yes, such hate. I fired again and somehow got him in the head. There was so much blood . . . I vomited, until the rest of the boys came up. A lot of them had been in the Sinai Campaign and it wasn't new to them. They gave me some water and said it's always like that the first time, not to worry. I found I had fired my whole magazine at him. It's true what they said: you grow more and more callous as you go along, and at the same time, you get used to the gun and miss less. But I'll never forget that moment. It just goes slowly through my mind all the time.

But as we went on fighting, I began to care less. For the whole three days that we fought I was sick and vomiting, but it meant less and less to me. All my friends were going down and I grew madder and madder. I wanted to kill them, all the time that I didn't want to see them. I wanted to get a wound and get out; that's what we all wanted — anything to get out. You just went from house to house, up the stairs, on to the roof, saying to yourself: one more house and I'll get out, then another. Gradually you get fatalistic. Either you'll be killed or you won't — there's nothing you can do about it yourself, so you just go on, scared and hating, so many thoughts going through your mind. Like the bullets, they were coming from all sides; you never knew where the next one would come from.

As we grew angrier, we stopped being human beings. You start out shouting, but by this time, we were all just machines for killing. Everyone's face is set in a snarl and there's a deep growl coming from your belly. You want to kill and kill. You grow like an animal, you know — no, worse than an animal. Things were happening . . . I can't tell you about them. Once, one of our NCOs gave a drink of water to a prisoner. The Jordanian drank and then he pulled a knife and slit the NCO's throat, like a chicken. Things like that. We killed the prisoner, you can't blame us. But you've got to understand what things like that did to us. We hated and hated. And all the time we were thinking what they would do to us and our families if they got us and we were going along thinking, you're out for loot, are you? You'd rape my wife, my sister. . . .

We didn't touch the civilians, though. You just don't think of civilians in the same way as soldiers. The soldiers, though, that's different. They don't seem like men to you. You don't think that they are people with families. You think all the time of your own family, but *they* are just insects to be killed. Until afterwards, when you realize that they had families too. . . .

Then we got to St. Stephen's Gate and we could see the Western Wall, through an archway. We saw it before, but this time it was right in front of us. It was like new life, as though we had just woken up. We dashed down the steps; we were among the first to get there, but a few had already got there and I could see them, men that were too tired to stand up any more, sitting by the Wall, clutching it, kissing the stones and crying. We all of us cried. That was what we had been fighting for. It goes so deep, this emotion we felt when we reached the Wall. What they did in Sinai and in Syria, sure it was marvelous, but it wasn't the same. Getting to the Wall meant everything.

That was about it, except that we had to go back and clean out the snipers. There were a lot of them — they killed a whole lot of women and children in the next few days, people coming to see the Wall. We had to clean them out and it wasn't easy.

The worst was after we had a rest. We couldn't eat or sleep, thinking about the fighting. We just drank and thought. I used to look at my Uzzi, lying next to me. It looked so innocent, just a piece of shining metal. So innocent. Like a person with a smirk on his face. Then we'd be ordered to get up and go in again. We were so scared, then. But we had to get up and face it again, somehow. You get a sharp pain in your guts, just like the feeling you get before you jump from a plane.

I think those three days aged me five years. My father used to tell me that until a man had been through a war he wasn't a man. He was right, I know that now. It's like a part of a man's education. But it's a part we're better without, you know. I know I'll never be the same person again. When I came out of it, everything had changed. Everything was fresh and new and wonderful – the sun, drinking, showering, walking. I still feel that way. All the things that used to bother me are so small and silly. I know what life is worth, now I've seen so much death.

I've got to respect the Legionnaires. They fought like tigers. They fought fantastically. They were fighting for their own homes, you see. But we were fighting for our existence, that's why we won, though they outnumbered us three to one in the Old City.

I came back without any joy. The victory didn't mean anything to me. None of us could even smile, though the people were cheering us when we came through the Mandelbaum Gate. But we had lost fifty per cent of our company. Another company – fifty men – came back with four alive. I never want to go back. I've had enough of the place. I'll tell you in two words what the battle was: murder and fear, murder and fear. I've had enough, enough.

We had to do it, though. That's all I know. But it must never, never happen again. If it doesn't then perhaps it will have been worth while. But only if it never happens again.

AN HOUR OF GREATNESS

From a discussion at Giv'at Haim

Amram: Did you feel any hatred when you were in Jordan?

Peter: No, there wasn't any hatred in us. I did come across a sort of general hatred on the Syrian heights, but not in Jordan. It was all a matter of fighting and advancing, work and fatigue. The enemy was anonymous. But in Syria I did notice signs of a general outbreak of hatred.

Amram: What do you suppose was behind it? The Syrians themselves or something they'd done?

Peter: Yes . . . the things they'd done recently. But apart from that, mass psychosis is catching, you know. You see three or four people infected, and suddenly the atmosphere's full of it.

Amram: Were any of your unit fighting for the first time?

Peter: Yes, lots of them.

Amram: How did they react to it?

Peter: Just like all the others, they weren't any different.

Shimon: There's a big difference between the men who're married and have kids and the younger ones who aren't married yet, who don't have their own families. I remember once when we were under heavy fire, I was behind some cover and I caught myself thinking at that very moment that I ought to watch out. We weren't on the move, just waiting under cover, we didn't have to advance and I thought I ought to try to improve my own position a bit, get some better cover so that I'd manage to make it home again, because

I had a wife and kids waiting for me there. I remember thinking about it.

Amram: Didn't you think that way when you were younger?

Shimon: It certainly bothered me far less. I don't remember worrying about myself so much. But I must add that I also had a feeling, and I think the others shared it, too, that I was ready to give anything, to do anything . . . I remember that when I was sheltering behind that rock waiting to move forward any minute, I didn't want to get hit. But I knew the minute the order to advance was given, I'd have to get up and run, and that then it wouldn't matter at all what happened. It was the same later on, as we continued to advance. I remember that on the one hand I was conscious of the fact that I had a wife and kids at home, and on the other hand, I knew that the whole war was really being fought for their sakes, and if I didn't come back that was for their sake, too. All these things which seem like platitudes, subjects for books and stories, kept flashing through my mind as we came under fire that night. I remember thinking that there wasn't any point in getting hurt for no good reason. But the minute it really became necessary — you had to do it. I'd have done it at any price, and so would the others. I'd have jumped from behind cover to save someone else, and I knew the others would have done the same for me.

Amram: You really felt there was some special link between you and the others?

Shimon: A very strong link. I'd no doubt about it. Take the matter of evacuating the wounded for example: just think how all the boys rushed round and dragged each other to safety. I remember it so clearly. That mutual trust that had grown up between us through the years of reserve training was very clearly felt right through the unit.

Amram: If we're discussing that point, Peter said that in his unit it was almost like a kibbutz — all the boys made up a team, linked to each other, explaining things to each other. I should think the atmosphere in your crowd was something like that.

Shimon: Yes, very similar, so much so that I remember the CO once saying, "I want to hear orders. When you give an order, that's that. But when you say, 'Come on, boys, let's do such and such a thing,' then it's friends you're talking to and you can't be so sure things will get done." I think that shows just how close we were.

Peter: The CO got the whole battalion together and gave us a talk. He really did a good job. He spoke about a relative of his who'd been in the Etzion bloc during the war in 1948 and had been taken prisoner, along with some of the others. He kept emphasizing the point that these boys had been taken into the home of one of the Arab Mukhtars so that they could later be turned over to the Arab Legion. Then along came some of the irregulars who wanted to finish them off. They told the Mukhtar to bring them out and hand them over — and he went outside with his gun and stood up to them and said: "They're my guests, under my roof, and I shall deliver them over to the Legion. Anyone who wants to do anything about it will have to finish me off first." He really saved their lives. The CO kept repeating this story, at every possible opportunity, and when the boys started cursing the Arabs, he used to say, "Okay, you're right up to a point, but there are good Arabs, too. There are Arabs who do know what honour and honesty mean, who do know how to behave." He used to explain to them, "We're going to have to live with the Arabs — if not now, then in another ten years' time. It's inevitable. Any cruelty we show now will simply arouse more hatred. Some people claim that if we behave properly to them, see to their wounded, give them water, cigarettes and treat them fairly it doesn't have results. But I think it can have results." And he convinced them. The boys believed in him. Once he'd talked to them, the problem was over. There wasn't any cruelty. A couple of them had some extreme views on the subject, and he felt it. He got hold of them and discussed it with them personally, very quietly and convincingly. And they accepted his point of view.

Shimon: Soldiers of all ranks used to spend hours talking about this question. In our crowd there were two boys — one from Giv'at Brenner and another from Tivon — who'd managed to crystallize two quite different attitudes to the war, and it was they who used to lead the discussions.

Peter: There was a man in the brigade who was once our CO. They didn't call him up, but he showed up all the same and went to HQ. A really exceptional man who's been secretary of Kibbutz

Yagur three times. He used to go from unit to unit explaining this point and seeing to it that there wasn't any doubt whatever. When he got to our lot, he could see that there wasn't any need to explain, we were all quite clear about it. But among some of the men in the rear, in the workshops and so on — they really had whole lectures on the subject. It was taken good care of.

Amram: The question is, how far do people who've been through a war lose their humanitarian standards, stop treating people as people, and begin behaving towards them as if they were some *Arabush,** or as if they'd ceased to see them as human beings . . . ?

Peter: I take a very serious view of things like this. I've got very clear ideas about hatred. You know, I've got a lot of experience in this business of hatred because of my own past experiences, and I've come to the conclusions that hatred is a matter of individual personality.

Shimon: Do you mean hatred in general, or hating particular people?

Peter: Real hatred, like any real and deep emotion such as love, has to have some definite focus. Someone who's done something to you, someone you've got an account to settle with — that's the sort of person you can strangle or do in. Someone who's done something to you, or someone who's close to you — a friend, a relative, someone there's some sort of personal connection with — that's the sort of person you can hate, too. But to say you hate Arabs, that's just talk. I can understand justifiable hate. Do you want to know why I'm so certain about the whole question? It's because I went into it myself, with the Germans, only a short while after the Second World War. I found I couldn't hate. I didn't want to talk to them, I didn't want to have anything to do with them: but it was still a long way from hatred. And even if I did use the word hatred then, I was quite certain that what I meant wasn't hatred. Hatred's far stronger. I wasn't at all sorry when they punished the Germans. "Fair enough," I said. But that's still not hatred. Whatever bestial qualities there are in man — the more primitive a man is, the more powerful they are.

*Derogatory diminutive used for Arabs.

Shimon: You could really see these things in the weeks before the war, because at that stage we weren't yet on a war footing, we didn't even know if there would or wouldn't be a war. You could see then, in the way people talked, exactly how they approached the whole question of war, just how they reacted to the Arabs. There were differences in how they felt about Jordanians, Egyptians and Syrians.

I don't think there is any difference here between people from the towns and those from the kibbutzim, or between people from kibbutzim of different political outlooks. I know boys from Hashomer Hatzair kibbutzim who've been educated on the concept of love for humanity and so on — yet some of them said that the only way they could see the Arab question was through a gun-sight.

Amram: It seems to me, from various stories I've heard, that this business bothered some of the boys from the kibbutz, but that they didn't have the moral strength to stand up for their own views, to withstand the pressures. . . .

Peter: As far as all that's concerned, I haven't got the slightest shadow of doubt what my duty is and what I've got to do. Apart from this, I didn't have any doubt about the opinions of all the old crowd in the battalion, from the CO right down through all the officers and men, just no doubt at all.

Amram: It's a question of about a tenth of a second in which you've to decide. . . .

Shimon: There weren't any atrocities among our crowd.

Amram: How did your boys behave over loot?

Peter: An army that starts looting is finished as an army. There's no control over it. Everyone starts running off into the houses. Anyway, apart from that, it's dangerous. From the point of view of morality, the Israeli army's different from others. We made sure the soldiers knew this. They knew that anyone caught at it was liable to be punished.

Shimon: I remember that in our case it happened for the first time just after the capture of Darbishiyeh. We took up positions inside their fortifications so that we could regroup against a counterattack. There were three or four houses there which we had to comb out. As we went through them, checking up on the situation, the boys started saying, "Look, cigarettes! Let's take some!" I was in a tough spot. What the hell, couldn't they take a few cigarettes? At first I said they couldn't take anything at all, later I decided to let them take a packet each. They'd been on the move for a few days by then, and they'd run out of smokes. Then, all of a sudden, one of them began "I want this . . . I want this. . . . " They began to open boxes. Actually, at first I didn't see anything wrong in it when the boys started rummaging around. At that moment I didn't imagine. . . . Only later on, when we'd advanced further, into abandoned villages, I suddenly thought, "What's going on here? They're getting out of control, snatching things." You see, the proportions get changed.

When we came down from the Syrian heights, the CO ordered all the loot to be returned. He got all the junk together, everything that anyone in the company had taken. Within two or three minutes everyone brought it all in and it turned out they'd only taken little souvenirs: handbooks issued to privates in the Syrian army, little cigarette holders, worthless things like that. There wasn't even a lot of it. It would all have gone into an orange-box. Anyway, there was a primus stove included in the haul. the CO spilled the paraffin from it on the heap of stuff, and set light to the whole lot. Somehow we felt that cleansed us, that it completely removed us from all contact with the sin of looting. But at the same time, it seems a pity that a soldier fights and sacrifices . . . he should have something left, I don't know: a Syrian army badge, the cover of a Syrian private's handbook, something he'll be able to take out in ten years' time and show his grandson and say, "You see this? This page, this book — that's how they used to train the Syrian soldiers. See, now do you understand why we fought them?"

Peter: You can do all that without that type of souvenir. I see it quite differently. . . .

Shimon: You can put it in another way: a unit that'll burn little things like that won't touch bigger stuff.

Amram: During the war, lots of boys used to talk about what it all meant to them as Jews, whether it was connected with the Western Wall or with the tremendous response of Diaspora Jewry. Did you come across the same thing?

Shimon: Yes . . . yes . . . I did. They used to talk a lot about there never being another massacre of the Jews like Hitler's. I remember them talking about it, and I remember feeling the same way; I felt that we were moving up to attack Jalbinah so that Jalbinah wouldn't be able to carry on harassing the Jewish settlements. It sounds like a slogan out of a book on Zionism, but I remember that I really did feel like that. I felt that tonight we were once and for all going to finish off this business of them shelling our villages. I'd say that the boys experienced some sort of national awakening.

Amram: They got less cynical?

Shimon: Certainly. Of course, when we got to the Western Wall, they weren't cynical at all. They went up to it and touched the stones, they were breathing deeply, sighing. There was something about it. Of course, it's true that we were also caught up in a special set of circumstances. You mustn't forget that we got to the Wall on the day the war finished. It was the climax of the war. When I touched the stones of the Wall, I knew it was all over, that moment, that very second, the war was over. . . .

Gad: You don't see very much when you're the tank gunner. I remember that I was terribly irritated by it all the time. It's difficult to sit there and travel along and not see too much, and your vision's very limited.

We were all quite pleased about things at first. When we entered Khan Junis the people started clapping us, and there were white flags flying. Then suddenly we started seeing the first of the dead.

When you see one of the ones who's caught it, you curse the whole damned war. You wonder why it's got to happen, why you've got to shoot. I started thinking about people; it seemed awfully strange at first. In the beginning you deliberately don't aim very accurately, it's awfully difficult to make yourself shoot. Then you do, and you get used to it. I remember how amazed we were at how much we'd changed. What have I got against an Arab? Even if I can see that he's got a gun? I don't know, it's awfully strange. You shoot at him, you know he's a man, that he's got a family, that's he's married. It all goes fine right up to the moment you see someone dead. That's when we began to curse the war. You're terribly frightened, you see burnt-out tanks. . . . I remember we thought about home all the time; all the time we thought that at home you could sleep in peace, you could work and eat, it was peaceful there, without this dreadful fear. You keep thinking about home, about the peace there is at home. . . .

We felt that there was a really strong people behind us. It was the same in the weeks before, too, you felt the whole nation stood together. All the papers ran a special page for us — the battle page — it was really nice, that's where you could see that everyone was trying to help, everyone was trying to do something for the next man, everyone was giving whatever he could . . . it was a marvelous feeling. They used to say the youth weren't worth anything, with their crazy dances; that there wasn't anyone to rely on; and then suddenly these same youngsters started showing what they were really made of, they were so marvelous that lots of people said there's never ever been anyone like them. I remember that during the war this feeling of being a special people was terribly important to all of us, we felt we were special, and that we'd better carry on being special. It was an hour of greatness, a great and unique nation.

For us tank people it was easier. If you hit a tank, you can't see what's going on. As a gunner, I could only see through the sights and from there it looks quite different.

Amram: A sort of clean war?

Gad: Exactly. You see it all as if it were happening on a TV screen. It occurred to me at the time; I see someone running and I shoot at him, and he falls, and it all looks like something on TV. I don't see people, that's one good thing about it. During the real fighting, we were in the tanks the whole time. Afterwards of course, the problems started. There were prisoners and that sort of thing.

I knew I had a right to conquer. But to kill? We boys of eighteen held their lives in our hands. They were much older men. And when you see a man of forty or so come up to you and start pleading for his life, when he shows you photos of his kids, and his wife . . . it was very, very strange.

WE'RE EVEN FORCED TO WANT IT...

From a discussion at Na'an. Interviewer: Giora Mossinson

Situated between Tel Aviv and Jerusalem, Na'an was the first kibbutz to be established by a group of young people in Palestine. Its founders were working-class youths, the founders and first graduates of the Working Youth movement. The kibbutz was a center of Hagana activity until 1948. Today Na'an has a population of more than 2,000, including a large proportion of children of the kibbutz among its members.

Participants:
Kobi, twenty-one, who was born and educated in Na'an, where he became a garage mechanic. In the Six-Day War he fought as a sergeant-major in the Tank Corps on the Sinai front. After the war he was one of the founders of Kibbutz Golan, a new settlement on Golan Heights. *Tamar*, Giora's wife, nineteen, was born in Kibbutz Alonim and became a member of Na'an on her marriage. She works in child care, with young children. Her daughter was born shortly after the Six-Day War. *Ayelet*, nineteen, born and educated in Na'an. On completing her education, she was called up and trained for administrative work in an armored unit. On the outbreak of the war she accompanied her unit throughout the conquest of Sinai. *Yiftah*, twenty-seven, married with two children. After his Army service he spent some years

78

working as a fisherman in a young kibbutz on the Red Sea. He currently works with the dairy herd at Na'an. During the Six-Day War he fought in a paratroop unit in Jerusalem. Others from Na'an who appear in *The Seventh Day: Yosef* (Yoske), born in Russia in 1910 and came to Palestine with his parents in 1921, where he was educated in Jerusalem primary and secondary schools. As a member of the youth movement of the Histadrut, he joined Kibbutz Na'an in 1930. He lectures at the ideological seminar of his kibbutz movement, and is married with three children (including Kobi, who appears in this discussion).

Giora: Ayelet, as a girl who was with a combatant unit, it would be interesting to hear what happened and what you saw.

Ayelet: Let me start with the waiting period before the war. It was quite a depressing place. It wasn't just that the boys were withdrawn and quiet; there was a feeling of fear. I remember one evening when the battalion commander came back from a briefing session, and from what he said I sensed that things were pretty bad. This was after Syria and Iraq had joined Egypt and were moving their troops up. We felt that the situation was very serious, and there were even moments when we were a bit panicky. But I for one didn't doubt for a single moment that we had no alternative but to win. There wasn't any other way out.

Giora: How did you feel, as a girl? Weren't there moments when you'd have preferred to be a man? After all, you knew that when it came to the point others were going to do the real job.

Ayelet: I could only say the blessing: "Blessed art Thou who created me a woman." I talked things over with some of the boys. They were really thinking about things very seriously: whether they'd come back alive or not. It was only then that I suddenly caught on that for them war was a matter of life or death. It wasn't like that for me at all. For a girl it's a unique experience to be in such surroundings — but not a question of life or death. I didn't feel that I'd play a decisive role. I was like an observer.

Giora: Perhaps you'll tell us some more about this waiting period? Was there really this backs-to-the-wall feeling?

Ayelet: In the beginning we really felt that way. We were being forced to fight a war that nobody wanted. But gradually this feeling became blurred. It became clearer that we wanted it to happen, and to get it over with. A real lust for battle, almost. That's as far as the pre-war period was concerned. It was so different from what happened afterwards, during the war. Then I think I was in some sort of state of shock: nothing was clearly defined. I'm still trying to push it all away from me. I don't want to think about it: I want to forget. I get an awful feeling of disgust and nausea whenever the subject comes up. It's because of all the dead and wounded, all the horrible things we saw there. If I saw things like that in a film I wouldn't be able to look, I would have to close my eyes. But there I looked at them in cold blood, and it didn't affect me. When I see a cat run over I can't look. But there, when I saw all the dead — theirs as well as ours — it didn't make any impression on me. I'd go further than that: I think I was a completely different person then. I try not to think about it too much, not to go back over it, not to explain it to myself, to put it all behind me.

Giora: Can you fix some point when you personally had the feeling that the war had really begun?

Ayelet: The moment we came across the first casualty. We'd crossed the border, with a great happy cheer, just like tourists. After a few hours we suddenly saw a helicopter, with a group of people near it. We knew that we'd got near the battle area. We waved to them from a distance, but when we got nearer we saw stretchers, bodies wrapped up in blankets and wounded men limping around. It gave us a terrific shock. We became part of the whole terrible business and it stopped being like a trip to the country. We felt a little frightened then.

We never travelled along the main highways, but always through wadis and over tracks, quite often through hilly regions where there was every likelihood that the enemy would be above us. The boys sat on the lorries and half-tracks with their guns pointing upwards. It was an opportunity for me to test my reactions. My spine felt prickly, and I imagined that's what's called fear. I must say I was quite pleased that I was able to look at myself from the outside, and not lose control of myself, even though I was frightened. Occasionally they shot at us, and we had to jump out of the lorries and find cover while bullets were whistling overhead. I was more surprised than frightened. I was fascinated by the scream of the bullets. Afterwards I thought a lot about death: for example, I thought that if I or another girl were to be hit it would be a pointless death, we hadn't come to fight and our death here wouldn't help anyone. It wasn't such a pleasant thought, that you might die there by mistake.

Giora: Did you manage to think even when the bullets were flying?

Ayelet: Yes: while I was hiding behind a rock and when I got an order to run and take cover. Yes, it made me think. It wasn't pleasant to have to hide, it felt like running away. There in the middle of all the shooting, all sorts of thoughts crossed my mind: that life is sweet, that it would be a pity to miss out on it.

At first we had two prisoners of war. I was very frightened of them. I thought they'd pull out a hand-grenade and finish us off. I was glad that we let them go. After the fighting in which Tally was killed, when I'd seen the bodies of some of the boys who were closest to us, who'd been with us right through our army service, I felt completely different. I felt that if I had a gun, I'd shoot every Egyptian I saw – to stop them killing us and to avenge the boys who'd been killed. I had murderous thoughts. I was surprised at myself, but I could understand what was behind it all.

While I was with the boys I did the best I could: first of all looking after the casualties, cheering them up, smiling. There were some really awful cases there. Some were in shock and others had quite serious wounds. We talked to them and tried to buck them up. They'd got all the wounded together in one place and it was there that I found Tally. He'd been in my class. I found that very difficult to get over. When he was killed it didn't affect me so much because subconsciously I'd been waiting for it to happen. If you're specially worried about somebody in particular you're always aware of this possibility.

In order to withstand the dreadful sights I was forced not to show any emotion. It was only once, a short while after I heard about Tally's death, that this whole business of death hit me and I felt that any minute I was going to cry. Somehow I forced the tears back and got over it. Here were all the boys standing around – and was I going to cry? I forced myself to get over it, and I did. But most of the time I was just numb, really numb; I can't explain it. There were two other girls there who didn't manage to react this way and I had to try and stiffen their morale a bit. I don't think I really caught on to the whole question of death. I think perhaps very few people can really grasp it, and perhaps that's why I managed to control myself; maybe I still haven't quite caught on. At home, for example, when I meet bereaved parents, I feel pain and pity very strongly, but it's more because of feeling with them in their sorrow than because of really having grasped the significance of this thing called death. Quite simply, it hasn't penetrated. I've got a block somewhere and it hasn't lifted yet. It must be because of this that the whole business didn't have such an effect on me.

Giora: Do you ever think of the dead with the sort of feeling that it's all over for them, there's no more life, no more family, nothing. . . .

Ayelet: Yes. It's just like that. When I feel good, or I see something beautiful, I think to myself that those who got killed won't be able to feel this way any more. But this feeling isn't strong enough to make you really aware of the full meaning of death.

Giora: Do you think it's a sort of shock that makes you push away all these thoughts, memories and feelings?

Ayelet: Look here, if anybody thinks war doesn't cause some sort of shock, then they're making a mistake, a very big mistake. Wars aren't a natural thing, even though they recur time and again, and you can't say that this is what man was made for. You can't say that any animal is essentially warlike. Our normal lives educate us to a completely opposite outlook, and the Six-Day War was a total reversal of all the patterns of my life up to then. After all, how old am I? Only nineteen.

Giora: Kobi, was the war a shock for you, too? How did you reconcile it with the education you received? Didn't your army training leave any room for doubt and questioning?

Kobi: My army training was technical, and I still love things like that because I like machines, tractors, tanks — it's all the same to me.

Giora: But if you'd thought things through to the end, they trained you to work efficiently just so that the machines could kill.

Kobi: It's not just if I think things through to the end that I realize this. In fact, there were moments: there was one moment, one night when I'd got deep into all the filth, and what I saw there . . . I came back to the tank and climbed up and I really thought I'd had it. I look at this tank a bit differently now. Even if I get on this tank in twenty years' time, I'll still smell that same smell and see the same filth. Afterwards I was amazed. After a day or two, I was at it again. War is so filthy, so bloody filthy, I don't think you can ask anyone to think about it calmly and analyze their reactions coolly.

Yoram: One of the things I forgot to mention before was a real physical reaction I had every time they shouted "Stretcher bearer!" The first time I heard it I reacted just as we'd been taught — they'd begun calling for stretcher bearers all around me, and I ran and brought one to one of the wounded. But later on, especially towards the end, whenever I heard that cry I felt physically sick. My stomach would tighten up. I didn't feel angry with anyone in particular. It was fury with the whole world. Together with a feeling of despair and exhaustion. You know it's just like in books — actually writers have had centuries of experience in finding the right words for it — every time there was a shout of "stretcher bearer" I felt like throwing my Uzzi down on the ground, screaming curses and sitting down right there, and saying, "Count me out, I'm not playing any more."

Of course I saw at once that this would have been pointless, it wouldn't have helped at that stage — but perhaps that's *the* thing to do. I went right on bringing stretchers, running around and trying to help. But the first reaction was certainly exhaustion, furious anger and nausea. When I kept on hearing that cry, again and again, it wasn't hate I felt, it was just — it frightened me. It can break you, a thing like that. Yes, I can fully accept that the war broke people up. I think the thing to fight is war itself.

Tamar: All our lives we've been educated against war and we've fought against the whole idea of war; and you can see that it doesn't help. Even now, we're already saying, "The next war, the next fight." You can see it doesn't help, it's something forced on us.

We're even forced to want it. I remember that all of us, that is all the mothers, were in the children's house. It was a week or two after we'd had our babies. Some of the girls said they were sorry they'd had a child. I was thinking all the time, "I'm glad I've got a daughter." It was in my mind right through the war. I also said, "I'm glad she doesn't know what's going on, that she won't remember it all." At the time I think I was trying to convince myself that there'd never be another war. But somehow I felt all the time that this wasn't the last, that history repeats itself and . . . really, perhaps we need lots and lots of children — we've just got to go on having children.

Yiftah: So there'll be lots of soldiers?

Tamar: So that if one person dies. . . . How can you bring up kids and show them flowers and all sorts of beautiful things when you know that perhaps in ten years these same kids — or even their fathers — because even they won't be so old. . . . Some people have already fought four wars. How can you bring people up that way? It's one big contradiction in terms. Sometimes the thought steals into your mind: perhaps it would be better to give up this country, to do away with one more war in the world, to get rid of one war area. I don't know. Sometimes I really had rebellious thoughts; in the shelter, for example, as I held my two-weeks'-old baby in my arms I wondered whether this was really necessary. Was it that vital that we could or couldn't sail through the Straits of Tiran? Now, as I analyze it, it's clear that everything was absolutely necessary and completely justified. But even then if Giora hadn't come back perhaps I wouldn't have been able to come to that conclusion.

Ayelet: I saw the hair's breadth that divides life from death; it takes a minute fraction of a second. You suddenly realize that life and death are of little significance, it happens so quickly and death suddenly becomes meaningless and empty. Perhaps one even begins to believe in some sort of destiny, some sort of fate which determines things. After this, I must say I was less afraid of death and of dying. Suppose I thought, "I want to get out of here alive, I want to stay alive," immediately afterwards I also thought, "But why should it be me that comes out alive, why not the soldier next to me?" So that wasn't really a factor. I remember thinking that it couldn't be that a person dies in this way. I would look up at the sky at night and try to see if there were more stars than usual: perhaps the souls of the dead were up there somewhere. It seemed to me as if, among other things, I'd never be able to eat properly again. You felt really sick there. Sometimes we forced ourselves to eat the dry biscuits we were given just to keep our strength up. It also seemed as if I'd never be able to sing again or be happy, or that if people were feeling happy around me then I'd be overcome by a feeling of sadness. It was a shock to me to come back and to forget everything so quickly, to be able to sing again and feel happy.

When those boys got killed, I thought that I must never forget their death and that I'd owe it to them to live a better, more honest life. But when we got home so quickly and I looked around and saw how people were already forgetting and I saw all sorts of things . . . suddenly I discovered that I too had forgotten, and it was a shock to me. But I didn't make any effort to remember; on the contrary, I tried to get away from it all, to put it all behind me, to forget it. But all the same I think that whenever people around me are enjoying themselves I'll always feel a bit sad.

Yiftah: Me too. I felt the same way about the dead and the wounded and for some reason this feeling has become blunted. Now it sounds rhetorical, I suppose, but I felt that we owed them everything. At the time, this seemed very clear to me, and quite natural. Again, I can't put it into words now, but then it seemed like blind fate. The first day after the war I began to be haunted by the memory of one of the boys who didn't reach the battalion in time. He chased us all over the country and finally caught up with us half an hour before we got onto the buses for Jerusalem. He was the first to be killed, just as it was all beginning. And he almost missed the whole show. . . . I felt that we carried a heavy debt — it was a very heavy price to pay — it almost overshadowed what we gained as a nation. And that's no exaggeration. I was obsessed by the feeling that we owed them everything. And yet — this feeling passes. For some reason or other it goes away. I always thought that somehow the dead give meaning to life. Now I think about it more than I've ever done before. There was a time when it really got hold of me. It seemed so obvious, and I found it a great help.

Kobi: I discovered that I hated two things: the boys who

behaved like animals — and Nasser. I didn't hate the soldiers I was fighting against at all. All the time I was shooting at them I was thinking: poor wretches; they're all burnt up, and everything; and they're really innocent. Who brought them to this? He did! This policy, this dictatorship, this stupid dictatorship in which his soldiers' lives mean nothing. I don't know Arabic, but I used to tell the boys to shout at them: "Look what Nasser's done to you!" And they screamed back: "We want to go home." Perhaps that's the Arab mentality, I don't know. They're simple peasants. I had a still greater hatred for those to whom the war was just like a game of chess. You got to know people when you were with them in the reserves before the war, and you mentally graded them: this one's like this, that one's very close to you, the other you feel no special sympathy with. After the first day of fighting, the whole picture blurred. One man whom I particularly admired, an excellent worker, very friendly — now I feel just the opposite about him. Another chap — someone I'd never even noticed before — suddenly I wanted to hug him when I realized what a really good type he was.

It was on the way back to Abu Ageila that I saw my first corpse, a charred corpse hanging out of a burnt-out pick-up truck. It turned me to stone. I shouted down the intercom of the tank, "Look, a corpse!" They all shouted back, "Yes? Where? How?" as if it were something unexpected. Later, there were so many of them that it began to be interesting — one lying this way, another that way. I used to ask them, "What are you staring at?"

Ayelet: I also surprised myself, the way I used to look at them, how I'd even search for them by the burnt-out vehicles, how I'd turn around and look back at them as we passed. It seemed as if I was being deliberately cruel to myself, it caused me terrific anguish and nausea, and yet I forced myself to look, I made myself do it. It occurs to me that there's a feeling of guilt at the root of it all. I don't know exactly, I haven't gone into it so deeply.

Yiftah: But Kobi said he didn't have to force himself, it simply interested him.

Kobi: You have to differentiate. There are somethings you think before the fighting, and others that you think afterwards. The question is what you actually do about things. It's not what you think that's so important, it's what you finally do.

Giora: For me, both are important.

Kobi: Look here, you judge a man by what he does rather than by what he thinks. The road to hell is paved with good intentions. What's important is whether humanity expresses itself in deeds. In my opinion, a man shows his true qualities in standing up to his problems and getting over them. That's what's meant by "the hero who conquers his desires." It may even be fear that stops him doing what he wants to do. But as I see it, it's the end result that counts, what you actually do in the end. It doesn't matter what you think. This avid curiosity that makes you turn around and look at the corpses is one of the factors in man's make-up which pushes him from one war into the next. If only he could master these forces within himself and not permit them to express themselves in actual deeds, then perhaps there'd be some hope that there'd be an end of war. I don't think that the test is in a man's thoughts or what goes on in his conscious mind, because you'll always find that that includes murder, killing, cruelty and sadism.

Yiftah: Quite right. People usually become a bit twisted at some stage or another. I was shocked at myself, or perhaps let's say, I condemned myself; no, it's better to say that I was shocked at myself when I suddenly discovered that I, too, had this thing that Kobi's talking about, this desire to look at corpses. It seemed impossible to satisfy this hunger until, at some point, there was a sudden feeling of revulsion, a feeling that it was all choking me.

THE FIELDS BECAME PRECIOUS

From a discussion in Mishmar Hasharon. Interviewer: Shlomit Teub

Mishmar Hasharon, situated in the coastal strip of Israel some 25 miles north of Tel Aviv, was founded in 1933, and is today a flourishing agricultural settlement with a population of some 700.

Participants:
Yoni, twenty-two, a bachelor, works in the fruit orchards. Fought as a lieutenant in the infantry in the Sinai. *Avinoam*, twenty-three, bachelor, works in the vineyards. Hobbies: sport, classical music, youth work. Sergeant; fought on the Sinai front. *Zvike*, twenty-three, bachelor, sergeant in an advance tank unit.

Yoni: You ask if life became cheap. On the contrary: the lives of others, of those close to me, became precious. It was my own life that seemed unimportant, somehow. That was one of the things that really surprised me. You ask if I discovered things in myself that hadn't been there previously. Yes, I really think that there were some instances where I behaved — where I endangered myself too much. Afterwards, when I tried to analyze it, I saw that it hadn't been very responsible behavior.

Shlomit: Didn't you try to balance all these feelings at the time?

Yoni: No. But they were the very things that led me to succeed in the battle; because I was ready for anything that might happen. Then there was something else that surprised me enormously. Before the war I always thought, at least I had the feeling, that all this talk about love of one's country was just so much empty phraseology. But during the war, I found these *were* the things that counted, the things that gave you strength: the fact that back there you'd got a home, friends, people who want to live, even that you yourself want to live in this country. You found that the fields became precious to you, that the lives of all the people you know, of all the Jews living in this country, became precious to you — you suddenly felt that there was something in all this. You know, the first few days after I got back, I kept talking about it all the time, about how I'd found out for myself that all these things that I'd once thought were just slogans, things like, "it's good to die for your country" and "love of one's homeland," they really existed. I think war is the most extreme example of what brings men to realize all this.

And it stops. I want to tell you something. During the fighting itself, it seemed natural to me that even our own soldiers should die. It seemed natural that people die in a war. After the war, when my CO was killed, it affected me much more. I wasn't desolate, but all the same I felt it much more than during the war. I asked myself what was the point of life. Now, after the war, I ask what's the point of death? That's the difference. It's only after the war that you understand what the point of life is, but then you ask the question, was it worth all those dead — so that I can live?

Shlomit: What I meant to ask was whether the significance of things remains with you afterwards — the significance of things like "the homeland," the things you used to see as mere phrases before all this?

Yoni: Yes. That will always remain with me, now. I discovered something then that was so powerful that it will always be in me.

Avinoam: Every time I endangered myself to the point where I was sure the next bullet had my name on it, I think an element of self-confidence came into it. You rely on some sort of superior power, you believe in your luck, in I don't know what. . . . But I never felt that I was going to die.

Zvike: I want to go back to something else we talked about earlier. This business of calling the dead "carcasses." It seems to me that in using a word like that there's an element of psychological defence protecting you from all the killing and murder that otherwise threatened to destroy your soul. When someone uses a word like this, it shows he wasn't psychologically ready for it. He'd always had a respect for life, so in an attempt, perhaps even on an unconscious level, to prevent such thoughts really getting through, he defends himself by using a term like corpses or carcasses. Later he loses all sense of proportion in the face of so many dead. It's like saying, six million Jewish dead in the concentration camps. Your mind boggles at the idea, it can't grasp it at all. When you say that one man got killed, two men got killed — that shakes you. But six million Jews — you can't talk about that, it's beyond our ability to grasp, it's too abstract.

THE REAL HORROR

From a discussion in Gat

Shlomit: Amnon, you told us that after the war you couldn't go back to reading detective stories all about one person getting murdered. You said it was because your sense of proportion had changed after all you'd seen and had been through. Did life suddenly seem cheap? Had your attitude to the sanctity of life changed?

Amnon: The value of our own lives didn't lessen, not even during very critical moments. The fact that we began to kill without being bothered by it all — retrospectively, this was an appalling experience. At first it was grim in itself. Later — how can I put it? — the enemy stopped being a person. He became just a thing opposite us. The day after the fighting we went into the battle area. There, lying next to one another, on the same battlefield, were our dead and their dead. Suddenly you realized that they were all the same. But that was just a passing shadow. The real horror began a few days later, when we were acting as the occupying force and there was a lot of time to think things over. People began saying, "I don't know how . . . I felt as if they were flies on a window screen . . . that's to say, they stopped being people . . . . " But I don't think the value of life lessened because of this. People were horrified at themselves, at how they'd been able to kill. I can't judge today. I think that for me my sense of proportion changed at different points during the fighting and I can't tell you, to this day, just what points these were. I only know that my attitude did change. But I can't pin-point exactly when it happened. I don't know. Today I'm less upset at funerals. No, perhaps it's not like that. I can't define it. But everybody's sense of proportion has been turned upside down, and they're all conscious of it.

Dan: I never had any problems about this. I'm no great sadist, but I never felt. . . . Look, we were in the thick of it as soon as we crossed the border. Most of our fighting was done in the first day or two. I'm sure after we'd taken Gaza and the whole business had quietened down, that if anyone had gone and killed one of them in the street, he'd have been put in prison, and severely punished.

Amnon: A few days after the war, I was standing by the road here, near Kastina, when suddenly a man was flung out of a car and just lay there on the roadside. He lay on the road just as I'd seen hundreds lie, back there. Everyone nearby started running around in a panic, but I found myself standing there quite indifferent to it all. The first picture that flashed into my mind was of bodies like this lying on the roadside. I really saw it like that — and I just stood there. Then I saw people dashing about, getting upset over it. All the traffic was brought to a standstill, there was an ambulance and sirens. Then, things came back into perspective for me, perhaps he'd fractured his skull, perhaps he'd die. But for that first minute, I just stood stock still, without budging an inch. Everyone else ran, but I stood rooted to the spot. Suddenly, I asked myself, "What are you standing here for?" And he was one of us. So if that's what you mean by life becoming cheaper, then perhaps. . . . It shocked me. I confess it shocked me that instead of seeing a man who'd had an accident, all I could see was a road covered with bodies.

YOUR MIND GOES BLANK

From a discussion in Mishmar Hanegev

Asher: One of the most difficult experiences I went through was on the first night of the fighting, when we went into Rafiah. I was attached to the striking force. There was shelling going on and you couldn't hear or take anything in at all. When it was over, the force moved on in the direction of the advance. In front of us there was another unit, with its casualties and dead. I went up and asked if they needed any help. "D'you remember Yossi? There he is — over there. This is Baruch, that's Uri and Ehud and Chaim and Moshe," the other doctor said. They were all wrapped up in blankets, naked and burnt. So long as you don't know the people personally, you can deal with them calmly, as doctors do. But when you know these boys, when you've worked with them for a whole year, when you've attended this one's wedding, and you remember how his love affair went with his girl, when you've shared so many common experiences: and then you see them lying like that, all wrapped up in blankets, laid out on the floor, then as well as the terrible anguish, you have the feeling — your mind goes blank. Actually that's how everyone felt, all the boys who were there and saw it all. The armored corps made the breakthrough and all the rear units were under fire from snipers and enemy tanks left behind. In fact, all the units fought, whether it was a supply unit, the garage hands, or our brigade headquarters unit. Everyone fought, that was what characterized this war. That's why we all felt the same way. We all knew that we had to destroy in order to live.

93

David: But when the Egyptians surrendered with their hands up, looking so wretched and all that, was there still the same feeling of hatred?

Asher: No. The hatred only lasted until the moment you actually came into contact with them. When they did arrive in that wretched fashion, suddenly all the feeling of hatred virtually disappeared. We just felt disgust at the sight of them with their hands up; it was really a feeling of repulsion. If they'd have fought, we'd have felt morally able to finish them off. You always respect a fighter more than these so-called heroes who aren't capable of putting up a fight.

TODAY I CAN'T SMILE...

This is the most immediate reaction to the war to be found
in this book: a page from a diary, written by a nineteen-
year-old girl soldier born on Kibbutz Usha, which has a
population of 600. It was founded in 1937, and is
north-east of Haifa.

El Arish, 6.7.1967. Suddenly, without knowing how or why, I found
myself in the very thick of the war. They woke me in the middle of
the night. "You're off to El Arish. It's no dream," they said. "See
you after the war...." And now here I am, in a little hut in El
Arish.

There's a heavy, thick blackness outside, and an awful noise. Not
the sort of noise you're used to, but shots, screams and short
frightening booms, then *boom* again, *boom, boom, boom,* and a
scream. All sorts of sounds like that, tearing at your ears, crude
sounds, without any harmony....

Enough. It's time it was all over. Enough. Today has already been
enough for my eyes and ears. There's been enough banging at one's
feelings, enough illusion and faith blown sky high. It's enough. The
existence of evil has been proved....

And they tell me that it's still not over; they say it's only the
beginning: "Look here, girl, you've got to understand ... there's no
choice," they say.

But I don't want to understand that there's no choice; that people
should get angry with each other, that they should slaughter each

other, and that while it's not exactly nice, there's still no choice. ("And anyway, it's time you understand that not everything in life can be controlled, and that everything isn't always nice . . . . ")

I know one's got to be strong. That one's got to know how to get over it. But no one shows me how to do all this. . . .

Be strong!!!

I knew that you dug a grave for the dead, and said prayers for them. But today — they're all spread out, torn limb from limb, blown up, stinking.

Be strong!!!

I saw a boy, the only soldier left from his platoon. All dazed, his eyes red and empty. He didn't smile. Just asked and hoped that someone else might have been saved. No, no . . . there wasn't anyone else left.

Your throat chokes, your eyes cloud over and you run outside, to get over it. But the wind that's usually so good, so refreshing, only brings in great gusts of stench from the dead and clouds of heavy black flies. . . .

Someone passed by and said *"Shalom"*! He smiled and asked, "How're things?" I got out a dry choked *"shalom"* and walked on.

I am not strong. I can't smile today . . . maybe tomorrow. . . .

Rivka Niedt

THEY'RE NO DIFFERENT FROM US

From a discussion in Kibbutz Tirat Zvi.
Interviewer: Amram Hayisra'eli

Tirat Zvi was founded in 1937, in the Beisan Valley. It is
the oldest, and still the biggest, religious kibbutz (population 800); its members are deeply orthodox, and educate
their children to continue this way of life. Close to the
Jordanian border, Tirat Zvi is still subject to frequent
artillery attacks.

Participants:
Micha, who is married, with one daughter, and who is in
charge of the fish-ponds. In the Six-Day War he fought in
Jerusalem as second-in-command of his battalion, and took
over from his commanding officer, who was killed during
the fighting. *Danny*, twenty-seven and the father of two
children, teaches physical education in the kibbutz secondary school. He fought in Jerusalem as a lieutenant and
company commander.

   Amram: Had you ever seen dead soldiers before?
   Danny: Yes, I had. We had some clashes with infiltrators when I
was on national service. But it wasn't the sight of dead soldiers that
shocked me.

97

98

Micha: Was it that life seemed to have cheapened?

Danny: It didn't only seem, it really had cheapened. This business of killing — I don't know if it's a plus or minus, but I'm one of those who didn't even kill so much as one Egyptian. I didn't see the need for it. Perhaps it's because I once looked at one of their identity cards and saw "age sixteen and a half." So as a teacher I couldn't help thinking: "What, am I expected to kill a kid like one of those in our own sixth form? How can I do it?" And they really were kids. They stood there shaking. I think at least a third of those we took prisoner had wet their pants. All in all, they'd only been in the army for six months. Six months in the desert. I just don't see myself as a great "killer."

Micha: Whenever I have any dealings with Arabs today, I can't for the life of me understand that saying "Honor him, but suspect him." They're human beings like anyone else. Nothing in my experience has convinced me of the truth of this saying. An Arab's nothing new to me. We're right on the border here and we see Arab peasants almost every day, sometimes we talk to them. I've never felt any hatred towards them, or thought of them as enemies. When I was firing, during the war, I didn't have any such thoughts as "He's a human being, too!" I didn't even think about the moral aspect of killing him. All those long years of training behind me have had their effect, I suppose. I saw a target, it didn't matter if it was moving or not, and I shot at it: my only thought was to get him — nothing else came into it. But on the other hand, when I saw POWs, I did think of them as human beings. In fact, sometimes I thought I was being too soft. I don't know, I just didn't like shouting at them. I felt uncomfortable. They're human beings just like me. It made me feel better about the whole thing when I felt I could believe what they said. For example, we went in to clean up pockets of resistance in the Old City. We were sitting by the Wall. There was a family there that had taken shelter in some hole or other. We didn't let any of them out because we didn't want anyone wandering around. The women said, "I want to go out to feed my baby, to get some water for her." The boys objected: "Don't let any of them move", they said, and perhaps they were right. "You never know what may happen! Don't let them out!" At first I'd agreed to let them go. It made me feel good to be able to believe them. People talk to you just like we're talking now. Let them — why not? They're no different from us. . . .

A MOMENT OF TRUTH

Discussion in Yif'at. Interviewers: Rachel Halprin and Avraham Shapira

Yif'at is a large well-developed kibbutz east of Haifa, with more than a thousand inhabitants who include the present Minister of Agriculture and many others prominent in public life and in the kibbutz movement.

Participants:
Amram, twenty-two, a youth leader who works with groups of under-privileged youth educated in the kibbutz. In the Six-Day War he served in the paratroops as a sergeant fighting in Jordan and on the Syrian Heights. *Lotan*, thirty, father of a six-months-old child, works as a surveyor. In the Six-Day War he fought as a sergeant in an advance patrol unit. *Haggai*, twenty-one and married a week before the war broke out, works in field crops. In his spare time he is a youth leader and an archaeologist. He was a paratroop sergeant but was declared unfit for service as a result of an accident during a practice jump. At the beginning of June, 1967, he "ran away" from home, and he fought during the Six-Day War with an infantry battalion in Jordan. Others from Yif'at who appear in *The Seventh Day: Aharon*, twenty-three and father of one child, works in Yif'at's factory. He served as a private in the paratroops, and fought

in Jerusalem. *Rafael*, twenty-five, father of two children,
fought in the armored division which took Nablus, and then
on the Syrian Heights.

Haggai: The night the fighting was over in Jordan, I was
stationed on the West Bank of the river. There was an order to stop
all movement in our direction from the other side of the Jordan, and
it was quite clear that we meant business. I was in command of a
small group of men on a certain stretch of road, and I knew that the
Arabs who came up this hill weren't usually soldiers. Groups of
people went past three times during the night, but I never gave the
order to open fire. Each time it turned out that they really were
civilians.

The next night we were moved on, to another point on the West
Bank of the river. There were reports of Iraqi troop movements on
the other side, and the orders to shoot were even stricter than the
night before. I don't know why — perhaps because I was afraid of a
clash with armed forces — but when we saw figures moving up from
the direction of the Jordan I gave the order to open fire immediately
after one warning. And we killed one of them. When it was all over, I
went to see what had happened. I found that the man we'd killed
was an Arab peasant, nothing to do with the army at all. I felt
absolutely lousy about it.

Perhaps what made the feeling worse was my impression of the
boys in the ambush who happened to do the actual killing. It may
have been because we were in a brigade that hadn't done any real
fighting for a military objective, hadn't met face to face with an
armed force, and this was a real opportunity for them to come out
of it all with some sort of pride in their own fighting ability. I
remember that when we got back to base I was questioned by my
CO. He could see that I was a bit upset. "You didn't do anything
contrary to your order," he told me. "You're fully covered.
Supposing an armed platoon had come up on you and you hadn't
opened fire, then you'd all have been wiped out." But somewhere
inside me I still had an awkward feeling that it wasn't fair. I don't
believe I'd have felt the same way if there'd been a fight with an
armed force that meant to finish us off. But how the hell could you
tell the difference at night?

Rachel: Asher, didn't you come across the civilian population in Jerusalem?

Asher: Well, I didn't actually fight there. But perhaps there's one episode I can tell you about. We covered the advance, after the boys had gone ahead into the city. There were a few heavy machine-guns around — a steady barrage from the hill opposite. They were firing at us all the time, and we were firing back. The planes came down on them once: then our tanks started to give it to them and they started to run. One of them didn't even bother to take his uniform off, like most of them. He just started running. He got about five hundred meters up the road, sort of out-flanking us. All our fire was directed at him. He *was* a soldier — that was clear — and he was trying to escape. I think we were justified in shooting at him. The bullets whistled round him and he still carried on running. He got away in the end. I can't exactly say I felt any qualms of conscience, but I *did* feel glad that he'd got away.

Amram: I remember something that happened on the first day, when we got to Latrun. The village was already quite empty. There was a very old man wandering round, bent over his stick. He crossed over the road. I was standing on the corner and he stopped close to me. He was quite confused. There'd been heavy shelling during the night. They were very frightened. I don't know Arabic, but all the same I said to him, just like that, "You asked for it? You got it!" Of course he didn't understand, but that was all I could say. I felt I had to say it. But it was very strange. For me, Latrun's* a place that's always been a bad spot for us, for the country, I mean. And now, suddenly we — here I am standing alongside this old dodderer and I haven't got a clue who he might have been and what he might have done a few years ago. And he's standing by my side for all the world as if nothing at all has happened.

Later, we were in position there, when a procession trooped out of the village with a chap holding a white flag up in the front. I don't know where the hell they came from, because we hadn't seen a living soul around except for two and a half miserable asses. But suddenly there they were and I must say that I found the whole picture a bit

---

* Area of heavy fighting during the War of Liberation.

heartrending. I don't know if any of the other boys felt the same way. I didn't say anything about it to anyone, I didn't talk to anyone, but it was a very depressing sight. After all, here we were suddenly invading them, whatever the reason. After a couple of hours in the village, we started driving along the road and we came across them again. They were just walking along. For a minute I asked myself. . . . I'm not just talking, because I really *did* think this way; perhaps it all sounds a bit up in the air, but I honestly felt this way. And it's interesting that as far as that old boy was concerned, although I felt sorry for him for being such a pitiful old soul, so alone, so out of it all, not understanding what was going on, at the same time I also thought to myself, who knows who he was or what he was doing when there was fighting here years ago. And then suddenly I saw that procession of pregnant women and crying kids. They hadn't really done anything. They were quiet and peaceful. Old people looking at you, begging for mercy, asking you: "What have we done? We're not to blame." You sit at your post and you can't help them, of course. I felt a whole mixture, a sort of clash of feelings: on the one hand, just because this was Latrun you felt you wanted to take revenge — I don't quite know how. On the other hand, seeing that procession. . . . I couldn't make up my mind exactly how to behave towards them, how to think about them, how to look at them. Nobody fired at them when they passed, but some of the boys threw curses at them. After all, we were quite angry and on edge, especially that first day. It was enough to shout at them in Arabic or just to glare at them. It made it quite clear how we felt.

Rachel: Did you feel that our soldiers hated them?

Amram: To some extent. We hardly talked to each other. There wasn't any opportunity, and it wasn't exactly the atmosphere for talking. It was very difficult. Some of the boys perhaps had a different attitude. What the Arabs would have done to us didn't matter to me then. It didn't interest me at all. Even though I knew they'd have slaughtered all of us. But when I saw them wandering around there, when I saw them as refugees. . . .

Lotan: I think this business of one's attitude to the enemy is connected with the education one's had. The less a man's education has some real basis, some real roots, the more he's inclined to project in his actions the same behavior he thinks the enemy would adopt. What I mean is this: some people don't behave in accordance with the dictates of their own consciences. Instead, they try to think what the other side would do. Since we knew very well how the enemy would have behaved toward us, they let themselves ignore what they knew to be right and behaved as they knew the other side would have done. The advantage our education gave us was that we had our own standards, we knew that our reactions were based on certain principles, and we behaved accordingly. The fact that the Arabs would have behaved differently to us didn't have anything to do with it. Our type of behavior was an exception to the ugliness of whe whole thing.

Asher: In Jerusalem, after we went in through the Lions'Gate, when the fighting had started inside the Old City, some of the boys had already got to the Western Wall and were dealing with snipers. All the vehicles were pulled up outside the gate and there were a lot of soldiers around. Out of the gate walked four Arabs — elderly people — and a woman. They were carrying a little girl, all wrapped up in a blanket. She was dead. They took her alongside the gate; a bit north of it, there's a cemetery. They dug a pit, put her in and covered it over. I think that was the moment of truth. Anyway it brought us back to a world of human feelings, far more than all the carry-on, the speeches and so on, which came afterwards.

Avraham: Perhaps we can get back to the question we were talking about before. Historic rights? Moral rights? Conquered territory? Liberated areas? There wasn't time to think then, that's quite clear. But how do people think about it now?

Asher: I can't tell you about other people. I can only tell you how I personally see it. For me, there's no problem. Jerusalem is ours, it's got to be ours, and it'll remain ours.

Rachel: But why? Because you conquered it?

Asher: Because I conquered it, and because I had every right to do so, because I didn't start the war. Everyone knows that Israel didn't want territorial gains. It's a good thing we had the chance, and it's a good thing we took Jerusalem and other places. There's every justification for hanging on to it all.

Rachel: From what point of view?

Asher: It's difficult to say. It's got a lot to do with history, and the awful things that happened during the War of Independence when the Jews were thrown out of the Old City, or before that, with all the Arab attacks on the Jewish Quarter there. And especially because of what they'd have done to us if they'd been the conquerors — and they'd have done it like a shot, I don't think anyone doubts that.

Lotan: I think you have to make a distinction between the problem of Jerusalem and the rest of the territories we're talking about. As long as security problems dictate that we stay in the territories beyond our previous borders, then we have to stay there. But the minute these problems are solved, then in my opinion we've no more right to stay there, at least so long as our only right is that of military success. And it's got nothing to do with who started the war, or the background against which it all began. But I wouldn't say the same about Jerusalem, because Jerusalem's got some far deeper meaning. It's something in our hearts, something to do with the way we feel. It was the source, the cornerstone of the whole Jewish people. Jerusalem really symbolizes our whole history, it's a thread that goes right through the story of our people. It was always the focus. Jerusalem's not just an idea: it's a whole world that embraces everything. . . .

Rachel: Perhaps I can ask you this: as a non-religious person, how do you feel about the holy places?

Lotan: When it comes right down to it, I think the question of emotion is the decisive one, for religious and non-religious alike. So even though I'm not religious, the Wall meant an awful lot to me. And again it was because I felt that the Wall wasn't just a wall, that it wasn't just a collection of stones, but expressed something. It's enough for me to know that it's served as an address for all Jews, whenever something hurt, whenever something oppressed them. It symbolizes everything. But to go deeper into the whole problem — that's a whole world in itself.

Avraham: Look, today's the Ninth of Av, the anniversary of the destruction of the Temple. Does that fact have any special significance for you?

Lotan: For a religious man the Ninth of Av means the

destruction of the Temple. But for me — I know that historical processes aren't crammed into a single day or even a couple of days. Everything that happens is the result of events that develop over a much longer time. So I can't take a single day and attach a specific event to it just because it happens to be a historical moment. For me, the Ninth of Av symbolizes a situation in which. . . .

Asher: That's it! It's a symbol, and only a symbol. . . .

Lotan: For me it marks a complete break in Jewish culture. I don't see it as the burning Temple, or the stones being scattered all over the place. What I see isn't exactly the religious side of it. It's not precisely what a religious person would see, but I think it's pretty much the same thing really; we just approach it from different standpoints.

From a long-term point of view, what importance do a few hundred dead have? Historically speaking, it's unimportant. The slightest earthquake finishes off thousands. It hurts. It's a high price. That's true. But if you try to weigh it up in the long run — it doesn't mean anything. It's a good educational point, it's a symbol of heroism, but it doesn't have any real historical meaning. Apart from that, my attitude is that conquest in itself doesn't give you any rights. Anyway, that's what I maintain about all the other territories. But Jerusalem is different.

As for the other territories, we've got to try to do the best for the people. Wherever it'll be best for them, whether it'll be called Jordan or Israel, that's where they have to belong. The minute the people living there suffer from the fact that they're in Israeli-held territory, then I claim we've no right to hold those areas. Of course, security considerations also come into it. It's important that we hold on to the Syrian Heights. It's important that the people in the settlements below should be able to live, because they can't go on as they were before. It's moral right that determines things. In my opinion, all this playing around with history — we were here, then before that they were and before that again it was we who were here — it just doesn't count. At the moment, what counts is who *is* there and not who *was* there.

THE WAR WAS A YARDSTICK

From a discussion in Mishmar Ha'emek

Mishmar Ha'emek, situated in Jezre'el Valley, some fifteen miles south-east of Haifa, was founded in 1926 by graduates of the Hashomer Hatzair youth movement from Poland. It was the scene of one of the decisive battles of the War of Liberation in 1948, when most of the kibbutz was destroyed during the fighting. Today its population is about 720, more than half of them born on the kibbutz.

Participants:
Menachem, member of the Editorial Board of *The Seventh Day*. *Avishai*, twenty-two, unmarried. Grandchild of two of the founding members of the kibbutz. Paratrooper; fought in Jerusalem and on the Syrian Heights. *Shmuel*, twenty-two and unmarried, is the grandson of a well-known literary figure of the late nineteenth century. He was born and educated in Mishmar Ha'emek. At eighteen he was conscripted into the air force and became a pilot in the regular army. He returned to his kibbutz a year before the Six-Day War, but remained a pilot in the reserves, and was called up as such. *Hanan*, twenty-nine, married with two children. In charge of the kibbutz poultry. Enthusiastic basket-ball player and violinist. Lieutenant in the armored unit which fought on the Syrian Heights. *Amir*, thirty, married with

107

two children and son of two of the founding members of
the kibbutz. In the Six-Day War, he served as a private in
the armored division which captured Nablus.

Shmuel: The war has completely changed my attitude to the
Arabs. I used to see them as something remote from me, but during
the war, when the Syrian television showed our pilots being lynched in
Damascus, and later, when I heard about all the other things — after all
that, today I hate them. Yes, I hate the Arabs, it's as simple as that.
After the war, my first reaction was pure jealousy of the paratroopers
and the infantry boys who'd been able to kill them with their bare
hands. In the last two days of the war, after I'd heard what had
happened to the pilots they'd captured, I just wanted to kill. Their
barbarity, their lack of the minimum of decency, their complete
failure to show any sort of respect towards enemy soldiers — it all hit
me very hard. Of course, in a way I expected it. Just a fortnight before
the war I'd read *Prisoner in Syria* — but all the same, it gave me a
terrible shock.

I think that the war brought lots of people I know to a great many
personal decisions about their future, what they're going to do,
marriage, and so on. I know that lots of things I've thought about for
years have suddenly resolved themselves; suddenly I seem to see
everything much more clearly.

Another thing: there's a quite fantastic desire for some sort of
tranquillity; nothing else, just wanting to be at peace, to be peaceful.

The war turned out to be just what we'd expected. The attacks on
their airfields, and then what followed. There was only one thing that
surprised me: the physical fear. Flying through anti-aircraft fire —
straight away, in the first flight, and before I'd even dropped the first
bomb — we ran into anti-aircraft fire, real fire and brimstone. I was
frightened. I have to admit it, I was really frightened.

It's quieter coming back. You fly over the sand, over Sinai. On the
way back you feel it wasn't so bad — especially when you realize
you're still alive and getting out of it all. But when you get back to
base and you hear that so-and-so got killed, then someone else, then
another one, that's when you feel really scared. It's not so much a
physical fear, more of an intellectual one. Later, that passes, too.

Towards the end of the war, in the last couple of days, I decided it was all a matter of luck whether I got out of it alive or not. I became quite apathetic. What I mean is, I knew it no longer depended on me, I realized that there was no statistical logic in it, and that was that.

I took the war very much to heart. Afterwards I dreamt about it now and then. And I'm glad I'm still alive. You know, I really haven't even managed to think, or even begun to work the whole business out yet.

Avishai: On the way north to the Syrian Heights we stopped somewhere to refuel and I met some boys from Katz's battalion. I didn't know that he'd been killed and I asked them about him. They told me he'd been killed. Then, when they told us to start moving up to the Heights, I said to myself, "I don't care if I get killed or wounded. Nothing matters. I'm going to take my revenge: every Arab that comes at me now will get it right in the head!"

When they decided that we weren't going in after all, God! I was so mad about it, because I felt quite simply that I was going to take a personal revenge for a friend of mine. . . .

There wasn't any special hatred during the war itself. That only came later, when you heard about the dead and wounded.

Menachem: And that shows in the way you feel about the Arabs today?

Avishai: I don't know if I hate them today, because we're so far above them. You generally hate someone you're somehow frightened of. I don't think I have any special hatred for them today. There's a certain attitude of the conqueror to the conquered, of the strong to the weak. . . .

Amir: It seems clear to me that people felt differently about the West Bank than about the Syrian Heights. There was a different attitude to the two enemies. People fought more humanely on the West Bank. But when they got up into the Syrian Heights, they hated the Syrians to the depths of their souls.

Menachem: How do you feel about going back to normal everyday life?

Hanan: There are lots of let-downs. For example, people are already saying they don't give lifts any more.

Menachem: Yes, Tel Aviv is still Tel Aviv, and in the kibbutzim they've gone back to talking about the same old problems. You sort of feel that the war didn't really do anything at all to change. . . .

Hanan: That feeling that Shmuel talked about — wanting a sort of tranquillity — that's very understandable.

Menachem: Lots of things I used to think were right before seem quite wrong now. In the fortnight before the war I was one of the few (at least in my unit) who thought the war could and should be prevented. I found out that that was nonsense. No one's going to do anything to save us. Actually, I've felt that way for a long time. After all, I've been through so many wars — even if I was a child during the Second World War, I took an active part in the other three. But all the same, I always thought that war could somehow be prevented. Today I'm sure it was necessary.

One of the most frightening things was seeing the refugees. The boys were horrified by it all. And that was something positive. But on the other hand, there were some very negative things. You saw them smashing down the doors with their rifle butts, in a sort of frenzy. They didn't take anything, they hardly touched a thing really, just broke things and threw them all over the place.

It's degrading, it degrades you as well. And you hate it. We're not professional soldiers. We just don't know how to take these things.

Shmuel: Before the war we were thirsty for battle — really longing for it. We waited and waited. They came to get me during the evening milking.

I smelt the smell of war and it was a sweet smell. We got to the base on Wednesday night and I went straight into the first formation — on alert. This was still before the war; we were terribly tense. "At the end of the week — that's when it'll happen." And then Eban went to the States.

We started worrying. Not for ourselves. We were so sure of ourselves. No. We worried about the armored corps, and the paratroopers, and all the rest of the crowd.

I'd sooner have a war now, with the borders we've got at the moment, than any state of phoney cease-fire. The present border lines really do give us maximum security.

Menachem: And what do you propose doing about the Arabs?

Shmuel: I'll tell you what to do with them. . . .

All: Go on, tell us!

Shmuel: Just a minute, take it easy, everything in good time. Anyway, as I was saying, we were thirsty for battle — and yet it just didn't happen. We were ready — there were days when the whole lot of us sat there in the mess and we thought this is it, the war! And that night, I couldn't close my eyes, I spent the whole time planning.

And when we finally went, there was a sort of tense silence.

Before the war, one of the boys always used to joke around, "You'll be killed — and you'll be killed — and you won't come back." He didn't come back himself from that first sortie.

It was such a great feeling when we took off — the whole airforce went off — and that fantastic silence. . . .

Their anti-aircraft were ready and started firing at us immediately. And then you saw their planes being blown sky high. The first two days were marvellous, despite the fear. The feeling that this was what you'd been waiting for, of giving it everything you had. All the time I felt terribly disappointed that I didn't see one of their planes in the air. I'd made my mind up that I'd shoot one down — and there wasn't even one there. Do you know what kind of anti-aircraft barrage we were up against?

After the war you began to feel sick. You didn't want the war, in fact at the end I fought only out of a sense of duty. . . . Two or three of my very best friends were killed — I felt terrible, I really hated war, and it went on for about a week afterwards. Today, I'm thirsty for battle. Come on, let's face it, it's a feeling of elation that you get.

Menachem: Listen, you kill people in a war. You destroy houses.

Shmuel: Don't you understand the difference between you and me? From the air I just don't see people dying.

Hanan: The worst feeling I had was at the beginning. I hated the war, I didn't want blood to be spilled because of tactical considerations . . . you felt that the Russians were building up tension in our area just so that they could turn around and say: "If you're going to do it in Vietnam, we'll do it here!" I said to myself: We'll fight for our country, we'll spill our blood. But to do it just because of intrigues between the Russians and the Americans? I didn't believe we'd succeed in changing the borders, and I didn't think that if we did, we'd hold on to them.

Menachem: And you believe it now?

Shmuel: I believe it now.

Avishai: We won't hold on to them long.

Hanan: One things's clear to me: we won't go back to the old borders, at least not on the Syrian Heights.

Avishai: I don't have any hard and fast ideas about it, because I think that what the Arabs on the West Bank think will be quite a decisive factor. And that's no small handful of people — there are nearly a million. I'm not a racist, but I know one thing: I read the statistics and for every thousand Arabs in the country there are sixty births as compared to twenty among the same number of Jews. You can make a simple calculation that within one generation — and that's worrying. The kibbutz is nothing to go by; today, in the cities, two children per family is the fashion. Okay, I say, very nice, so we'll have a bi-national state, but we should be the majority, otherwise it won't be a Jewish state. Look, two years ago there was all that trouble in Belgium with the Flemings, and they're not such a depressed minority, so what might happen here in the next hundred years?

Amir: The problem is — what's feasible? You can't talk about a viable peace if you're going to hold on to borders that aren't yours by international agreement. It's not just a question of not being *able* to hold on to them; I don't think we *should*. Today it's perhaps justified to hold them as a bargaining point.

Shmuel: Look here — friends of ours who've just been killed may well have been killed by the people we didn't finish off in the Sinai Campaign. People you didn't kill now may well kill us in the next round.

Amir: Shmuel, there's one thing you've got to understand: people are born and people die. A parent dies and when his son grows up he in his turn becomes a soldier. There'll be another round, he'll kill someone, you'll kill him. If, at some stage, you can break this chain, by ceasing to kill — then perhaps there'll be a chance of peace. Otherwise there isn't any chance. No chance at all.

Shmuel: You won't get peace by following humane practices. I'm quite sure that the Arabs really hate us. Look, a crowd of Arabs near Cairo who'd never seen a Jew in their lives grabbed hold of an Israeli pilot and lynched him. Even before the war had properly begun. Do you know what that means? That's what propaganda does. There's one saying I keep remembering: all's fair in love and war. Do you think they'll love you just because you didn't kill them? I know for a fact that there were lots of cases where they surrendered with their hands up, and when our boys turned their backs for a moment the Egyptians whipped out guns and shot them. That's how it is, because that's the Arab mentality. You want me to tell you exactly what it was they did to the body of one of our pilots? They just don't know the meaning of the world humanity!

As far as the future's concerned, there are two different answers. One: a beautiful peace, with trade relations and secure peaceful borders. And there's another view: that we keep the borders we've just won, which are good for our security, and put a military government into the West Bank. Perhaps I'm being cynical, but I think it can be done.

Amir: I don't want just twenty years of peace, I'm not interested in a mere twenty years of quiet. I'd rather there was a war in another ten years — and then a permanent stable peace. Better that way than a war every ten years and never peace.

Shmuel: I don't understand how you can see Arab soldiers and not kill them. . . .

Hanan: It wasn't just that we didn't kill them, but when we came across their casualties we saw to their wounds and brought them—

Shmuel: But they were prisoners. I'm not talking about prisoners. Soldiers have to kill. . . .

Amir: We're not talking about war. But we are talking about giving them water, about attending to their wounded, and about the fact that you're a human being and that it's not possible—

Shmuel: I remember coming back after the war. You say everyone was very upset here. But it's not true. They were all a bit upset, but I was in the depths of depression, utterly finished. And I got back here, and, you know how it was? I was astounded. Two of the boys had been killed and people were carrying on normally. I was completely broken up. I remember asking someone: "How come everyone's so cheerful here?" And now, all this business with the political parties and all that stuff — I tell you, I'm just glad to get up in the morning and go off and work till I'm bone-tired, and talk to people a bit, and get irritable, and enjoy myself a bit, and that's it. . . .

Amir: When it comes down to it, the war was a sort of yardstick for everything. I must confess that I've got different ideas about all sorts of things now. If you're talking about politics, then it seems to me that what's going on now is the absolute height of pettiness. I used to think the same way before, but now I'm incapable of understanding it. I think everything that's going on at the moment is only fractionally on a higher level than all the pettiness that surrounded the coalition negotiations. Shmulik said that he was shocked by the off-hand manner of the people at home. In my case it was just the opposite. Perhaps it's a question of age. I was simply dying to know what was going on in Mishmar Ha'emek. News of home became a real symbol for me.

Avishai: One person's away in the army, someone else is doing his duty back home. In just the same way as Jerusalem the Golden became a symbol of the war, so this continuity of our life here was a symbol for me. I came back on Monday, two days after the war. Suddenly I could see a sort of tension in everybody. And they told me: we haven't heard from this one, we've got news of so-and-so. Then I knew that the worst place of all to be was at home. Horrible. . . .

Menachem: The happiness they felt about those who came back safe and sound was greater than the mourning for those who didn't, despite all the sadness. They were saddened by the wounded, and there wasn't anything you could do to comfort their families. But the joy they felt about those who came back! When a hundred men go off to fight out of a big family of four hundred members, it's just not possible to spoil the joy of their return.

Avishai: I think I was the first back after the war. I couldn't understand why everybody came out and shook my hand. . . . You might have thought I'd won the war single-handed.

Amir: I spoke to a boy from our unit today. "Hallo," I said, "How are things?" "Listen," he said, "it's awfully difficult to get back to everyday life!" He was only a mechanic. "I don't know what's going on," he said. I told him not to worry, none of our lot had been able to get over it for a week after they'd gone back to work — and that's a fact. It was the same for everyone.

WITH MIXED FEELINGS

From a discussion in Mishmar Hanegev. Interviewer: David Alon

Asher: A lot of Egyptians were roaming round among the dunes. We were almost out of water but, nevertheless, our boys gave the Egyptians, who were almost dying of thirst, drinks from their water-bottles. They'd been wandering around, over the hills and through the dunes, since the first day of the war, and they were almost completely dazed. They didn't have any strength left, so they'd decided to come back on to the road and they were wandering along in despair. We'd been ordered to help them as much as we could and told to aid them in getting to the other side of the Canal.

I remember when we were going along the road towards Kantara we saw an elderly woman walking along with a child in her arms. Her husband was walking alongside and there was a second small child trailing along behind. We were travelling along with the unit's reconnaissance squad, which had suffered a lot of casualties during the war. They'd fought hard. We passed by the couple and the kids, and as we passed there was a feeling that maybe we should take them along — at least that's the way I felt, and later I found that lots of others felt that way too. The first jeep stopped, reversed and picked up the woman and child. Then I saw that everybody had been asking themselves the same questions. There wasn't a lot of room in the jeep, it was packed with stuff. Nevertheless, we took the woman, the child, the husband and the other kid. Everyone produced sweets and gave them to the kids. They gave them all water; the kids were keener on the sweets than the water.

Two kilometers along we came across a repair unit half-track with only the driver in it. "Here, boys, what are you doing?" he said. "I need help, they shot at me, and now you're giving Egyptians a lift." The moment he spoke and we got out to find out who'd been shooting at him, the same question flashed through our minds: "Were we really educated properly? Were we acting in accordance with outdated principles? Or is this a humane, rational way to behave?" You look at this blond lad of eighteen and you think that he could have been killed in his half-track, and then you suddenly turn around and look at these people, at these Egyptians you're dragging along with you and you say to yourself, "What are you doing it for? Why do you have to be so humane and kind-hearted?" And nonetheless, you go on doing it.

These doubts continued to plague me after the war, too. Let's be frank about it. I saw those wretched people streaming along the road, poor miserable souls, carrying their bundles, all sorts of bundles. They were soldiers, each with a little pack on his back, bare-foot, some of them already with sores on their feet which they'd bound up with rags. There were some who could scarcely stand — and they were thirsty. One of them urinated into his water-bottle and then drank it. It's difficult to believe. I looked to see if it was water or really urine, and it was urine. Until that moment, this had been something I'd only read about in books. I began to think about the Jews wandering through Europe and other places. One immediately rejects this idea. God in heaven, how can one compare the two things! Deep inside of you, you still have the feeling that it isn't quite like the wanderings and sufferings of the Jews. I think that these doubts and questionings went on for a long time: should we or shouldn't we help them? You see a soldier, not such a youngster, trudging along keeping himself upright with difficulty. He looks like a drunkard (that was one of the signs of sunstroke or dehydration — we can recognize these symptoms among the soldiers), and as you pass him you know that if you leave him he'll drop down dead. You give him a little water, a little food — he'll rest a bit and perhaps he'll live. It was clear at this stage that we weren't going to have enough water for all the Egyptian soldiers: it had to be rationed between the older ones, the weak, and the wounded. It was a problem deciding who was going to get it. We helped them as much as we could. But each time we helped them we heard of some incident. A fellow would come along and say: "They're shooting at me over there, come and help!" And you went and saw that those same wretches on whom you'd just had pity were among those who'd started shooting now.

We were approaching an oasis. A large number of Egyptian soldiers came out of a big house, formed ranks in surprisingly good order, put their hands up — and that was that. Suddenly, I noticed that one of them could scarcely stand. He was on the point of collapse and had an infected wound in his right leg. I called him over and told him to lie down (we hadn't managed to have a wash all through the war. Now, of course, it was after the war, but we were still filthy. I was fully armed, and none of the Egyptians knew that I was a doctor; not even all our boys knew). As I called him over, there was a sudden silence among the Egyptians. They thought he was going to be killed, or if not that — then something pretty serious. Then they saw me put him down on the floor, open my pack and take out bandages, alcohol, and clean the wounds and try to do as much as possible for him. Suddenly they saw something that they didn't understand. An Israeli officer kneeling on the ground, attending to an Egyptian private who was filthy, full of pus; not simply an officer attending to a private, but an enemy officer taking care of his enemy. This was something completely beyond their understanding, and just as previously there'd been dead silence among them, now they suddenly shouted: "Ya'ish Israel!"*

On the one hand it was disgusting, on the other hand this was perhaps the only occasion that I felt some sort of sincerity in this cry which I'd heard before. I'd never seen a scene quite like it, and I had mixed feelings about it. It was disgusting, perhaps, the way they were behaving without any national pride; but on the other hand you could see they weren't used to being treated like human beings. We tried as much as we could to help and attend to their wounds, but even as we did it, we had mixed feelings about it.

David: What did it feel like to be a victor?

*Long Live Israel.

Asher: Actually you didn't have to look at it that way. You didn't sit down and say, "I'm a victor." All sorts of other feelings came into it. I was very busy. For example, I had to identify the dead — I can't even begin to tell you how terrible that was. When you knew the ones who were killed, and you saw them, mutilated and charred in the most horrific way. And that's what I was doing. Again, unfortunately, emotionally you can't only concentrate on one aspect of things, you're torn between all sorts of different duties. Anyway, it was my duty then to deal with the dead who were hardly identifiable.

David: What went on inside you when you saw these boys whom you'd known?

Asher: First of all, it hurts. In the beginning it's difficult to believe. You'd seen them just a little while before, perhaps a day previously or even a few hours before. And now you saw them stretched out and sometimes externally they looked untouched, all in one piece. And then it was very difficult to believe that that was the way it had all ended. It couldn't be. I must tell you the truth: I always used to take a good look, perhaps they really weren't dead, even though logically I knew that they must be. I used to tell myself that I was being a fool. But that's one of the feelings: the feeling of disbelief. Then comes the anguish, and that's unbearable. Looking after the casualties presented no problem. I don't have to tell you about all the horrors — shattered legs, arms, whatever you want. But that wasn't a problem, I'm used to it. Perhaps in the first moment — but after a quarter of an hour I forgot all about it and worked automatically. Perhaps it's a defense mechanism, it may very well be so, this working automatically. But when you see boys you knew, it's very difficult, very difficult indeed. Sometimes you felt so choked up, you couldn't talk. If only I could have cried, it would have been better, but I couldn't.

David: Now, two months later, how do you feel about the dead? Are the memories still as alive, or have you managed to bury them?

Asher: I still feel the same way about the ones I really knew. Each time I remember them I still get that same heavy, dull feeling of pain. At the time, I felt the same anguish about those I hadn't known, but today it's. . . .

David: How did you react to the Egyptian dead?

Asher: The full horror of war was really borne in on me when I saw the mounds of Egyptian dead. Enormous great mounds of them. Young and old mixed up together. And then, I don't know how to explain it, there was some sort of inner compulsion to go along and see if perhaps there wasn't a picture to be found on one of them, a child, a wife, something of that sort. But if you had found it, you would have left it immediately, you didn't want to touch, to have anything to do with it all, as if you personally weren't to blame, as if to say, "I didn't do it." I don't think there's anything out of the ordinary about this feeling. In fact, you felt that everything that had happened was somehow all their fault.

As for the present, the mood changes as far as individuals are concerned. For example, if there was a wounded Egyptian soldier, I'd feel about him — even though I didn't know him — just as I feel about the patients I treat in the hospital.

A LOUSY FEELING

From a discussion in Gat

Shlomit: How did it feel being conquerors in Gaza? How did the boys react to it?

Dan: It's an absolutely lousy feeling being in a conquering army.

Amnon: In Sinai — in the last round — I was in Gaza. One picture sticks in my mind. We were going along the main street and the whole lot of them, I mean the locals, were standing in the doorways clapping their hands slowly and steadily, like this. It was an unpleasant thing to see — it reminded me of all the films I've seen about conquering armies. A really stinking feeling.

Dan: This time the situation was quite different from the Sinai Campaign. This time Gaza fought hard and suffered a lot. And there was fighting in the town itself. When we took it, it was desolate. Everything was closed. Afterwards we got ourselves organized — went out on lots of patrols — there were curfews. It was a lousy feeling. I remember, as soon as they told us our objective was to capture Gaza, spontaneously, right that minute, most of the men said: "Give us anything else to do, any other positions to take. We're prepared to do anything rather than be policemen!" We just didn't want to carry out police duties.

Shlomit: Did this unwillingness show up in your behaviour there? Did people do the necessary minimum and nothing else?

Dan: Most of them did act that way. But there were some who felt very much at ease in that sort of job. As Amnon pointed out, most of them were those who hadn't managed to see any fighting, or weren't so keen on fighting. That type had an access of confidence, they suddenly considered themselves tough when they got there. And there were a few, mainly those with inferiority complexes, who found this a good opportunity to play top dog.

I remember once, we were carrying out a search in some section or other of the town. There was a crowd of people following some distance behind the soldiers. Suddenly a woman appeared out of the crowd. She had a lot of little children with her, and she ran to the bus, began to cry, grabbed hold of me, and tried to hang on to the side of the bus. She said she had seven children — they were there with her. Her husband was the family's sole breadwinner. If we sent him away to Egypt, she said, there'd be no one to support the family and they'd die of hunger. He was in the bus we were evacuating them in. It was a horrible episode. You could see that the boys were thoroughly shaken by it. Nobody was able to go and get rid of her, no one felt up to it. They just stood around and felt terrible. In the end, I went up to her and told her to go away. Finally, an officer with a higher rank than mine arrived, we talked it over, and took her husband out of the bus and let him go. He began to move away with his family — perhaps he thought we were letting him go only in order to get hold of him again. When he was about twenty meters away, he realized that we were really setting him free. He began to kiss and hug his children. It was a very touching scene, afterwards, to see how he embraced them; very moving.

Later, the second-in-command of the brigade came over and asked what I thought of it all. "I'm only asking for one thing," I told him. "Get us out of here. It's a horrible job, really horrible. I'm a kibbutznik. It's not for us, we haven't been brought up to it. We haven't been trained for it." Perhaps the army should train people for this type of thing so that they'll be up to it. We shouldn't have to do this sort of thing. It was a difficult period because there weren't any regulations yet. A little later an ordinance was issued which distinguished between a state of war and a ceasefire. It's not a good feeling. Above all it destroys human dignity. It destroys the semblance of man. I felt it happening to me, felt myself losing my respect for people's lives. A fortnight after the capture of Gaza, I was with another officer just near Ashkelon. We saw a cart travelling along the road and holding up all the traffic. And he said to me: "Isn't it a queer feeling? This is the first time we don't have to push on and kill. Suddenly you've got to stop. It's a human being – and you mustn't touch him, you mustn't kill." It was such a dramatic change.

NINETEEN LOST YEARS

From a discussion in Hulda. Interviewer: Amos Oz

Amos: Obviously you don't need to tell us again how much you hated the feeling of being the conqueror, but what about the people under you: immigrants from North Africa, people who'd been in the country for years, people from immigrant towns? Do you think they enjoyed being conquerors?

Shai: I don't think I can link it to different classes or particular parts of the country. I think that here and there in the battalion there were a few people who got some satisfaction from the whole business. Of course anyone's glad not to have lost the war. But some of them actually seemed to enjoy dealing with the whole business of sorting them out, deciding who should go to Kantara and who should stay at home.

Amos: Before the war we all read a lot about the refugees, and we talked about it, discussed it in the youth movement and so on. You've been in a town where there were lots of refugees. Did you feel involved in it in any way? Did it affect you somehow?

Shai: It's a very complex business. When the refugees get their rations from UNRWA, they come in "districts" — the districts they once lived in. Each day it's the turn of a different district. One day the ones from Beersheba come to get their food, the next day the ones from Zarnuga, next from Rehovot. I remember that the first time I asked one of them where he came from, he replied: "From Beersheba." Then I asked another and he said he was from Zarnuga. I was furious.

123

Amos: Why?

Shai: I couldn't grasp it. Nineteen years had passed. Today I do understand. This was their whole existence. They were living an illusion all the time. How dare they say that they're from Zarnuga? From Beersheba? From Rehovot? They still live grouped according to the places they once lived in — the Sheikh of Zarnuga, the Sheikh of Rehovot — in their refugee camps. It made me very angry.

Amos: And now?

Shai: Now I understand them completely. First of all, they kept a spark of hope that they would return. I think this was a result of that waiting. All the Arab states inflamed their feelings and hopes and kept them isolated. They didn't let them assimilate into the other Arab states. One part of Rafiah belongs to Palestine, the other part is Egyptian. People living on different sides of the town have different papers; there's a border, and people from the Gaza Strip couldn't leave it for Sinai. They lived in hope for nineteen years and now I can't feel angry with them. I can only pity them. In effect, those nineteen years were wasted. Completely wasted. Nineteen lost years, in inhuman conditions, with hopes that were never fulfilled.

Amos: Didn't you have some sort of feeling of respect for people who remained faithful to their homes and their ancestral birthplaces? The same sort of theme runs right through our own education. We've got the same background. We, too, have been brought up to keep faith with a place, with a home, with the soil of a lost land. Didn't you ever connect the two?

Shai: Today when I try to analyze it for myself, I say that on the one hand it's quite obvious: their tragedy really is a tragedy. We've never tried to conceal the fact. In my opinion, there's nothing to prevent them living with us today. The treatment of the refugee problem has already become a political issue, but there's also the more fundamental issue of how you can create some contact between people, between the two peoples. Yet, I don't see any reason — even today — why there shouldn't be Arabs in Zarnuga or Beersheba who look on it as their birthplace.

SHAMEFUL—THAT'S THE WORD FOR IT

From a discussion in Yif'at. Interviewer: Rachel Halprin

Aharon: Whenever we took a place, we were always relieved by people from another brigade who were generally older than us. Every place we left, they followed us in. What grated so much was the difference between them and us.

We were sitting right up on the walls just before they relieved us in the Old City. The jeeps were spread out along by the walls and they were standing below us. We saw a few men moving around in the village of Shiloah down below. We didn't know why they were roaming around like that. Afterwards we saw that they had sacks on their backs. I took a rifle from one of the boys and began shooting, not at them, but just in front of them. They got a terrific shock. We shouted down: "Bring everything you've got!" So they emptied the sacks by the wall, and we shot again — just missing their hands — and they scuttled back to their camp.

Though it's difficult to say that there was no looting at all in our crowd. I know that they took cigarettes and that an order was given to break into a grocery store so that the boys could get something to eat. For example, there was a platoon quartered in the Ambassador Hotel in the Old City. Their CO, who was killed later, Giora from Tel Amal, said to them: "Boys, you're not taking anything!" No one took a thing, apart from some food, even then they didn't take more than they really needed. I think that all in all the whole question of looting depends an awful lot on the officers.

125

Our CO really took a strong line over it. For example, here's a story that illustrates my point. This CO of ours — he was born on a *moshav*. When the war was over, we came back to Jerusalem. We made a trip through the whole of the West Bank and we had just pulled up somewhere — they were telling us about the Dotan Valley. We got off the buses and sat down near an orchard and a vegetable field to hear a talk about the area. Then we saw a jeep with an officer in it, about to pass us. But it was too much for him to pass us on the road! So he went into the field over the vegetables and through the orchard. This CO told some of us to move our vehicles forward and block him off. There was an officer in the jeep. He started to look for the person in charge of us. At last he found out who it was — talked to him — started to plead and then to threaten. We didn't move. And it wouldn't have taken much for the boys to have beaten him up. Because really, even though this was enemy territory, Arab peasants' land, and the devil knows what else — and during the war, tanks had come across this way — even so, now, when we saw that he was driving over a field, it mattered a lot to us.

Hagai: I'll tell you an odd story about looting. In my company we had a religious CO from Kibbutz Tirat Zvi. On the first day, after we'd gone through Jenin, we moved on to the objective and found all the Jordanians had gone. We dug ourselves in there because there were reports that they might mount a mortar barrage, and we stayed there until later that night. Then we went down into the village. While we were up there the administrative personnel had gone into the village. When we got to the base we found the storemen and the cooks — all that lot — absolutely rolling in things that they'd looted from the village. Wrapped up in carpets, women's jewellery — it was a horrible scene. At that moment, everybody thought: for God's sake, what do they need all that stuff for? Then, I remember, the CO got the whole company together, formed them all up in a semi-circle and stuck all the storemen and cooks in the middle along with their loot. Then he started quoting them chapter and verse of the Bible: "Thou shalt not plunder! Thou shalt not . . . ! Thou shalt not . . . !" It was really impressive. After he'd finished, one of the storemen got up and asked him, "What about that bit in the Bible: 'And when Jehosophat and his men came to take away the spoil,' what do you make of that, then?" So the CO began to explain that Rashi,* commenting on the verse, says that it should be taken to mean that a conquering army takes only what it really needs during the fighting. That's to say, if they have no food, and since they have to live somehow, then they take what they need, but nothing more than that — no property. I stood in a corner and I thought to myself, "What a peculiar army this is, standing there and listening to all this stuff." But there really was something in it.

After that parade, there was no more looting in our company. No one touched any booty. The example set up by the CO and the officers influenced them all.

Let me mention one other small point that occurred to me following on from what Asher said. After the war, the brigade had a parade before we all went home. It took place in Jenin, in a big empty space where we were all formed up in open formation, with the cars parked nearby. Between the parking area and the parade area, there was a field of cucumbers. It was completely fenced in and signs had been posted there saying: "Mines!" Actually there weren't any mines there at all. How do I know? Because we saw soldiers ignore the sign and wander around the field. What impressed me so much was that we'd posted mine-warning signs there simply to stop the soldiers from treading all over the cucumbers.

Amram: Another thing, I remember. It made me shudder; why did I feel so disgusted? At the sheer lunacy of it. Straight away they had to parade around in Legionnaire's trousers, wear their *keffiahs*: really sick. Really — perhaps shameful is the best word for it. I told myself: "In another hour I've got to attack alongside of him, and here he doesn't even belong in the war at all. We don't belong together...!"

Lotan: We went into a village, which was an antiquities center. We were among the first who went in to Sebastiah. You could feel that the whole village was stunned. The village notables, and the people in charge of the antiquities, came up to us and tried to invite us into a restaurant. "Help yourselves, please. Have a drink. Take some postcards — as many as you want!" So we said: "Okay, but

*Medieval Rabbinical commentator on the Bible.

only on condition that you let us pay the full price for anything we have."

Rachel: What do you mean by "we"? Do you mean the soldiers said this on their own initiative?

Lotan: Look, the boys who were there were rather special. A small unit — a really fantastic crowd. And, I repeat: it hasn't got anything to do with whether they're kibbutzniks or town boys. In this case I wouldn't make the distinction that some of you made. We said: "We'll be happy to have a drink. We'll be happy to have postcards, but only if we pay." I remember that we paid five *agorot* for each card. We didn't know the exact price, but we reckoned that was about the price we'd have paid in Tel Aviv. Later, an English-speaking tourist guide in the village came over and said something like: "When I see this type of behavior I realize how much we were fed false propaganda." Coming from him, this was like being given a victory award!

Asher: Tell me, do we owe them anything? What's all this about paying?

Lotan: We looked on them as civilians. . . .

Asher: Huh, I think you really were a special unit. . . .

Hagai: I don't think one should be so impressed by the sort of pretentious words you heard from that guide. There were things like that wherever we went. Everywhere it was the same sort of thing: "Nasser can go to God knows where . . . and Hussein can go to somewhere else . . . They all lied to us." I always forgot that only two weeks earlier those same people had taken part in mass demonstrations in Jenin and Shechem and all those other places. They'd demonstrated against us and they'd nearly thrown Hussein out because he wasn't tough enough.

Lotan: You've got to differentiate between lip service — you understand? The guide was sincere.

Rafael: We were in a reconnaissance unit, and we'd been pushing forward all the time — actually, right up to the end of the war we were tensed up for an encounter with the enemy, and right up to the end we didn't take a thing we didn't need. Actually we came out of it all pretty poorly off — we needed certain equipment to keep the vehicles on the move. But the minute the war was over, there was a sort of outbreak — not a gradual thing. We finished up in Syria, and there the problem was a bit different. I don't think we'd have reached this stage of things in Jordan, because as I see it, in my unit we didn't hate the Jordanians. Me neither! I did what I did under orders, not because of hatred. But it wasn't like that in Syria. Anyone in our crowd who tried to take anything went straight to detention, there weren't any half-measures.

ON CONSCIENCE AND MORALITY

From a discussion in Giv'at Hashlosha. Interviewer: Yariv Ben-Aharon

Yariv: From the newspapers it seems as if there's a sort of moral arrogance in the country: we fought the enemy because it was vital to do so — but we don't hate them. But does the reality of the war, as we see it now, three months later, bear out the truth of this attitude? Weren't there some moments when there really was a feeling of hatred for the enemy?

Zvi: Right throughout the war, I felt an awful repugnance about pulling the trigger. There were times when it was almost absurd; times when it was absolutely essential and when I still hesitated. I'm convinced that it had nothing to do with fear; it was simply an unwillingness to kill. On the first day, when we crossed the border, we saw an Egyptian jeep in retreat, and a tank firing at it. They were quite right to be firing at it, and yet the first thing I said to the others was, "Why's that idiot firing? They're not firing at us!" I just didn't see any justification for killing or shooting unless there was real danger. And I had the same feeling all the way through the war.

Ehud: That feeling of hate that you sometimes have towards people — that awful feeling of being unable to control yourself — I didn't feel that sort of hatred at any point during the war. You felt that both you and the enemy were taking part in some clash of forces on a much more generalized scale. When he fired at you or you fired back, it wasn't meant personally — even if you did aim specifically at him. You didn't know the man. I know that later on,

130

when we started collecting the documents and photographs, pictures of women and children, we felt awful.

Yariv: Look, there are masses of descriptions in books about how the Russian soldiers really loathed the German invaders . . . hated them. And they didn't know them personally either.

Ehud: They hated them because of everything that had gone on before, because of the whole background. They hated them because they'd actually seen the awful things the enemy had done.

Hillel: There was a different sort of hatred for the Arabs during the War of Independence.

Yigal: Yes, they hated them because they'd wiped out villages, murdered, killed and raped, they'd done every horrible thing that can be done in a war. They had a good idea of everything that had gone on before. You can't say the same was true in our case. There haven't been any incidents between us and the Arabs bad enough to make us hate them.

After we'd cleaned up the whole of the sector, right up to Ismailia, there was talk of a commando unit at large in the area, and this was in addition to the tens of thousands of routed Egyptians, many of them still armed, who were also wandering around there. Our aim was to outflank them and herd them towards Kantara so that they'd be forced to cross the border. In no case — and I emphasize this — in no case, with just one exception, did we open fire, even though we were travelling in jeeps between hundreds of armed soldiers who, in most cases, didn't put their hands up, but crouched behind the bushes out of sheer fear. They lay there, and you didn't know if they'd fire or not. Each time, we'd go up and order them to put their hands up and hand over their weapons — and not a shot was fired.

Yariv: All of us agree that both our fighting spirit and our strength in this war sprang from the certain knowledge that the Arabs were bent on a war of annihilation. In other words, basically there wasn't any difference between the Germans, who did what they did, and the Arabs, whose intentions were quite clear. Didn't we expect a war of annihilation? If they'd won, wouldn't we all have been wiped out? How can you say that there was going to be a war of annihilation and at the same time also say that our army's strength wasn't based on hatred?

Yigal: What we're talking about here is how soldiers felt towards the enemy. They could read in the press about the Arab leaders' desire for a war of annihilation. They could also understand that the Arabs facing them weren't exactly fond of us, or even that they hated us and that they really intended to wipe us out. But the feeling wasn't one of hatred for the Arabs.

I don't think anyone believed in it or thought about it as a concrete possibility. We knew they weren't strong enough or capable enough for it. After the war, when we saw them without arms, hungry, thirsty, at their last gasp — then it was pity, not hatred. And during the war there was a feeling — a sort of feeling of superiority, sometimes even carried to the point of endangering human life.

Yariv: Why do you talk about "battle discipline"? You know, in the days of the Haganah and the Palmach there used to be a concept which they called "purity of arms." Is that the idea you're driving at?

Yigal: "Battle discipline" is a technical term. In the Haganah and the Palmach, the morality of war was part of their background; they thought about it, discussed it, were educated towards it. What I'm talking about — especially in the armoured corps and the Air Force — is more of a technical term. For the officer who gives the order to open fire; this is "battle discipline." And the same goes for the gunner who fires. "Purity of arms" — that's more suited to the individual soldier facing his enemy with a rifle. It's not appropriate to this last war.

Yariv: I thought you were coming to the conclusion that there couldn't be any such thing as "purity of arms" in a war such as this last one.

Yigal: I didn't say that. I just want to say: "pure" — you can talk about arms being justly borne, you can talk about them being defensive weapons, but you can't talk about them being pure. What can be pure about them when there's blood and____?

Hillel: But the fact that the war was fought for some principle makes it pure. In which case, the arms are pure, too. Of course there's dirt wherever you go. The borderline between murder and killing in war is very blurred.

Yariv: Tell me, Hillel, don't you think that people went along with all the killing during the war partly because of a feeling that this wouldn't be the last one? It influences your feelings when in fact you know that you're going to fight this army and this people again. Don't you think that knowing this negates all the usual rules of the game: first the war, then prisoners, then a cease-fire and so on . . . ?

Yigal: You don't play around during a war, you don't make calculations like that. There were Egyptians soldiers wandering around there fully armed who hadn't surrendered. Whether you shoot them or not — sometimes that's a matter for the individual soldier to weigh up. It has no connection with that idea of "purity of arms." It may well happen that in just a second he'll find himself face to face with an Egyptian soldier who'll manage to surprise him. I know of several cases in which tank commanders were wounded or killed by wounded Egyptian soldiers firing at them. Sometimes we had to attack the Egyptians just so that we could prevent them from making surprise attacks on us later. Of course, I'm not talking about soldiers who came out with their hands up. The dividing line's very blurred. In cases like these you don't start conferring with other people. Everything you've been inculcated with — none of it stands in any sort of relationship to what you feel when you actually take part in the fighting. Your standards change. As far as that's concerned, you can't discuss it with people who've not taken part themselves. And that's it. You can neither justify nor blame someone for firing or not firing.

Hillel: That concept of "purity of arms" doesn't exist today as strongly as one knew it from the stories of the War of Independence. There are precise orders — what to shoot at and what not to shoot at. And that's it.

Someone shot a dog and killed it. It made me feel sick. And the corpses — you certainly don't hate your enemy. You don't even know who he is; you don't care. You don't see him at all: You fight in a tank — in a block of steel. Now, as far as "purity of arms" is concerned, I think we were too careful. We tried to be too humane, and it cost us quite a bit.

Ehud S.: As far as I'm concerned, the calculation is quite a clear one: one isn't prepared to endanger oneself. I don't want to say that

I always worked on this basis, but sometimes I regretted not having done so. I had all sorts of reservations: I couldn't fire at an unarmed man, or at a man who looked beaten. There were a lot of people in our unit who were wounded and killed by Egyptians soldiers who left their positions with their weapons raised above their heads. There wasn't any time to bother with them, so we left them. And they went back into their positions and carried on firing at us. Sometimes they even fired at the last tanks in the column. Now, coming back to this question of "purity of arms," I fought in a built-up area, in Khan Yunis — and that's where it really shows up. In the desert, it was quite clear that it was one army facing another. But in our case — in a town — I remember one episode when, in the middle of the attack, a company officer suddenly reported to the battalion CO that he'd gone into a room and found eight wounded children there, would the CO send someone immediately to get them out. It made a tremendous impression on me. I almost shouted at the battalion CO, "Tell your officer that he's an idiot! Hasn't he got anything better to bother about?" At the same time, as far as our concept of "purity of arms" was concerned, I think that's clear enough proof. I might add that this didn't occur when we were winning, but at a point when we weren't able to advance, right in the middle of the fighting.

Hillel: Don't you think that in the light of modern warfare conditions it would be an idea to cancel out that concept of "purity of arms"? Couldn't we forget it, and stop confusing ourselves?

Zvi: It's a concept that counts as far as a man's life is concerned. The thing to do is to redefine it.

Yariv: Perhaps we are talking about a concept that's altogether out of place. There are two words used in this idea — "arms" and "purity." The whole concept belonged to a period when the arms were different. Let's see if you can still associate today's arms with the idea of purity.

Zvi: Our personal weapons were hardly used. Okay, so the concept of "purity of arms" is also a relative one. Perhaps one could say that today, because of the developed state of arms, the relativity of the concept is even more pronounced than before. But the concept itself still does exist. You can't do away with it.

Hillel: It's expressed differently now. Today, when you've got to direct an artillery barrage on an objective, then the concept of "purity of arms" dictates that you don't shell a settled civilian area.

Ehud: This is war on a larger scale, involving greater destruction.

Zvi: I'd put it another way: as weapons become more sophisticated, so this concept takes on an increased significance. As weapons develop, they become capable of wreaking total annihilation. It gets more difficult to pick out specific targets, and that's when the whole thing becomes far more significant. You have to weigh things far more carefully because weapons of this sort kill far more people.

Yariv: Perhaps you can say that in modern warfare the moral considerations are decided by far fewer people. For example, the decision as to which objective to shell. It's not every soldier that has to decide this. Yet all the same, there wasn't a single soldier who didn't, at some stage, have to decide, to choose, that's to say to make some sort of moral decision — to choose between different possibilities of action. If what we're talking about here is a moral question of choosing between different lines of action and attitude, then it seems that in this war, quick and modern though it was, the soldier, for all that, was still not turned into a mere technician. He had to take decisions that were of real significance.

JUSTICE AND STRENGTH

Discussion in Geva. Interviewer: Amos Oz

Geva was founded in 1921, in the Valley of Jezre'el, by pioneers from Russia and Poland. It is a classic example of the *kvutza* — the small, intimate kibbutz which emphasized group solidarity as one of its main aims, and the return to the soil as a moral principle. Today it numbers about nine hundred, but in many respects retains its close-built social structure.

Participants:
Nachman, forty, father of seven children. For the past ten years he has taught in the joint secondary school of the kibbutzim in the Harod Valley, and he is now its headmaster. He is a welfare officer in the army, and served as such during the war. *Uri*, thirty-seven, father of three children, the eldest of whom is eighteen years old. For many years he has been in charge of the sheep in his kibbutz, and he works as a youth leader in his spare time. In the Six-Day War he was in a commando unit. *Eli*, thirty-seven, father of two children, is in charge of the citrus grove in Geva. He is a member of the Histadrut Central Committee. In the war, he was a tank officer. His young brother was killed on the Syrian Heights. *Gili*, thirty-seven, father of three children (one born in May

1967), was born and educated in Geva. He is in charge of the large dairy herd and acts as a youth leader in his spare time. During the Six-Day War he fought in a tank regiment which captured Nablus, and then fought on the Syrian Heights.

Nachman: Anyone who can't kill the enemy, who can't destroy a house, had just better stay at home and not go to war. Of course it's all the most dreadful experience. Destruction itself is a horrifying experience. Certainly for those of us who all these years have been concerned with building, with construction. When you see such a vast force as that, entirely directed towards destroying houses, wiping out villages and killing people, when the tanks roll across the fields and wreck the plantations and blow up irrigation pipes . . . the whole business of war is terrible. And you've got friends who are being killed all around you.

During the war, everything takes on a different significance. A man's life has a different value. A man I spoke to only two hours earlier — suddenly he's no longer alive. And I find that it doesn't horrify me so much. "That's it, that's the way the war goes — that's the natural course of events," I think. The conclusion I come to then is that we're at war, and that men at war live according to the rules of war.

When people ask whether we came back happy, or whether the country was or wasn't happy — I don't know if people were happy after the War of Independence. Who was happy then? Who was happy after Sinai? I remember that when the State was proclaimed, there was happiness and joy in the streets, yet it was quiet, because the war started immediately afterwards. It seems to me that there's a general undertone of sadness for those who died. There's scarcely anyone who wasn't connected in some way with someone who was killed.

Amos: There's another undercurrent, too: that we did to the enemy what they planned to do to us. Why don't you think about that aspect?

Nachman: Yes, I'll talk about that, too. It's not a question of being happy about it, because we're not a people that glories in war.

To the extent that there is a question of battle readiness, or what they call security-mindedness — I don't know. Perhaps it's different with some people, or maybe even with some political parties, perhaps there are some people who do see war as an ideology. But for us, the need for continual preparedness, the possibility that war may break out at any moment, is all simply a a matter of facing reality. And that's the sad part of the whole business.

If you want to put it this way, then all Zionism is terribly tragic right from the beginning. The way the Jews came here, the way our people came back to the land of our fathers. The only way our people could survive involved a clash with the people who were living in this country. There are Arab villages all around our area — Nuris and Maazaar and Komi — and they're not there any more. Do I have to put up with qualms of conscience all the time? Do I have to cry the whole time because they're not here any more? No! The return of our people to its land met with opposition from those who lived here at the time. It didn't come about through any agreements. The whole business was determined by force, not by agreements, or goodwill.

When we were talking about the war in the dining-hall on Friday, I said that for me one of the toughest of my experiences was coming to a certain intellectual conclusion: right goes along with might. In other words, right without might is meaningless. And anyone who wants right to be something more than simply an abstract idea — anyone who wants to live by that right — has got to be strong. That's the law of our times. It's cruel; but all I can do is regret it. And I'm not prepared to have a bad conscience if I'm compelled to implement that right by force, because I haven't any other course of action.

Amos: And does that remain the same right as it was before you implemented it by force?

Nachman: It begins with the whole issue of Zionism. The existence of the Jewish people and any possibility of its returning to this country involved a conflict with those who were living here. If you think you shouldn't have pushed anyone out — then you'd have had to go on living in the Diaspora. And you'd have been slaughtered there. No one came to our defense anywhere. No one did the job for us. We were slaughtered while everyone stood on the sidelines. And you mustn't forget this. I'm deliberately putting it harshly. For heaven's sake don't think that I rejoice in our sacrifices. But we're faced by a frightful reality. And it really is frightful. . . .

I just want to remind you of how things began to develop even in this last chapter of the Six-Day War. Remember the beginning of Nasser's troop movement into Sinai and towards our borders. Look at the closing of the Straits of Tiran, remember the pact between Egypt and Jordan. And, as the ring closed in on us, the other countries were all against what Nasser was doing — at first! Afterwards they began to draw back. No one dared send a ship to test the blockade of the Straits of Tiran. The Americans said they'd send a ship as a try-out. But did they do it? Did they deter Nasser in any way? He displayed authority and force and effrontery. It was quite obvious: no one was going to come to our aid!

Gili: Haim Topol came to put on a show for us and he told us how in England and other places they all felt sympathy for the little country that was about to be wiped out!

Nachman: And from this you get the question of the war. That's to say, you're right to defend your life by force. Very simple. And if there's a war? By all means, if there's no other answer. If you won't fight for your life, they'll wipe you out. They say so quite specifically, and we can see it in all the drawings in the Arab schools. And we all saw it on the Syrian Heights — all those earthworks, all those trenches, a whole country entirely devoted to attacking you.

Amos: I think you're making it a little easy for yourself. Of course everything you've said is quite true. We really did fight for our lives, and there are no regrets over that, no question at all. A man fighting for his life fights fiercely and with everything that comes to hand. On the fifth of June I felt that the flood waters would sweep me away if I didn't push them back with everything I had. On June 10, I suddenly found myself in Hebron, in Jerusalem, in Bethlehem, and Sharm el Sheikh. Never in my wildest, most fantastic dreams before June 3 could I have imagined such a thing. Perhaps I was short-sighted. But there is a certain disproportion, a certain gap that the imagination can't bridge, between a war which began as a war of defense, a war in which we were fighting for our very lives, for the lives of our women and children and the situation that exists today. It's difficult to get used to this rapid change.

Nachman: For years we've been saying that if war were to break out we'd carry it into the enemy's territory. Do you think we said things like that just to give people something to talk about over a cup of coffee?

Amos: But we never said we'd take it into "liberated" territories. . . .

Nachman: Wait a bit, Amos. I know all about this business of terminology turning into ideology. Now — the war itself was a just war. And I say this because there are lots of people who claim that the whole of Zionism is an injustice, that it's immoral and so on — they feel guilty about the very fact of our being here. But I don't see how we could have done things differently. Things happened the way they happened, and we found ourselves with these wars on our hands. It's very tragic. Tragic, indeed, but that's fate. That's the cruelty of fate.

The war went beyond the armistice lines. But those lines were also drawn by chance. Why chance? Because they're the lines that mark the end of the War of Independence. So they remained there. Points of Jewish settlement suddenly became non-Jewish areas. The Etzion bloc and Beit Ha'Arava, for example — what greater right do the Arabs have to Beit Ha'Arava than we do?

As far as the business of territorial expansion is concerned (the "liberated" areas) I'm quite familiar with the line that we've liberated them from a foreign conqueror. That's just chauvinism. But what should we have done? Should we have stopped at the armistice lines? Should we have left the Syrian Heights in their hands? I don't know what you want. Why should we regret having won, almost as if winning was a catastrophe? The war achieved more than was hoped for — and it's good that it did. As far as the rest is concerned: what to hold, how to keep it, how to run things there — that's something that has to be decided on the basis of political and security considerations.

Now let's go on to something else. A very striking thing showed up during this war, and that concerns the new immigrants. We call them new immigrants even though they've been here since the War of Independence. Especially those who came from Arab countries. This whole section of the population, which is perhaps the majority in Israel, now feels itself on equal terms with the veteran population of the country. Because of the part they played in the war, they now feel an equality with the older-established Ashkenazi community — and that's something very important.

I want to point out one of the things that impressed me most about this war: the way everybody played his part. Not only the front-line troops. We won this war because people fought and did what they had to do with all they had, "with all their heart, with all their soul, and with all their might." Look at the way the service branches worked; look at the second-line troops who were so vital to the front-line. It was such a fantastic example of devotion and complete loyalty.

You remember this spirit of unity that was felt everywhere; every car stopped to give lifts; restaurant owners let you eat for practically nothing. The whole nation was united, at one, inspired . . . It was a wonderful display of unity and national comradeship.

Amos: You must remember that somewhere along the line the debit side of catastrophe involves the negation of man.

Nachman: Maybe you're right. But the fact remains that things did happen as I've just put them. There was a sort of inspiration, a renaissance . . . . There is something positive within us all, within all these people, throughout the whole nation.

The big problem is one of education. How — despite the fact that from our point of view this was a just war — are we going to avoid turning into militarists? How are we going to retain respect for human life? This is the contradiction, this is the paradox within the whole business. What we've got to avoid is cheapening life and becoming conquerors. We mustn't become expansionists at the expense of other people, we mustn't become Arab haters. The problem is how to avoid turning our soldiers and our children into cynics who say, "Justice! There's no such thing. The UN? Nonsense! Honour is a relative term." It's very difficult. It's something we'll have to pay attention to, to think about and to fight for.

Gili: I was one of the first into Nablus after the tanks had gone in. People were gathered on the pavement. A tremendous crowd.

Soldiers with rifles, and civilians, dancing in the streets and cheering us on. They were expecting an Iraqi battalion. A lot of people were armed — hundreds, hundreds. I asked the battalion CO, "A lot of them are armed, should we fire or not?" He said, "Don't fire!" It might have prevented some of the losses we had later if we'd gone straight in and fired and the town had surrendered immediately. Perhaps some of the boys would still have been alive today. Perhaps it wouldn't have made any difference at all, though.

Anyway, the fact is that we went in without firing a single shot. The battalion CO got on the field telephone to my company and said, "Don't touch the civilians . . . don't fire until you're fired at and don't touch the civilians. Look, you've been warned. Their blood be on your heads." In just those words. The boys in the company kept talking about it afterwards, I heard it from every one of them, right down to the drivers. They kept repeating the words, "Do you remember that 'Their blood be on your heads'?" they'd say. By the way, that particular CO is a member of Kibbutz Kabri.

Uri: It'd be interesting to know if this was his own on-the-spot decision or if he was following directives.

Gili: Look, that's all very well, but we could have gone in and started firing immediately. It could have happened unintentionally, because all our weapons were at the ready, safety catches were off and the first platoon had its shells ready for firing. Something could easily have gone off. The fact is that we went in quietly. They caught on that we were Israelis. Instead of waving white flags — we didn't fire — they went up on the roofs and climbed Mount Gerizim and began firing at us. The fighting went on till six at night — and people were killed.

Sometimes you make a cold calculation . . . I think some cruel things happened too, but we mustn't forget for a minute that had the boot been on the other foot, then they would have killed, smashed children up against walls, raped and done everything in the cruellest possible way. We mustn't forget this. That "their blood be on your heads" was something quite fantastic, you won't find it in any other army. I'm certain of that. And "when they rose up against us to destroy us," we behaved as we did . . . We had no desire at all to fight against them. They used to say in the army that the army orchestra, armed with drums, would guard the Jordanian and Lebanese borders.

Amos: Have you been to Nablus since the war?

Gili: Yes, three times. Once I went with the widow of one of the boys.

Amos: How did you feel about Nablus after the war? Was it the same as you felt about being in the Old City? Or as you might feel in a conquered city? As if it were a foreign city? As if you were abroad?

Gili: I don't know . . . It's difficult for me to say, very difficult. I didn't feel as if I were in a liberated city; I've no illusions on that score. I didn't feel any differently from the way I feel in Nazareth, an Arab city.

Amos: And supposing we make peace and give Nablus back to the Arabs, to an Arab state, that is. Will you be insulted, or sorry about it, or hurt?

Gili: Nothing of the sort. It certainly won't hurt me.

Amos: You won't think you've been betrayed or sold down the river?

Gili: No, no. . . . By the way, one of my uncles sent me a declaration he wanted me to sign: "The soldiers oppose the return of the liberated territories." I'm not going to sign. We're trying to achieve peace, and we still don't know how to do it. If returning Nablus will help . . . But to me, at least, it seems quite clear that there are some places we can't give back. The borders will have to be changed. They're going to have to make some arrangements about military security; perhaps returning the territories to Jordan with the proviso that the Jordan army is kept out of them; that's to say, that we'll keep the Jordan river.

As far as the Syrian Heights are concerned, or at least that part which overlooks our settlements: if they're given back, it'll be a crime second to none. If we reach any agreements there, then as I see it, that border will have to be changed. It's not natural. I don't know whether we should keep Kuneitra, but we won't have such a bad border if we keep the old Syrian military positions. Twenty kilometers isn't such a bad thing, I can tell you. Though if we do return it, even with a real peace treaty, I know I wouldn't trust the people we're giving it back to. When I went up there, I was amazed at how the settlements in the Galilee were able to exist there so long. The only reason people feel depressed is because of the feeling that we'll have to fight again in another few years.

Eli: What bothers me is the behavior of some of the men who were with me. There were two sides to the coin. On the one hand, the treatment of civilians. We were responsible for the civilians, and they were really well treated. There was even a woman who'd just given birth — she was given milk and we looked after her. On the other hand, it was very strange. I don't know how to explain it; I was never close to any feeling like that — I saw a lot of dead people, and I killed some of them myself — and I never felt like that at all — there were isolated episodes where the soldiers wanted to demonstrate their own strength and degrade the Egyptians. Of course the officers didn't permit such behavior, and anyway it wasn't anything like widespread: but in my opinion this is a feeling that's much more degrading than hatred. Once we were combing out a village and we found out that the Egyptians soldiers were coming back there at night from the mountains. We were ordered to send them off in the direction of the Suez Canal. We caught two there and they were apparently soldiers. Some of the boys who caught them wanted to beat them up. I didn't allow it. I wouldn't agree. They wanted to put the wind up them, to see them shake with fear. I still can't grasp it. I've thought a lot about it — I've always been so far from things like that — and I still don't understand. Afterwards they themselves said: "Don't think we were serious about it." So they themselves felt . . . I don't understand them. I thought perhaps it was because they'd been educated differently, that perhaps we'd grown up in a different period.

Uri: Didn't you ask them? Didn't you talk to them about it?

Eli: I talked a lot. In the end, they didn't want to talk to me about it.

Gili: And they didn't explain to you? You couldn't manage to get an explanation out of them?

Eli: There was some sort of stumbling explanation. They said, "Look here, he's laughing in our faces . . . He's making fun of us . . . Look how he's behaving. . . . " It was nonsense. He stood there and shook with fear like. . . . It's true he was laughing, but it was the sort of laugh that the devil himself might give.

Amos: Tell me, Eli, you've been in Sinai before, and in more or less the same places, too. Didn't you have a strange sort of feeling that the clock had been turned back?

Eli: The first time in Sinai, when we reached Sharm El Sheikh, there was a night fight, and some of us were wounded. The next day we got the order to advance to Tiran. There was a parade at Sharm el Sheikh — I wasn't there because I'd already gone to Tiran. That's when Ben-Gurion sent that famous letter about how we'd come back to the place where King Solomon had been and all that sort of thing. There and then, I told my friends: "You'd better realize that it's not ours. We had to do it. We had no choice. But all this talk about history, about how it was ours. The whole world belongs to the Jews, because there are Jews everywhere. Not every place that we conquer can be ours. Don't drivel on the way they do." That's exactly what I said to them. That was in the middle of Sinai, the first time we were there. This time I said what I feel now: that we fought for peace and not for territory.

Amos: Don't you have some sort of feeling that you may have to go and fight there a third time?

Eli: Yes.

Nachman: And that's not a happy feeling.

Eli: No, the philosophy I developed after the war is much more extreme than the one you put forward. That's to say, I can't see any solution to the whole problem. That's our life, that's how we've got to live and that's how we've got to educate our children, and perhaps we should have a few more children. There'll be another war — it's out of our hands.

Amos: And do you think we can live like that?

Eli: Yes. I don't think we can live any other way.

Amos: Well, God forbid that it should happen, but don't you think that perhaps the third or fourth time the whole business will break you? The question is how long we, as ordinary flesh and blood, can bear it. Can we go on holding the sword in one hand only? Nachman, how can you go and talk to them about education towards kibbutz life? It seems to me that there's some sort of contradiction here. There's something here that contradicts the basic tenet of kibbutz life which says that every man has his own world and the right to fashion it. The question is whether this really applies to every man as a man, or whether it only holds good for the man who's also a kibbutznik and a Jew and an Israeli? Is it only people in this category who have a right to create something? There's a contradiction here. Particularly after this great victory, I think there's a very, very, serious danger. . . .

Uri: I asked you an entirely personal question, Eli. I asked if you don't think that in the light of your very pessimistic outlook there's a danger that there may come a day, in another two years, another four years, when we may have to go back for a third or a fourth time and that you'll lose your capacity for saying "no" to these men under you that you were telling about.

Eli: Look, among all the men I met there was a feeling that they weren't fighting to kill, but quite simply because their backs had been pushed against the wall. There was no choice. But that can have more than one effect: it can produce militarism and it can produce the opposite. The desire that it shouldn't happen again, that there's no choice, we have to do it — that's one attitude. Anyone with a little bit of an education, who sees this, doesn't enjoy killing. Ninety per cent will arrive at this conclusion. Perhaps ten per cent will think just the opposite. I don't think there's any such danger as you mention, perhaps even the opposite.

Amos: I'm afraid of one thing, that simply out of weariness or despair. . . .

Eli: It's not despair as far as I'm concerned, by the way. There's no despair. It's just realism.

Amos: But can you live that way forever — with the feeling that every few years we're going to find ourselves with our backs against the wall? With the feeling that every few years foreigners are going to be intent on killing you? Can you imagine living this way and still being the same person, the same nation in a few years' time? Can it be done without our getting to the stage in which we'll quite simply hate them? Just hate them. I don't mean that we'll take a delight in killing, or turn into sadists. Simply deep bitter hatred for them for having forced such a life on us.

Eli: My feeling is that this war in effect added rather than detracted from moral values.

Amos: Some of those soldiers you were talking about become officers, sooner or later. They're younger than you are. What'll happen then? Will they be like you, or like they are now?

Eli: The minute they become officers they'll become more responsible. As I see it, if they'd fought before, they wouldn't have behaved like that. I think that accounts for the tremendous differences there were between us. I tell you, I think that when all's said and done, the war heightened our values. The basis for the war was completely moral and a lot of very positive things happened — at any rate that's how it was in the long run. An incident like the one Gili mentioned — I'm sure the same thing would have happened in our crowd; an officer would have thought and thought to try and find some way of not killing. When all's said and done, our battalion behaved the same way, too.

Amos: I want to ask you a very difficult, perhaps even a heretical question, about what's been said here tonight. It sounds as if almost everyone agrees that the war brought out the best in a man. That's very obvious in what Nachman said and in what we see in the press, too. All those who condemned our young people and emigration and the crisis in moral values and all that, had their words thrown right back in their faces by the reality of what happened. It was proved that we're far better than we thought ourselves to be. But personally, I've got some rather heretical doubts about all this. My question is this: Let's say that a criminal, a thief, a robber, is sitting at home with his family, and suddenly people armed with knives come along to kill him. In his fury, he seizes the first broom that comes to hand and without thinking of the danger — without working out how many of them there are and how many he's up against — he goes outside and lashes out at them. Let's say he acts with energy, daring, courage and success. Does this put him on a higher moral plane, does it mean he has some moral standards?

I have the feeling that what we did in this war was to go out in our fury, in defense of our women, our children and our homes. Can you say that this is really a proof of our enlightenment, of some inner hidden strength that we didn't know we had? Doesn't it rather testify to the sheer instinct for survival which even the lowest of creatures possess? We're not the lowest of creatures — I never thought as badly of us as some people did. But I'd still like to ask whether the war really proved anything? Does the fact that people sacrificed themselves to the last ounce, even gave their lives, prove our moral strength?

Nachman: Don't try to make me out to be a militarist. Let's not think that war uplifts the nation and reveals its moral values. But, nevertheless, the period *did* reveal examples of comradeship. I don't mean bravery. There were revelations of what people really were, in terms of what we call interpersonal relationships. People were sensitive to each other and formed relationships with each other — and it happened just because they all faced the same danger and the same possibility of annihilation. Defending ourselves doesn't make us into moral beings — but I still say that the war was essentially a just one, because we never had any intention of annihilating or conquering or oppressing other people. On the contrary, it was the Arabs who had these intentions and we who defended ourselves, and that's why we're in the right. But there *is* the question of what will happen if it all just repeats itself in another ten years. I tell you, it may well happen. Someone looked into it and discovered that if we start from the period of the riots in Mandatory times, then starting from 1920, you get first the 1929 riots, then the Arab revolt of 1936, then 1945, then the War of Independence, then the Sinai Campaign — just about every nine years. The question is, what alternative could there be? Let's look at it from the opposite angle: What if we don't fight? Can we give it all up, surrender, make peace? What else can we do except increase our strength: economically, educationally, culturally, and militarily, all at the same time? There's almost nothing more trite than what I'm saying. But I'd like to know if there's anything more true! Here we are asking ourselves, nagging at ourselves again and again, worrying about what effects it will have on us. What scars will it leave? How are we going to educate the youth? Won't they all be very militaristic? But what else can you suggest?

It really does look as if we're living a contradiction, exactly as Uri put it. Here in the kibbutz we talk about wanting to see a world in which human life is valued, in which people respect each other, in which there's tolerance and so on — and at the same time, as far as the Arabs are concerned, as far as our surroundings are concerned, there's aggression. But what I say is this: we're offering them equality, not supremacy — and they don't want to accept it. What can you do with this sort of psychology, this sort of situation? And from their point of view it has a certain logic. That's what's so tragic, that's what this business of Zionism is all about, because as far as they're concerned, our being here in this country is seen as a conquest, while for us it's a matter of life itself. We say we've got something to give the area: culture and enlightenment. They say: leave us alone, we're not interested in your culture, we've got our own culture, we've got our *pitta*, we've got the clay from which we build our houses, we wash our clothes in the running water that flows in the wadis — and that's real life. We don't want your culture. We don't want you here. It's tragic. It's very nearly thesis and antithesis. But there's no other way out. . . .

We have to live with it. It was a long time ago that people first began saying, "It's hard to be a Jew." I agree. It is hard to be a Jew, physically, morally and intellectually. It's hard to be an orthodox Jew and it's hard to be humane when you live with all this constant preparedness for war. There are a lot of contradictions here. But you can't let yourself be broken by them. I think we sometimes sink into a sort of melancholia about it all. We've got to be aware of the dangers that a wrong sort of education may create, just as Uri said at the beginning. That's really the point. There really *is* a danger that the youngsters will start seeing the Arabs as *Arabushes*, not as men. And we may find that there are episodes like the one Eli described. But what we have to do is try to educate our own people to behave like the boys who captured Jenin: on the same day as they saw their friends killed alongside of them, they also saw long lines of refugees streaming past in cars. They gave them water and sweets and all their food — their own battle rations. That's another contradiction. Policy is dictated by the need to exist, and it happens to include some cruel things, too. I want to tell you, I saw those abandoned villages and the awful sight of work left in the middle — and what's more valuable than work for us who were educated on that concept?

There were orchards standing deserted, empty barns and cattle wandering around, mooing and bellowing terribly because they'd nothing to drink. That's one side of it: I see a thing like that and I think: "That's war." War isn't a kid glove business. But what can you do? That's the way it is. So it hurts me. And because it hurts me I'm sure I won't become cruel. In point of fact, I'm reconciled to the whole business, right through to the end.

What about you, Amos? Do you think we have a right to be here? Starting with the first pioneer who came to this country with its strange scenery, its unaccustomed climate, its foreign people — what about all that business?

Amos: Look here, I was born here.

Nachman: But, Amos, just a minute, if you're consistent about all this, then you must conclude that the whole business is unjustifiable and it's not possible. . . .

Amos: I'm not consistent, because in essence I too have to use your word. In essence I think it's all a tragedy. What's a tragedy? It's tragic when both sides are a hundred per cent in the right, from their own points of view. I'm condemned to be inconsistent. But if you ask me, then it'll cost me a lot, but I'll answer, yes. I tell you that I'm prepared to visit the Western Wall as a tourist, just as long as there's peace.

One of the men from Hulda died during the war. He was a paratrooper. Perhaps you knew him. He was killed in the attack on the Police School. A young man, also in the reserves, just two classes below me. About twenty-four or twenty-five. When I came back from the war, I went to see his parents. A few of the kibbutz members were there and the mother was crying. The father was biting his lips to hold back his tears. One of the older members tried to comfort them: "Look, after all, we've liberated Jerusalem," he said, "he didn't die for nothing." The mother burst into sobs and said, "The whole of the Western Wall isn't worth Micha's little finger as far as I'm concerned. . . . " If what you're telling me is that we fought for our existence, then I'd say it *was* worth Micha Hyman's little finger. But if you tell me that it was the Wall we fought for, then it wasn't worth his little finger. Say what you like — I do have a feeling for those stones — but they're only stones. And Micha was a person. A man. If dynamiting the Western Wall today would bring Micha back to life, then I'd say "Blow it up!" That's how I feel about it.

Eli: What matters to me is quite simply that we *do* have a history, and we've learned something from it. It's a pity. I'd like to be able to reach them. I'd like to be able to talk to the Arabs. But I've no more desire to acquire other people's land. Really, we've done enough of that. We can live in the country. Just let's ensure that there'll be peace. I've no more desire to take other people's lands and property — no desire at all.

Amos: I want to correct something I said, Nachman: I want the Jews to be able to go to the Wall and pray there. But it doesn't matter a fig to me if in order to do so, they have to get a Jordanian stamp, just so long as it's all being done within the framework of a peace settlement. That's to say, today it matters more to me than it did before, because I've been there. But a man's life? Jew, Arab, whoever it is! Today, I'm completely opposed to all this myth of lands crying out and places calling for liberation. It's worth dying to liberate *people*. But to liberate places? It's not worth anyone's little finger.

Eli: The whole country, all the newspapers, everyone's talking about "liberation". "Look, we're there" — "These places are ours" — "After two thousand years" — "It's ours" — "The Cave of Machpela"* . . . Ezer wrote me a letter: "Listen, you can't imagine how moved I was when I got to the Cave of Machpela," he said. Yet I didn't feel a thing when I was there.

Amos: Listen, I was moved when I was at the Wall. But I was a thousand times more moved when I saw Shai, my best friend in Hulda, alive and safe after the war.

Uri: I don't know, I must say. I love the Bible, and I've learned all these things. When I went to Sebastiah, Hebron, ancient Jericho — all the things I learned, history, the Bible, archaeology. I tell you, that's my feeling: from an emotional point of view it was just like, let's say, coming to the Crusader castle at Montfort, when I'd learned to know it properly. It's mine. . . .

*Burial-place of the Hebrew patriarchs, in Hebron.

Amos: That's what's so strange about all these historical places. There are historical sites that are part of the country's history. But there are other places that are part of your own history. I'll give you an example: there's a town in Israel called Holon. It's not mentioned in the Bible. The Patriarchs weren't buried there. It's not in any historical record. It's just an ordinary little town that's risen out of the sand-dunes. And yet, you know something? Holon happens to be the town where I first ever fell in love with a woman . . . Holon means much more to me than Hebron. So, say what you like, for me it's more of a historic place than Hebron. If I can't make a sentimental pilgrimage to Holon once in a couple of years, if I can't get to a certain little corner, certain spots in Holon – that'll hurt me far more than not being able to make a pilgrimage to the Cave of Machpela which I first saw only two weeks ago. Perhaps it's not nationalistic, but it's – I don't care how heretical you think this sounds, but I don't have any feeling that Hebron's part of my homeland. But I do feel this about Holon.

Uri: I want to say something: before the war, you knew in advance that people would die. You knew that people who were with you one moment could be dead the next day. And you went. You can say that those lives are important and dear to you. But there are things that are even more important.

Gili: In my opinion you can't compare the Cave of Machpela and the Wall. Every nation has some sacred sites. I think that for the Jewish people, Jerusalem and the Wall mean far more than a first love.

By the way, one of the least pleasant duties that fell to the officers was visiting the bereaved families after the war. I was very careful about what I said in consoling them. I told them the straight truth. I explained just exactly how it had happened, and I was very careful not to use terms like "for the sake of the homeland," and so on. I was very cautious. Once the CO came with me. In this case, he got tongue-tied, and came out with something like, "We felt – we wanted. . . . " The wife couldn't contain herself and burst out: "But he was at home, and he said it would be better to wait and sit it out another two months and not fire a single shot and it would all work itself out and we wouldn't go and fight. That's what he said, and you – don't you tell me that it's. . . . "

But as far as Jerusalem and the Wall are concerned, as soon as it comes to the personal aspect, I'm not going to get into an argument with anyone — if his friend died . . . As far as the Jewish people are concerned, I think it's a national symbol.

Perhaps free access and a stable peace — free access to the holy places. But what the Jordanians did on the Mount of Olives, what they did over there . . . I tell you, it's a good thing that it's in our hands now. It was worth the price.

Eli: I don't want another people to have to leave their homes again as a result of war. I heard a Minister speaking on the radio one day. He was explaining about the Wall, who it belongs to, and who it doesn't belong to. He said that it's only for believers: the non-believers come there just as they go to Caesarea, as tourists. They come to see it, nothing more. I thought to myself, that man doesn't know what he's talking about at all. He has no understanding of this nation's soul.

THIS IS WHAT WE'RE FIGHTING FOR

From a discussion in Mishmar Hasharon. Interviewer: Shlomit Teub

Avinoam: I think one of the things that characterizes us is the tragedy of being victors. We're simply not used to it. It's got something to do with our education. Look, I saw the Mitla Pass and it made a deep impression on me. At first glance, you could say perhaps: "Look, just see how the Jews have smashed the Arabs. We went to war, they wanted to wipe us out, and just look, how marvelous. . . . " I admit that it left a deep impression on me, though. You mustn't show young people a thing like that. Anyway, you mustn't show it to Israelis because all our education is orientated towards building, and it has been ever since the first pioneers came here. Everything's been geared to construction. And here there's destruction. A classic example of destruction.

Yoni: It's destruction with a view to construction. I don't understand your attitude.

Avnioam: Maybe — but in absolute terms it's destruction. I'm glad that I can stand here on the remains of an Egyptian vehicle and that it's not an Egyptian that's standing between Beersheba and Yeruham. It's a splendid feeling to be able to wander around Sinai as a tourist. It's marvelous. But in absolute terms, when you see it, it's destruction, and it's depressing. It's depressing to see millions of pounds just thrown away. When we went past, we kept saying to each other, "Look, what you could do with this! What you could do with that!"

154

Yoni: It's destruction for existence. That's what I'm trying to explain to you.

Avinoam: I agree, but even so! All the men who were with me going through the Mitla Pass — all felt that way.

Zvike: You're talking about the destruction of war weapons?

Avinoam: The destruction of everything — armor, the road, the lot. They bashed them from the air there. . . .

Another thing. We took some volunteers in the direction of Banias. As we went up they said they couldn't see where the war had been there. I showed them a field of tomatoes that hadn't been picked; "Look," I said, "can't you see? This is where the war was." — "Where?" they said. It was a bit difficult for them to catch on to things like that. There was quite a big field of rotting tomatoes . . . that's where you see that there's been a war.

When we crossed over the jumping-off points in the south on the first evening, we passed over the Negev fields. The wheat was standing high, it looked very beautiful. We were flying low to keep out of their radar range. We were in helicopters, so we could see everything we passed over. Perhaps I was trying to find some sort of justification for this war, although what I recall is having no feeling of hatred for them. And I said: "Look, this is what we're fighting for, so that all this won't get burned up."

Yoni: That's love of the country.

Avinoam: I don't know what to call it. For example, I was furious when they had a go at the fields around Nahal Oz and there was a fire there. They burnt up fields, and it drove me crazy. I'd flown over there in a helicopter a couple of hours earlier. There were enormous stretches of field-crops. "Look at that," I said. There's never been a year like it, everything growing so tall and golden. . . .

Shlomit: But doesn't war also bring out the animal instincts in people? Don't people surprise themselves and discover the existence of forces within them that they hadn't known of before?

Avinoam: Definitely! Like all other living creatures, we have primitive animal instincts which in daily life we firmly repress. They're kept at bay and held in check by a thousand and one different influences — our surroundings, society, education, values and morality. But they exist somewhere and at a certain moment, in a certain situation, they will burst out. In my opinion, war is one of the best forcing grounds for such an outbreak, because the struggle is so much fiercer than anything in one's daily life, it's a tooth and nail fight for existence. In these circumstances, our natural defenses — morality, values, etc — melt away. They can't stand up to these instincts; and they in their turn take over and burst out. But it's just in those very moments when these instincts come to the fore that we are capable of overcoming them. That's to say, it's only then that we really face up to them. In normal everyday life there's no such opportunity.

Shlomit: Are we conscious of these forces?

Avinoam: I firmly believe that because of our fear of these things we consciously suppress them. In other words, we're conscious that they exist in our subconscious. Animal instincts exist. I think that the only opportunity we really have to face up to them in all sincerity, to struggle with them in our own hearts, is when they come to the surface. Then we are in control, or at least, we have the chance to strike back at them for once.

Shlomit: Once and for all?

Avinoam: No, not for ever. . . . But this is the only occasion when you can try to achieve control of such instincts, and overcome them. Not all of us are capable of this. Those who aren't behave in a barbaric manner — according to our daily standards, of course. What do I mean when I say "we overcome them"? Despite the fact that we're fighting for our very existence, for our very lives, we fight decently and morally, suppressing the sadism and the instinct to kill which is in all of us. We don't descend to the level of those we're fighting. As I see it, in their case, these instincts aren't suppressed. It's only when they are, that we'll be able, perhaps, to achieve peace with our neighbors, the Arab states. There's no point to the war, and to love of one's country, if the guiding lines are not essentially the desire to live in peace with them. In my opinion, peace is the first thing to strive for; and it precedes love of one's country and all the other things which are so important in themselves.

PART 4

GENERATION TO GENERATION

PEOPLE AND COUNTRY

Discussion at Ramat Yohanan. Interviewer: Avraham Shapira

Ramat Yohanan, founded in 1931, is a kibbutz of some 650 inhabitants, a few miles north-east of Haifa. It is known throughout the country for its part in the revival of Hebrew folklore, and particularly the agricultural festivals. Its economy is mainly agricultural, but it recently established a plastic factory. This is the kibbutz described by Bruno Bettelheim in his book *Children of the Dream*.

Participants:
Matitiyahu, Elisha and Amitai. The biographies of this family are given in some detail in this discussion. Matitiyahu is a very well-known figure in the kibbutz movement and in Israel. He was one of a small group of pioneers who reintroduced the rearing of sheep to the country, and he has worked with the prize flock at Ramat Yohanan for some forty years. He is equally well-known for his part in the revival of Hebrew folklore, and founded and supervises the Institute of Rural Folklore in his kibbutz. He is also a composer, whose songs have become part of the general cultural heritage of the country. Elisha is in charge of the banana plantation. Aged thirty-eight, with three children, he is a colonel in the reserves and commanded a paratroop regiment during the war. Amitai is twenty-five,

159

married, with one child born a week after the war. He works in bananas; he is a lieutenant in a paratroop regiment and fought in Jerusalem.

Matitiyahu: I spent a lot of time thinking in the two weeks just before the war. When I used to take the sheep out to pasture I couldn't think of anything but what was happening at the time. I thought to myself: I haven't had any really serious illness in all these years, my life hasn't been in any bodily or organic danger. On the other hand, as a Jew, and only as a Jew, I have survived many critical moments, both before I came to the country and since. These dangers derived solely from the fact of my being a Jew.

And here again, I mused, we are confronted with days of danger, days of challenge.

There are three aspects to what I felt. One aspect is common to the Jewish people, to the state of Israel and to us as citizens of the State. A narrower aspect is the place where I live, the kibbutz and its members. The third aspect involves my two sons, where they were, what happened to them and so on. They are both in combat units, while I took no active part in either attack or defense.

What goes on in each of these three aspects is tied up with Jewish destiny. We have to defend ourselves as Jews. At the time, I used to think a lot about the concentration camps, about what might happen, about almost anything that a sick imagination could devise, and about all the things I'd seen down through the years: the riots in 1929 and the riots of 1936. I know the Arabs, I've seen a lot of danger, up to and including the War of Liberation. I used to think a lot about the recurrent pattern of our lives . . . I went backwards in my thoughts, to the time before I came to Palestine, way back to my childhood.

In those days, in 1918, there were still pogroms. We were living in the Ukraine. The Jews had already begun to organize in self-defense in the towns and villages, and there was a readiness to stand up and fight. My father, a teacher who didn't even know how to handle a gun, had a fighting spirit. He was the head of the self-defense group in our town. There were arms hidden under the floor in our house.

When the pogrom began, they came to call my father. He went

first. I was only a child, but I can't forget it to this day. As for my
mother — her reaction was that father shouldn't go under any
condition. She wouldn't budge. Father was in a ticklish position. He
didn't know what to do. On the one hand, duty called, and on the
other, there was mother, a simple woman, incapable of grasping why
Jews should dare to defend themselves in a normal fashion. Jews
didn't do things like that. The incident made a deep impression and I
remember it well. It was a fairly uncommon phenomenon among
Jews then. I've often had occasion to discuss the gas chambers,
especially with Amitai. He would always get excited and end up
shouting: "How could they? How could they go like sheep to the
slaughter?" I told him to read more about it, to try to understand.
It's the Jewish way, Jewish optimism: "Ah, we'll get by. There's no
point in getting the *goyim* all stirred up." True, this was a failing. We
should recognize it.

It's interesting how my thoughts just before the war followed a
kind of repetitive pattern, referring back to those days, then leaping
down to the present. I sensed a kind of continuity. I felt very close
to the boys, as if I were in their place. I was sure that if I had been
their age I would have done exactly the same thing, might even have
fought in the same unit, taken part in the same kind of operation.
Home was my first source of inspiration. That's where I got my love
for the country, my feeling for Hebrew, my ties to my Jewish roots,
that was the primary source. I was in a youth movement, of course,
but my first attachment was formed in my father's house.

At that time, during the 1920's, I saw whole nations stirring and
awakening, yearning for national independence. And I asked myself:
"Where am I and what am I?" The many who felt they had no
future in Poland looked around for a country to go to. This was no
solution for me. For me, there was only the land of Israel. And it
answered all the questions I asked myself.

I can also tell you where I got my desire for a life on the soil. It
didn't come from the youth movement or from books. It's simply
that as a boy, I was drawn to a farmer's life, village life. I thought
that it was good, beautiful, attractive. Of course this was the
principal task in the upbuilding of the country at the time I came
here. The goal was to settle on the land, to strike roots. And that's

how I got to the kibbutz, to a life of work. In all these things I felt I was part of a whole continuum — past, present and future were links in an unbroken chain. This continuity gave me satisfaction, made me proud, made me love my sons, and during the waiting period, made me anxious about them.

I remember once when I was a boy some Poles caught me and tried to make me say: "Long live the priest, death to the rabbi." They abused me. They shamed me as a person, as a Jew. And they knew it even then. They did exactly what the Nazis did. And I didn't want to knuckle under, couldn't, my self-respect wouldn't let me. But I was only a child then and they threatened me. And then one of them took a whip — I still bear the scar here on my face. Every time I see that little scar in the mirror, that sign, it brings out the Jew in me. At the time, not long after, there were also pogroms. There was one moonlit night when the entire village cried *"gevalt"* like a flock of geese. It was ghastly. Winter, snow on the ground, moonlight and a whole town shouting *"gevalt."* You could hear the cries from one house to the next. I heard footsteps, and in another few minutes the rioters would have been at our door. What could we do? It was a low-built house, with no basement. I remember that instinctively I grabbed an axe and stood behind the door. I was determined that if they came into the house, I would let them have it.

Somehow, through some trick of fate, luck, they skipped us. They broke into another house instead of ours.

That was my consolation in those miserable days before the war: the feeling of continuity, that all of us were together, doing the same thing. My grandfather wanted to bring about redemption in his own way. He abandoned the things of this world, and studied *torah* day and night in the Rebbe's court. That's how he thought redemption would come. My father rebelled against this attitude and this closed-in world.

Avraham: Was your father religious?

Matitiyahu: Yes. He went to *yeshiva*, but only for a while. When he was sixteen he kicked over the traces, went wild. He was full of life. His Zionism welled up inside him; it came straight from the source. He was my inspiration. He was my model, my standard of perfection. And afterwards, I came to the path I was to follow, and as a continuation of that, the path the boys chose.

Elisha: There was a get-together of paratroop officers this week. Moshe Dayan spoke. He analyzed the history of Jewish settlement in Palestine, and noted in passing that warfare is rapidly becoming the dominant *motif* in Zionism. While the battle against the desert and disease may have been the central concern of Zionism years ago, war has become the central element of the past three decades. And when he said that, I thought to myself that this just about covers the span of my life.

And really, ever since I can remember, ever since I opened my eyes, there's been war in the air all the time.

Among the earliest memories of my childhood is the recollection of the fires on the oil pipeline, the flares in the night. There was a bay window in the kindergarten. When flares were lit, when the oil pipeline burned, we used to stand there in the window and look, then there were shots. I distinctly remember, my first memories of childhood were of "you can't go out" — "be careful" — "don't go far."

Then there was the World War, the bombings (Ramat Yohanan isn't far from Haifa), and the radio talking about war, morning, noon and night. Next came the news from the ghettoes, then the War of Independence. I was fourteen then, and we had all sorts of secret plans to run away and join the Palmach.

I remember during the fighting at Ramat Yohanan in the War of Independence; we had two platoons from the Palmach, and there was a boy of sixteen in one of them. We ran around to find him, to try to worm out of him how he ran away, how he managed to enlist. That's how we grew up, and there was no getting away from the feeling that this was one of the really decisive things. As a child I must confess that I was pretty scared. I remember that during the attack on the kibbutz I worried mostly about Dad. I wasn't worried about the outcome, I didn't think that the Jewish people would lose, but I knew that Dad was running around out there near the barn, from trench to trench, and I was simply afraid he'd get hit. We stayed below in the shelters, yet boys only two years older than us were already taking part in the fighting. They were runners or carried ammunition.

The War of Independence, which, as I say, I didn't take part in, left a deep mark on the atmosphere, the songs, ways of expression, our whole style of life. I never managed to fathom what effect the destruction of the Jews in Europe had on me. It was so big, I could never digest it emotionally. I remember as a boy trying to absorb and understand it, but I didn't feel it strongly. Mass slaughter made less of an emotional impression on me than the minor insults done to the Jews. What hurt me as a youngster wasn't that they killed Jews, but that they insulted them. Today, too, whenever I hear anyone say "*Arabush*" it reminds me of terms like "Yid" and that's why it grates on me so much. It's easier to understand hatred for the Arabs than to reconcile oneself with a term that implies a feeling of superiority to them. As long as I've been old enough to think, that expression has driven me mad.

Avraham: In connection with the gas chambers, or in general?

Elisha: Nothing to do with the gas chambers. In general. Especially before the massacre of the Jews. Through the stories that Dad used to tell about when he was in the Diaspora. I remember the scar on Dad's face very well. As a child, I liked to hear that story over and over again.

I enlisted in the army in 1950 during a relatively quiet period. The War of Independence was over. The World War was over. The riots were over. There was a State of Israel. There was an air of comparative peace. My strongest feelings date from the time of the retaliation raids, overshadowing the two wars (the Sinai Campaign and this war). There are a number of reasons for this. The retaliation raids were my first combat experience, and first experiences are apparently stronger. I didn't have the feeling then of being cornered, and it wasn't a war in which every Israeli took part. A reprisal raid was like a private war waged by a small group of people. You could, of course, draw the broader Zionist conclusions, it was a simple intellectual exercise. But as far as your feelings went, it didn't ring altogether true.

More than once I did some very serious thinking. There were quite a lot of operations over an extended period. The losses weren't heavy, but they kept on and on, this one dead, then that one – and then the wounded. And every time I'd think it over seriously. I must say that what frightened me most in all the fighting, and I was wounded twice, was the fear of being wounded and left an invalid. Getting killed is hard to grasp and hard to describe. It was no deterrent, or at any rate less of one. On the other hand, the invalids that I saw . . . when I saw those broken bodies a long time afterwards — not when they were still heroes, shown off at parties and rallies, but afterwards, years later, when they're wrecks no one remembers — the invalids pay a high price, maybe the highest you can pay. The rewards may seem ample at the time: glory, admiration, patriotism. But when you look at it from the long-term view, you can't help feeling that those fellows made a bad bargain. This bothered me for a long time.

And, at least from this point of view, I had a much easier time of it in the Six-Day War and Sinai Campaign. There was no need for soul-searching. It was clear that this was Armaggedon, that everyone was in it, and that "whatever will be will be."

Today, when I look back — it's easier to look back today — on the reprisal raid years, there was a bond between the people who took part in those actions. That bond meant a great deal to us. And to this day it still gives me something. It added another dimension, increased the depth of human feeling and experience. There is a corner of my heart which is sacred to those boys and that never-to-be-repeated period in our lives. Perhaps the greatest satisfaction comes from the special kind of relationships which evolved then and which still survive. There are no ties like them.

I find it hard to say where what people call Zionism fits in here. I'm sure it was a factor. It's no secret that our generation looks askance at Zionism, the Congress kind of Zionism, maybe because we've been fed too much of it. But I'm convinced that the Zionist impulse showed itself again and again in different forms. I have a deep attachment to the country. A physical sensation of attachment to the land. In the war, the last one, for the first time we felt as if we were really fighting for our country. This time, much more than previously, I felt that I was going out to fight for my country and my life.

At the time, the boys in our unit talked a lot about our attitude to the enemy. It was all theory. I must confess that I never felt hatred for our enemy. I didn't have the faintest trace of hate. It's hard to say how such a feeling affects your capacity to fight or your combat effectiveness. I used to read books about the concentration camps, and I could drum up some emotion of hatred for the Germans or for those who butchered the Jews, but as to the Arabs (maybe because they are more real to me than all the other enemies of the Jews, who really are only enemies by hearsay), I could never hate them in the past and I still haven't succeeded in hating them.

During the waiting,. we used to listen to the radio a lot. There was a lot of martial music, particularly from Cairo. It sounded sort of belligerent and cocky. I liked to hear it. For the first time, possibly, it used to make me want to . . . it wasn't hate though. It was like something evil hanging over you, and you suddenly want to get up and drive it away, smash it to smithereens.

For the first time I felt something resembling hate, a desire to get up and smash something to pieces.

Avraham: Several times — and I don't think this is altogether accidental — you emphasized the tie you felt to your country, your love for the country. You said that in this war you felt for the first time that we were really fighting for our country. Would you say you were fighting for the country alone, and not for the people?

Elisha: It's hard to differentiate between the people and the country. But again, it's probably totally subjective as far as I'm concerned. My attachment is chiefly to the country. I don't think it's at all accidental that I expressed myself the way I did.

Matitiyahu: I have to add something in connection with what Elisha had to say. I never hated the Arabs. I've had a lot to do with them, and they've caused me no little trouble. Yet I never hated Arabs. On the other hand, I can remember the hatred I felt towards the Russians and the Poles and all those. When people talk about the slaughter of the Jews, I can never forget the part played by the Ukrainians, the Poles, the Russians. Them I remember, and I remember them with hatred.

As to the country and the people, though I wasn't born here, for me the people and the country are indistinguishably blended together, a total merger.

Elisha: It's been my experience that it's the people who are new to the country who tend to hate Arabs. The people who have had nothing to do with them hate them. There's a close connection between hatred and fear. I was never afraid of the Arabs, and I'm not afraid of them now. There have been a lot of wars, but thank God we've always beaten them.

One of the people who works with us in the banana plantation went through the camps, through every kind of hell. His wife and children were killed. He says: "The Arabs are worse than the Germans." We've been talking about it for years. We would ask him: "But what do the Arabs do? What have they done?" And he would answer: "An Arab can come and murder you at night, stick a knife in you." The unknown frightens him. Hatred is all mixed up with fear.

There's one other little thing that I've only now begun to feel. In every war in which we were engaged, in all the stories we were told, we were always the weak against the strong, the few against the many. Now, for possibly the first time, we are the strong facing the weak. For me, this is a new feeling. We were always like David, and we always overcame Goliath.

Amitai: The people who spoke before me all talked about the distant past. My past isn't so long, but it also begins with wars. My first memories are of wars. To this day, I remember the games we used to play before the War of Independence. I was six at the time. I remember the fighting here very well, and I'll begin from there.

My bitterest recollection from the war is being evacuated from Ramat Yohanan. The next class above wasn't evacuated. One of the things that always used to bother our age group was the feeling that somehow history had passed us by.

From what I heard in the army, I found that this feeling was not at all local but nationwide. I grew up in the shadow of my family's history, in the shadow of my parents' lifetime of pioneering, in the shadow of Elisha, who was a veteran of the reprisal raids and all that. There was always the feeling that my generation was through with fighting and had retrogressed a little, become artistic. Yael Dayan once wrote that our generation isn't attached to anything. That's how I felt all through the years. In fact, only with this war did I put myself at ease on that score. I felt, and discovered that others felt the same, that we, too, want to contribute something, have to contribute something. And our chief contribution as far as the country and the nation were concerned was in this war.

We are the children of people who persevered through every hardship to achieve fulfilment here. These people resolved to carve out their own destiny, broke off completely from Diaspora ways to a life dedicated to building up a country and a nation. This generation, our parents' generation, is an élite. I used to ask myself: "And where are we? How do we express ourselves? If this is the stock from which we spring, then we too have to be some kind of élite." This stuck with me all the time, and I always had the feeling that we were lacking somehow, that we weren't fulfilling our historic mission.

I'm not the least bit surprised that Elisha emphasized the country and not the people. His direct attachment is to the soil on which he lives, to the land. I think that's why he spoke about his attachment to the land and not to the nation.

Avraham: Do you feel differently about it, then?

Amitai: No. On the contrary. I understand how he feels because I think the same way. Part of it derives from the education we received, from the books we read, the whole tenor of our education. We were brought up on heroic times and heroic people, on self-fulfilment. This education was common to all of us and made each one of us ask himself where he fitted in. I grew up in the shadow of war; or, more correctly, in the light of war. The wars that took place when I was a boy were fought by heroes. We won them all. On the other hand, what depressed me was the destruction of the Jews by Hitler.

That's a subject that has always interested me and still does. I am a product of what we can call the reprisal raid generation. A generation of strength, of war, of "a tooth for a tooth." I could identify wholeheartedly with the reprisal raids, but when I thought about the gas chambers, it seemed so horrible. I couldn't understand it and even today I'm still incapable of understanding it.

I lived through the "tooth for a tooth" period. And its principal expression was the reprisal raid. I think that one of the reasons that the State of Israel went over to reprisal raids can be expressed in the saying: "It doesn't matter what the Gentiles say: what counts is what the Jews do." I think it derives from some kind of feeling of inferiority or from the deep shame we've experienced throughout history. For me, the "final solution" is the essence of that shame.

Avraham: Do you feel there's any connection between the feeling of shame suffered by the village Jews which your father told you about, and the feeling of shame about the "final solution"?

Amitai: I didn't hear very much about what Dad suffered as a Jew during his childhood. I only heard about it much later, at a time when I was not very much interested in what had happened to the Jews. I knew the story of the scar. — Dad told me about it once when we spoke about the concentration camps, but not before. I was born at the time of the liquidation of European Jewry, during the Second World War. The sense of insult and pain may have been one of the unconscious reasons why I joined the unit I did. For as long as I can remember, I never had the slightest doubt that I would have to face some such challenge . . . and then I used to see Elisha, and hear about his exploits with that unit.

I didn't think in terms of "showing the Arabs" or "giving it to them." My thinking and my motives had their starting point in the destruction of the Jews in Europe. To "show" the Gentiles afar, and not those close at hand.

Avraham: The fate of European Jewry was always in your thoughts?

Amitai: When I think about it today, it seems to be one of the things that attracted me to the paratroops. I remember how as a youngster I wanted to join the corps. Not only that. When I think about the festivals for instance, my favorite, the one I feel closest to, is Hannuka. And the chief reason is the story of the Maccabees, the proud Jews, in their own country, the Jew rising to defend himself and stand on his dignity. We used to read a lot of books of this genre.

My generation found an important outlet in this last war. At long last we too were given an opportunity to make our mark on the history of the Jews in their own country.

Avraham: Earlier, you spoke about your personal connection with your father and your brother. After the war, didn't you have the feeling of "Here, I've brought home my diploma, I'm a man like my brother and my father?"

Amitai: Yes. That's how I felt. People didn't hesitate to run risks in the war, and they were real risks. They had the feeling that they were about to perform the greatest deed of their lives. I got a lot from my parents. It seems to me that a good deal of the education that children get in the kibbutz comes from their home. At the same time, I sometimes instinctively disbelieve some of the things Dad tells me. It seems as if he's trying to cover up for something. Dad and I have talked a lot about the ghetto, and I sometimes have the feeling that he doesn't altogether believe what he tells me, but he says it anyway to cover up for his generation. He feels he has a part to play in my education. The very fact that he chose to become a pioneer here and not stay there is proof enough that he doesn't go along with everything about the Diaspora and the background to the gas chambers and all that. I was deeply moved by books about the destruction of the Jews written by people who had been there, and probably the principal motive behind my joining the paratroops, my eagerness and all that was the feeling of insult done to our people throughout the generations. A deep feeling of insult.

Avraham: Did you read a lot about the annihilation of European Jewry too, Elisha?

Elisha: Hardly anything. Not from lack of interest, maybe for lack of time. In any case, to the extent that I'm familiar with the titles and the names of the authors, much of it seems to consist of stories of heroism, stories of partisans and ghetto revolts.

Amitai: I had an argument with Dad after the memorial day for European Jewry two years ago. It annoyed me that they turned it into a heroes' memorial day. In fact, only a handful rebelled and fought. We had a real argument right here in this room. I don't like to read about the ghetto heroes, maybe it's some kind of masochism. On the other hand, I liked to read the horror stories, like Ka-Chetnik's books.

It's my impression that the overall picture is not one of heroism. That's what bothers me. Today it seems to me as if the tales of courage and valour have some kind of educational objective behind them.

I don't have any feelings towards the Arabs, neither love, nor hate, nor repulsion. We live together with Arabs. The Arabs beyond our borders don't live with Jews, and they'll swallow any kind of distorted picture of the Jews you paint for them. We live with Arabs. We see them every day. We have Arab workers in the banana plantation. They don't work for us, they work together with us. That's why when the war came I didn't have the feeling that I was fighting against the Arabs as a nation or as a race, but against some kind of threat that was hanging over us. And as soon as the war was over, the thought of having fought against Arabs melted away.

When I realized after the war that I was going home, I understood that I was going back to everything that home meant: family, wife, work and the people I work with. I wondered how it would be when I met the Arab who works with us for the first time. I really like him. When I came up to him, he grabbed my hand. I didn't know what to say, and here he was holding my hand and saying: "*Mazal Tov*." I was taken back a little. And then he went on and asked me why I didn't bring him any tobacco. And the truth is that in Jerusalem, in the thick of the fighting, I spotted a large bag of tobacco on the body of a Jordanian soldier. And while I was looking at it, I thought about my Arab friend and wondered whether I should take it to him, and then I thought it wouldn't be nice if I brought him tobacco that had belonged to a dead Legionnaire.

Matitiyahu: I'd like to say something more about what we were talking about before. The awareness of the land that the boys spoke about is only natural. They were born and brought up in the kibbutz. Naturally, awareness of the land and the soil is more meaningful to them. Nevertheless, there may be another factor in this strange equation, a factor of which they aren't even aware.

I brought my parents to Palestine. For them, being here was a supreme happiness. My father was an outstanding teacher, with many years of experience and standing in the profession. When he got here in the 1930's, he couldn't find work. It was easy to understand how he felt. At the same time, I noticed something very strange, the thing that kept him going during these hard times. On several occasions, I took him for trips around the country, and it was then that I sensed what it means to talk about a person coming back to his homeland, a man returning to his homeland after thousands of years of exile. It's more than a phrase. Wherever we went, you could see right away that he knew the spot and its history well from his thorough knowledge of the Bible. Every settlement and every historical site aroused personal memories, as if he had actually been there and knew them from before. He would tell me what we were looking at, what had happened there. He would tell me, and not I him. The places we visited, and the biblical associations they aroused, revived him, put him back on his feet after all he'd been through. He made his living from all kinds of part-time jobs, and he didn't have a very easy time of it. But every time he came home from work, he would report that "on such and such a street, they've added another storey, and on such and such a street, they're building a new house" — and he would straighten up. This deep sense of participation was central to his experience. He lived in everything that was created here. He was rooted in the land as if he had never left it, not he and not his father and not his father's fathers.

I believe that things like this never go to waste. There's a kind of heredity that passes on these personal values. It's a powerful force. If after thousands of years it could come down to a particular individual, my father, then it can certainly be passed on from him to his immediate descendants.

Avraham: You would say then that for Amitai's grandfather, the land of Israel was sanctified by his spiritual heritage, the Bible and subsequent Jewish history, while for the boys, the land of Israel exists independently of Jewish history.

Matitiyahu: The two things are interlocked. In the beginning, the concept of the land was transformed into something spiritual and in this way it survived. Now, the actual land of Israel produces a spirituality of its own. This devotion to and love for the country that the boys feel — it's hard to believe that such an attachment can be created in a single generation, without some deep roots that existed previously. For instance, we know that the Jews lived in Poland for eight hundred years, but is Poland engraved on the heart of any Jew? Jews go from country to country as if — as if they were moving from one apartment to another without a sign to show for it.

Elisha: They move out of this country as well. Look at the emigrants. . . .

Matitiyahu: Now, this real concrete country produces its own spirituality.

Avraham: But the question remains whether Amitai feels the things you're talking about.

Matitiyahu: He doesn't know how to express it. But this war is proof that the boy's attachment is not to the country alone. The tie is national, real, physical, and at the same time spiritual.

Avraham: But earlier Elisha said that it was no accident that he spoke particularly about the country, the country and not the people.

Matitiyahu: We saw how everyone suddenly felt a deep attachment to Jerusalem. This isn't simply feeling for a city. It's something spiritual which burst forth. . . .

Amitai: There's been a lot of talk about territorial expansion, and someone even called the war the "Land of Israel Campaign." I have a feeling that we've lost something terribly precious. We've lost our little country. My first reaction during a trip through the West Bank just after the war was, "Fellows, we've got to get back to Galilee as quick as we can and show ourselves that our country – I meant the country we had before the war – is good and beautiful." I have a feeling of disappointment about losing that little country. I have practically no emotional ties to the broad areas which we hold today. We used to travel around a lot before the war. The special feeling we had for the country was also partly a result of these excursions, of our close personal familiarity with the countryside. Our little country seems to get lost in this vast land. My feeling for the country doesn't derive from the knowledge that it's the Promised Land. There's nothing equivocal about it. I was born here. And this is the difference between me and Dad. Dad came back to the country. I didn't come back, I was born here.

Avraham: Do you have any special feelings for Jerusalem?

Amitai: When I got to the Western Wall, I gave no outward sign of my emotion. Some people put on a show, but in my case I didn't let on anything I felt, in spite of the fact that. . . .

Avraham: Earlier, you said that this was a special feeling . . . Maybe you could put it into words.

Amitai: We had a sense of mission — you can call it a sense of national or historic mission; but when we were standing there at the Wall, our feelings were mixed with a large dose of curiosity. . . . Our attachment to the country runs very deep, or at any rate mine does. But not because I arrived at it through any conscious process. . . .

Avraham: Because you were born here?

Amitai: Yes. Because I was born here and, to tell the truth, because I learned to regard the country as mine. Every nation fights for its country or lives in its country. There's nothing special about the Jews in this respect. Every people has a certain territorial pride.

Matitiyahu: But Amitai, every people dwells on its own land. The Arabs have been here for generations. But they haven't been here for thousands of years and they didn't produce the Bible. They dwell here, but the Arabs lack something that we have, we who haven't resided in this country for many generations. The Arabs are inhabitants of the country, and that's about all. . . .

Amitai: I'm not sure that the Arabs' attachment to the country is any weaker than the tie the Jews felt to the countries from which they were expelled at one time or another.

Elisha: I'm certain it's no less strong.

Matitiyahu: They can only fight through hatred. And if hate is lacking, what will they fight with? Did they ever evolve a tradition of love for the country or of creativity, a culture all their own? From them, this country was a district, one of many districts in a wide region.

Amitai: I'm not so sure it's like that.

Elisha: Don't bank on it being like that, Dad.

Matitiyahu: That's the difference between patriotism and nationalism. They are possessed by nationalism, and we by patriotism. That's the difference between us. And there's another thing. It's hard to put your finger on it, but I'll try. Take myself, for example. My complete identification with the land of Israel isn't accidental or fortuitous. I came to the country completely broken up, shattered, without any feeling for what I had known in my childhood. I was searching for an identity. I had no deep roots anywhere. When I came to Palestine, I felt that I had been born anew. From that moment I began to live.

Elisha: I would like to subscribe to what Amitai said, contrary to what Dad's been saying. My sense of attachment to the country isn't historical (though I'm well grounded in history and I like to study it). I acquired it during the years I've lived here. When I toured the occupied areas, I had no sensation of returning home. I don't share Dad's feeling that we developed a sort of spiritual land of Israel, which was transformed by the act of physical contact. The logic of that is that we've just returned to the same areas with which we have a historical connection. Now I have a fairly good background in history, and I'm familiar with the historical, biblical background of the country. But when I went through the Dotan Valley, I didn't have the feeling of having come home. Despite the fact that it's the same country, the same sun, the same hills and sometimes even the same views that I know from our side of the border. . . . True, I always had a very special spot in my heart for Jerusalem.

Avraham: Always?

Elisha: Always. But I think much of it was acquired. Here too, the attachment grew out of my experience. But with Jerusalem possibly — not possibly, almost certainly — I have some historic tie. I must confess I felt it for the Israeli half of Jerusalem; the incomplete Jerusalem, or let's call it the non-historical Jerusalem, was quite enough for me. The attachment I felt rested to a large extent on my acquaintance with the city I knew, not only from history, but because during my short life I happened to have been there and I learned to know it as it is — as well as on the connection with history and the nation. There are two levels to our history. The first deals with the nation in its country before it left for exile and the second with the exile. There have always been people, and possibly Dad among them, who thought and dreamed that the generation born here would link up somehow with the distant past. That this generation would be the natural continuation of the Maccabees. . . .

Avraham: Bypassing the Diaspora?

Elisha: Bypassing the Dispora. The historic ties I feel were evolved through reading. And through reading I have a stronger link with the Diaspora. Ideologically, I have no use for the Diaspora. I could be "half a Maccabee" as far as my opinions go. Emotionally it's not that way at all.

Avraham: What is your emotional connection with the Diaspora?

Elisha: I love to read Diaspora literature. I love the works of Singer, Opatoshu, Shneour and the rest.

Avraham: And their world has something to say to you?

Elisha: Definitely. The people who wrote about this world lived it themselves, and they succeed in passing on what they felt to the reader. The way the Diaspora looks, the village atmosphere — the very things that Dad broke away from — have something to say to me even though I never saw them. I've read so much that, paradoxically, there have been times when I used to feel homesick for certain places — places for which Dad has no nostalgia. Strange as it may sound, I feel that I have some kind of special tie with the Jewish townlets of eastern Europe. In my thoughts, I return to the landscapes of eastern Europe . . . the snow, the birds nesting in the chimney pots, the rooks.

Avraham: What appeals to you? The actual scenes or the Jewish world of eastern Europe? The snow, or the ramshackle houses standing in the snow?

Elisha: I am drawn most to the landscapes and less to the people there. This is a very subjective kind of reaction. When I think of France, England or Western Europe, I feel a stranger. But I'm at home in the tiny villages, with a bridge barely making it from one side of a little rivulet to the other and a goose girl minding her flock. It's something very special even though I know that these scenes have long since vanished, and that modern cities stand where they once stood. More than once I've wished I could transmigrate somehow into that world. I have a special attachment to it, thanks to literature. Despite all the distortions. The carter in the story by Shneour is more of a hero to me than Judah the Maccabee. Possibly because in reading the story I felt the insult to the Jews, and the heroes there seemed to . . .

Avraham: Did you feel that the carter was an heroic figure?

Elisha: Yes. More than Judah the Maccabee. The carter, this Noah Pandre, and the other characters: for me, they're living Jews. My attitude to Judah the Maccabee and his generation is historical.

My feeling for that Jewry, the Jewry of the villages, is personal.

Amitai: I have no feeling for the Diaspora. Or to be exact, my feeling is antagonistic. On the other hand, I am drawn much more to the heroes of Israel, like Judah the Maccabee. I had no desire to read about heroes of the Diaspora and the ghetto revolts. In my reading about the Diaspora, I looked for the bad things.

Avraham: You would say then that you appreciate only physical courage, or heroism in war?

Amitai: No. I'm attached to the country, to its nature festivals, to the things that have been done here. I have no attachment to anything that happens in the Diaspora. I'm convinced that education plays a very important role in forming a person's attitudes; and this is how I was educated. I'd read a great deal. I wasn't so interested in the Cave of the Machpela or the other "holy places." But when I got to Wadi Kelt, I felt like Dad says, as if I'd come back to Wadi Kelt. I'd never been there in my life. I'd only read about it, and I remember that one of the dreams of my life had been to go to Wadi Kelt and walk through it to Jericho. I was more deeply moved there than at the Western Wall. Just as Elisha was affected by what he read about the Jewish townlet, I was affected by what I'd read about Wadi Kelt.

I remember we drove down the Wadi in our jeeps. We pulled up at every spring. Covered the canyon from top to bottom. For me, this was the high point of my trip through the West Bank. I'm sure that if I'd had a religious education, I would have been moved and affected by other spots. I hadn't been brought up to feel anything special about the Western Wall, the Cave of Machpela and all those places. What interests us is visiting Wadi Kelt and climbing to the top of Mount Gerizim. One of the things I most want to do, that I've dreamt about all my life, is to climb Mount Hermon. That's my greatest dream. The Hermon, and not Bethlehem or Hebron (though I was interested in Hebron because Dad had told me he'd spent some time in jail there once). I'm convinced that it's all a question of education.

Avraham: Do you say that as a statement of fact, or as a criticism?

Amitai: I have no criticism to make.

Matitiyahu: Can you explain your attachment to the country simply by the fact of your being born here?

Amitai: The fact is that the whole Jewish people returned to Jerusalem. Why? Because they'd all been educated to it.

I KNEW THAT WE MUST NOT FORGET

Discussion at Ein Hachoresh

In this discussion, there is a confrontation between a number of the initiators of *The Seventh Day* and a representative of a generation older than themselves, but younger than Matitiyahu: Abba Kovner, who was educated in the Jewish community of pre-war Vilna, himself experienced the Nazi conquest, and became a partisan leader. A number of the younger members of Abba Kovner's own kibbutz, Ein Hachoresh, also took part in the discussion; two of them speak in the extract given here.

Participants:
Ishai, thirty-one, was born and educated at Ein Hachoresh. He is married, with two children. He usually works in the orchards, but has also held a number of administrative and educational posts within the kibbutz, such as youth leader, chairman of the cultural committee, and secretary. His army rank is Major. After the war, he joined the regular army at the request of the kibbutz movement, and he is currently Education Officer to the Nachal agricultural corps. *Yehuda A.*, twenty-six, married, with two children. Works in field crops. Lieutenant, fought in the battle for the Syrian Heights. Biographies of Abba Kovner, Ofer of Giv'at Haim — whose letter is quoted here — and other participants, are

179

given in the note on the Editorial Board or on their own kibbutzim. Other participants: *Amram Hayisra'eli* and *Yehuda G.* (Giv'at Haim); *Avraham Shapira* (Yizre'el); *Menachem Shelach* (Mishmar Ha'emek).

Menachem: I felt uneasy about being a victorious army, a strong army. If I had any clear awareness of the World War years and the fate of European Jewry it was once when I was going up the Jericho road and the refugees were going down it. I identified directly with them. When I saw parents dragging their children along by the hand, I actually almost saw myself being dragged along by my own father. This was perhaps one of the immediate experiences that brought an association with the war years. It wasn't so noticeable in times of action, but just at those moments when we felt the suffering of others, of the Arabs, against whom we fought. This was perhaps the tragic thing, that the identification had to be with the other side, with our enemies.

People who have gone through a number of wars feel a profound fatalism. How much longer will we have to fight? At any rate, I've been in four wars, I've gone from war to war. People flee, destroy, everything. How long will this go on for? It's also connected with the massacre of the Jews by Hitler, this feeling of the tragedy of Jewish existence. It isn't anything conscious. But it's there.

Yariv: I have a feeling of tragedy in enormous dimensions: that was my experience both intellectually and emotionally: and it includes the confrontation with war and the consciousness of the fate of the Jews – the interminable wars, the feeling that we weren't fighting for territory but for our lives.

The Jewish aspect of the war applies to each one of us. Something in our education has made us very conscious of this Jewish tragedy. The war was a link in a chain of actions that derive from this tragic feeling. Our opponents, the Arabs, are really equal partners in this tragic conflict, have undertaken to struggle for survival. We've reached this conclusion through a process that's been going on for hundreds and thousands of years. The Arab has no understanding of this fateful – fatal – process, which results in refugees, in destruction.

It's true that people believed that there we would be exterminated if we lost the war. They were afraid. We got this idea — or inherited it — from the concentration camps. It's a concrete idea for anyone who has grown up in Israel, even if he personally didn't experience Hitler's persecution, but only heard or read about it. Genocide — it's a feasible notion. There are the means to do it. This is the lesson of the gas chambers.

Abba: Did you really have the feeling that extermination could happen here?

Yariv: Yes, without a doubt. I remember that a few days before the war, I got my company together. They wanted us to say something to the men. The situation was tense, but they kept postponing operations. And when I spoke, I used this historical parallel. Yes, we spoke about it.

Abba: So there were moments during that time when you actually conceived that extermination was likely here?

Yariv: Yes, certainly. I think it's an idea that everyone in Israel lived with.

Abba: The War of Independence, the establishment of the State, its twenty years of history couldn't guarantee that it wouldn't happen here? Is it really true that you, an Israeli, feared a repetition of Auschwitz in this country?

Yariv: It's true. My own personal view is that any Israeli feels that all these things are part of his life, but also feels — I do, at any rate — the relativity of their existence. I don't look at this just from the angle of military danger. The fact of Jewish existence in Israel isn't yet unquestionable. Historically, it's a very short-term phenomenon. It's also comparatively small numerically, as regards the proportion of Jews who actually live here. So one can't help asking to what extent the rebirth of Jewish life in Israel is alive and firmly rooted? I feel this problem very deeply. I think that many people had the feeling that we might not win.

Abba: What do you mean when you say that we might not win?

Yariv: Had there been a different balance of forces, a different army — Arab strength could have been concentrated as it was in certain places in the War of Liberation. There might have been places where the war would have resulted in slaughter of civilians or military defeat. But I don't believe that this would have created refugees or brought us to surrender.

Menachem: Why not? Don't Jews know how to be refugees?

Yariv: Perhaps, after all, my feeling is mistaken, perhaps in different circumstances we'd have behaved as Jews did elsewhere, but I certainly felt — and I think many others did, too — that all our achievements in this country would lead people to behave differently.

Abba: Behave differently? How?

Yariv: That people would do anything, as long as they were alive and able to fight, to defend what they'd created, their lives and their families.

Amram: An Arab from the Old City came to visit us in Giv'at Haim. He asked each of us, "Do you believe that we, the Arabs, would have slaughtered you if we'd won?" When he talked to my little daughter, and asked me, "Do you believe that I would be capable of killing a child like this?" it was a very disturbing moral question for me too. I answered, "Perhaps I can't believe that you personally would have done it." But my daughter gave a much better answer. She said, "I'm afraid of bad Arabs." He asked, "What are bad Arabs?" "Bad Arabs are the ones who come to fight us." "And how do you know who's fighting you?" "The ones with guns. The good Arabs are different."

I agree with the distinction my daughter made. But I'm convinced that we all believed, or feared, that a large proportion of the Arab masses were capable of behaving as they did, for instance, in the Etzion bloc.*

Menachem: Not only Arabs. In Indonesia they're slaughtering one another. In the Congo they're slaughtering one another.

Ishai: I behaved in the war as though I belonged to a normal people. In my conscious mind there was no idea of extermination. The question didn't bother me at all. I was educated and reared as a normal Jew, who lives on his own soil, who was born here. I hadn't a shadow of doubt about our victory. I feel that I belong to a nation

---

*Where Arab irregulars tried to slaughter the Jewish settlers, against the orders of the Arab Legion.

healthy in spirit and body, a nation that can't lose because it's better than its enemies. And not because it fought for certain values or for a heritage handed down through the generations. From the first moment I was convinced we'd win. I disagree with Yariv's and Amram's approach.

I behaved like a normal person, in a normal country. In my opinion, what I did was simply the duty of anyone living in his own country, who fights to defend its honor under provocation or under siege. I couldn't come to my men and tell them that we were facing a serious threat of extermination. And I definitely didn't fight for the honor of our people. Perhaps there's some connection with the past here. It may be. Later on I may have thought of this. On the other hand, the war gave me an outstanding lesson in what's called Jewish consciousness. And this through two experiences I had.

The first experience was Jerusalem. In my unit we heard the news on a transistor radio. When we heard of the conquest of Jerusalem there wasn't a single one who didn't weep, including me. Then, for the first time, I felt not the "Israelness" but the Jewishness of the nation.

The second experience was when we had to evacuate the inhabitants of a village. We didn't only think about this business, I remember, we didn't only feel it with our senses and our emotions. I remember discussing it. It wasn't a matter of identifying with them, as Menachem did with the refugees. Whatever the reasons, however justified the evacuation was on rational grounds, when you come to carry out an order like that you have a very uncomfortable feeling. The Arabs said to me, not once, but two or three times, or more: "Leave us to die here." And it's very hard, simply on the human level.

I don't want to say a lot about it, but for me these two experiences reflected a high level of Jewish consciousness. If up to now there was a gap between what I knew and what I felt, now I've changed, and that's very important indeed. I remember that on the day we had to deal with this business I didn't know what to do with myself. I remember the CO sent someone to call me four times. I agreed that it had to be done, I just couldn't stand being on the spot. I took my jeep and drove off, there and back.

On both of these occasions, I felt — I thought then, and still think today — that there were two forces at work within me, pulling in different directions perhaps; and perhaps they'll eventually come to some sort of resolution.

It may be that this feeling of "Israelness," of being and acting like a normal healthy people, is connected with the past, with Jewish self-respect. Perhaps with the partisans as well, and with Jewish martyrdom.

Amram: This feeling of normality that you speak about worries me. Our people, our soldiers, have a special spirit that's liable to be distorted under the conditions of a conquering nation.

Abba: Perhaps you'll repeat your sentence, and consider whether you mean a conquering nation or a conquering army.

Amram: Perhaps a conquering army. But it wasn't by chance that I used this expression. I had the feeling that it's not an army we're discussing, it's a nation. An army of conquest, but this army is actually the nation, it belongs to the nation. And what the army does, it doesn't do alone: the whole nation does it. Wherever any of us goes, he has a national responsibility. He can't say: "They sent me" or "They told me to do it." Some of the things that happened undermine the moral basis of our position. They caused many of our best men a great deal of emotional distress.

It may be said that there was no alternative. It's said that we were forced to adopt severe measures, because under war conditions it's difficult to control every soldier. Also because events moved so swiftly that it wasn't possible to plan ahead effectively.

It can also be argued that with all our shortcomings and imperfections we have moral standards second to none among the armies of the world: and, in any case: "What would have happened had things been the other way round?"

All these arguments are, in my opinion, no justification. They don't hold water. To begin with, we believe that our army was and will be unique. It's different from its enemies and even from the armies of enlightened nations. Secondly, there were so many wonderful expressions of a really humane attitude, even under these very conditions, that it's definitely possible to demand such behavior all along the line.

Abba: The fact that this moral conflict exists is very important.

The question really is whether it isn't possible to refuse to carry out an order that's morally wrong. Of course, Israel had no policy of extermination, and the government had no intention of turning the Arabs of the West Bank into refugees. But it isn't always possible to run to a higher political authority to clarify the situation or to prevent any undesirable act. But this still doesn't solve the problem. The specific question is whether the individual — the soldier, the deputy commander — bears a personal responsibility for an act which offends his moral consciousness and the spirit of the Israeli Army. Do you think that obedience to an order, or the knowledge that "this is higher policy" absolves you from moral responsibility for your actions? Where, then, is the point at which your conscience obliges you to say "No!"

Ishai: There was the problem of refugees infiltrating back through the lines at night. We had orders: no one was to be allowed to cross the Jordan except by the bridges. I know that we carried out the spirit of the order without harming anyone.

Amram: And you still say that this is a normal nation and a normal army?

Abba: We mustn't forget the moral of the terrible thing that happened in Europe. It was not only that murderers without any conscience attacked us, but that people with consciences, sensitive and moral in normal circumstances, preferred not to get involved in a risky situation, and remained aloof from the bloodshed. Was our behavior really no different?

Ishai: There are all sorts of cases. I know that there are people for whom this war was great fun. I know it.

Amram: I can't accept what Ishai said before, that we're a normal people. Ultimately, there's something definitely "abnormal" in the sensitivity he expressed. The men I saw around me behaved in the most humane manner possible in such a situation.

Yehuda G.: The destruction of European Jewry is the most important and most fascinating chapter in the history of mankind. I've been preoccupied since I was quite young with the experience of the Jews during that period. It's difficult for me to say to what extent it influenced me during the war. It's clear to me that I did have it in my mind, but in an unconscious form.

During war you don't have humane feelings out of principle or because of other people's historical experience. It's some little thing that arouses your humane feelings at the height of the war: the look in the eyes of a refugee, a mangled horse. . . .

Abba: When you keep on saying "What happened there, won't happen again," you unwittingly reveal your consciousness of the fate of the Jews of Europe. What seems strange is that *your* association should bring it up. Something you thought foreign to you is apparently hidden deep within you, and comes to the surface at a time of action. As for me, this phenomenon doesn't surprise me. But I can't get over certain other ways in which Israel-born soldiers expressed this association.

Quite a lot of people in Israel and abroad, who read the news or watched the television, saw us in those memorable days between May 15 and June 5 as a beleaguered nation. Two million beleaguered Jews.

Beleaguerment is a traumatic Jewish experience. But this time it was happening here, on Israeli soil. I won't mention the names of those who played a major part in building the country, who led the struggle to realize and defend the Zionist ideal, and who even so experienced those pre-war days in terms of memories inspired by the period of Nazism. They envisaged the dangers of the imminent war in terms of the ghetto and tried with all their might to avoid a war of desperation, a recurrence of the Warsaw ghetto revolt.

I won't go into what I personally felt about things, what it was that made me think differently and why I was so perturbed by the very possibility of any parallel of this nature. It's more important to understand your reaction. I'm amazed that *sabras* could see what was happening as a beleaguerment. Did you seriously see things in terms of the ghetto and the danger of annihilation?

Another point. The State of Israel, by its very nature, is regarded by world Jewry as the prime guarantor of the life and safety of the Jewish nation. Then, suddenly, it wasn't a Jewish community in the Diaspora but the people here, in Zion itself, who faced a serious threat to their very existence. What is your reaction to this paradoxical situation?

And last of all. The war is over now, but there are still some question-marks. But what are they? There's a feeling — a conviction even — that this wasn't the last war. Was the Six-Day War simply one of the wars we must go through or was there something in it which established — and not simply in our subjective consciousness — a decisive historic change? In other words, no matter what dangers of hostility and armed struggle the future may bring, one danger at least will never recur.

Do you believe this? And if the answer is yes: on what do you base your faith, for there must surely be a difference between us in this respect?

Yehuda G.: What you've said has illustrated our hidden link with the destruction of the Jews. As far as I'm concerned, at least, it does exist. No one who hasn't been through such an experience can understand its significance. All he can do is to analyze it rationally and use that analysis to arrive at an understanding of national honor. The honor of the people consists in its *élan vital,* in other words the ability to react when threatened with destruction. The thing I found frightening in this war, on the eve of the war, was the last week before war broke out when it seemed as if no decision was going to be taken. I felt quite clear on one point: if we began it, we would win. What I wasn't at all sure of was whether we'd win if we waited for them to start. By the way, not all the war was fought on their territory. On the Syrian front, it started on our territory.

Abba: It seems to me that at this point we come up against Jewish history. It's not a question of honor, whether personal or national. It's something much more significant. What does our historic responsibility demand of us when danger threatens a Jewish community or the existence of the people as a whole? Does one go out and meet the enemy, and take action at the appropriate moment, despite the dangers and the possible way to preserve the *status quo,* even by making concessions?

A new Jewish society has been created in this country. And even so it would seem that the 2000-year-old dilemma still exists. It's clear to me that there isn't and wasn't any responsible national body which doubted the need to fight. But implementing this policy in concrete reality wasn't always so easy. Look, up to the morning of June 5, Nasser won one victory after another without firing so much as a single shot.

We stood alone. This time, as always, our fate depended on our decisions. And I stress this, it depended not on our decisions, but on *a* decision, just *one* decision.

And as you know, there were people in the country who seriously doubted our ability to maintain an armed struggle alone against the united might of the Arab states and their allies. You've got to draw some conclusions from this.

I don't have any definite information about this, but I don't think I'm wrong in saying that what really helped the government arrive at their momentous decision was the spirit of readiness displayed by the army: and, when all's said and done, the army embodies the spirit of readiness of the people.

Generally speaking the army didn't have any feelings of contempt for the enemy. Before the fighting, our men never lost sight of the sheer weight of technological force facing them which was revealed by our reconnaissance patrols. They even tended to exaggerate the seriousness of the coming struggle. Yet, for all that, what characterized the army camps was a clear recognition that if we had to face them, we would hold our own. What puzzles me, and what I'd like to know from you, is whether this high morale sprang from the military set-up, or from some other spiritual source?

Amram: You have to distinguish between two things: the feeling of personal danger that existed then and that has in fact existed all our lives, and the sense of danger as far as the general situation was concerned. Both the "final solution" and the War of Independence play a tremendous part. Our generation seems to feel very deeply about them.

I think there's some mystic element here that's difficult to explain. We heard children give spontaneous answers over the radio to the question "Who'll win?" And even kindergarten kids said unhesitatingly that we would. This feeling is based on the knowledge that everyone may have to take part, that each of us may have to put himself in a position where his life may well be endangered; but if he's ready to do anything for the sake of the common cause, then the common cause can also withstand anything. There's some deep factor at work here whose educational effect we didn't appreciate properly.

Yehuda A.: I don't accept Ishai's approach. Perhaps my

circumstances were a little different because, as a member of Kibbutz Dan, I was one of the very few who fought near their own homes. Those of us who were in Galilee during the first days of the war felt very uncomfortable. In fact, we didn't do anything at all. We just sat there being shelled — we had the feeling that we could have reacted, but we weren't doing anything about it.

I don't know if people did think about the parallel between our situation and the Nazi period. What bothered me all the time was how my parents were managing in Dan. Someone suggested that if the Syrians did invade, we should let them advance a certain distance and then kill them off. No one would accept that idea with much enthusiasm, even if it was a military possibility. No one could imagine us letting them into Gadot, for example. Because if we had, they would have slaughtered every last person there.

We discussed this question. We said a thing like that couldn't happen. The Jewish people would never forgive a thing like that — letting them in to wipe out a whole settlement. Perhaps that's our link with the Jews of Europe.

Abba: I'm sure there is a connection. I want to understand it.

Menachem: It's a subject one doesn't think about consciously. But for all that, it does have a role to play. In fact, though we can't consciously grasp the magnitude of such a tragedy, we can't permit a similar thing to recur. The memory and the lesson of the gas chambers are part of our national honor, part of our lives here.

Abba: Perhaps you'll read us a letter we've heard about, written by a boy from Giv'at Haim who fell in the war.

Avraham: This is a letter which Ofer wrote to his girl-friend in 1963. He was a member of Giv'at Haim and he was killed during the paratroopers' battle for Jerusalem in the Six-Day War.

My dearest Yael:

I am writing this letter to you because there is no other person in this world to whom I am able to describe what is happening within me now.

There's jazz on the radio. The singers' voices are lively and enthusiastic.

I have just finished reading a dreadful book on the holocaust, *The*

House of Dolls, and I feel with all my soul the horrors of this terrible happening. I know there are some people who would sneer, ridicule, and think me eccentric if they were to hear what I am saying now. That's why I'm saying it to you alone.

I wouldn't presume to say that I have the same feelings as these condemned people who lived hopelessly under the shadow of death. But I can sense the loss and horror reflected in their Jewish eyes, wise with the knowledge of suffering, looking out from behind the electrified fences. I can never forget it. We visited the memorial building for the victims of the Holocaust in Kibbutz Lochamei Hageta'ot, and as I looked at the pictures I understood everything! Others didn't understand, couldn't grasp the meaning, said it was impossible for them to grasp it; and after we had left they laughed, and behaved as if nothing had happened.

I understood, I grasped, I knew that we must not forget!

I remember when we were still in Czechoslovakia, in Prague, our gentile maid was foolish enough to take us to see a film which portrayed the bestialities the Nazis perpetrated upon Czechoslovakian villages. Even then I was so shocked by what I saw that my soul could find no escape from such horror. That experience has left its stamp on me. I sit at the memorial evening for the victims of the Holocaust, staring into the eyes of the survivors who are sitting near me, and their entire being expresses helplessness and hopelessness.

Out of all this horror and helplessness I feel arising within me a tremendous will to be strong, strong to the brink of tears, strong and keen as a knife, composed and terrible and dangerous. This is what I want to be! I want to know that never again will those vacant eyes stare from behind electrified fences! Only if I am strong will they not do so! Only if we are all strong; strong, proud Jews! Only if we never again allow ourselves to be led to the slaughter.

Whenever I see a terrified Jew, a picture or a word that reminds me of all this, I regret every minute that I wasted in the army, and didn't take the fullest advantage of to become more efficient, more dangerous.

When we were advance reconnaissance scouts we were like that. We were quick, strong, and silent, like fiends. We walked powerfully through long nights, climbing mountains in the knowledge that we could conquer them. We did things that no one believed we were capable of, and we were confident in our power. Is there any better feeling for a soldier than being silent, alert and dangerous? We used to pass through villages, over mountains and fields, like shadows, and nobody knew that we had been there and disappeared.

I stood to attention at a passing-out parade, and found myself gazing at the clouds above, looking for the same proud power. My eyes dropped from the clouds, and fell on the officers who were passing in review. They were more than just a parade of officers. I felt confidence in their capabilities.

Abba: A few days ago we had a discussion very similar to this one in Kibbutz Ramat Yohanan between Matitiyahu, his wife and their two parachutist sons. Elisha, the older brother, said, "What hurt me as a youngster wasn't that they killed Jews, but that they insulted them. Today, too, whenever I hear anyone say *'Arabush'* it reminds me of terms like 'Yid' and that's why it grates on me so much. It's easier to understand hatred for the Arabs than to reconcile oneself with a term that implies a feeling of superiority to them. Ever since I've been old enough to think, that expression has driven me mad."

I don't understand this attitude: it bothered him that Jews were insulted, but not that they were killed. He doesn't like the expression *"Arabush"* because it reminds him of "Yid." But it's not because "Yid" has any association with the gas chambers, with annihilation, but rather that it's an expression of insult. In other words, the whole basic motif here, if I understand him properly, is: "I don't understand annihilation. What concerns me is dignity." Jewish dignity is more important for him than the very existence of the Jewish people.

And in this discussion here, Ishai has put forward a very similar approach. This feeling is foreign to me.

Every one of us expresses the yearning for peace; I think that's common to most of the Jewish people. But what if it turns out that this yearning is just an ideal, and, like every ideal, it can't be realized overnight? What if fate has decreed that there should be "peace in the land for twenty years" as it says in the Book of Chronicles, or "for ten years," or "for forty years," and no more?

What if your generation has to teach your sons and your

grandsons that we are fated to fight for our existence? What will happen then? Do you think that you and your children will be able to educate your sons like that? If your sons and grandsons have to go through the same thing, will they be able to bear it with the same strength of will as my father and my grandfather bore the same burden?

The Six-Day War was a turning point in history, a new stage in a continuous process. But was it such a profound change? In the Diaspora fathers didn't bring up their sons to commit suicide, or to despair. No one brought up his son to abandon Judaism. They taught them that it was their destiny to be persecuted; but, at the same time, they educated them to life. There has been a change here in this country, especially during these six days. But is it such a profound change? Has it really affected the mentality of this generation, the one now fighting? Will you be able to stand up for your Judaism like the generations which preceded you, who knew what it was all about and educated their children to it?

Menachem: The Jews of Diaspora lived a life based on a religious ideology which offers solutions over and above human life. Things get more complicated when you're dealing with a secular ideology such as we base our education on.

Ishai: Abba, earlier you brought up the idea that the danger to the Jew is far greater here. That would never have occurred to me at all. I still think that the danger was far greater there than it is here.

Nurit: I've often asked myself what would happen if we really did finally achieve peace here. It's interesting that as I see it, if the Arabs really do want to finish us off, then the best thing they could do would be to make peace with us. I'm not referring to questions of natural increase or anything like that. I think it's a question of Jewish fate.

Abba: I was talking about the spiritual character of the people: What direction are you going in? What are you going to tell your children? What sort of life are you going to offer them?

Amram: I want to go back to Ofer's letter. Ofer talks about identification with Jewish suffering and degradation. It's the same sort of feeling that Elisha had when he thought about those who went like sheep to the slaughter on their last journey in life.

Without expressing the deep link he felt with those people, with that entire world — so close to him and so far away — that they represented, he was trying, in his own way, as a young Jew, to give some expression to that feeling of restoring the nation's dignity.

That's why, for me, his letter lacks something: the other aspect of his attitude to that world which no longer exists. Most of us here don't know how great a part his grandfather's home in Safed played in Ofer's life. His grandfather was an orthodox Jew, a profound symbol in Ofer's life. Just before he was Bar Mitzvah he insisted on going to spend a week there, really learning how to go through the religious ceremony of being called to the reading of the Law.

Some of his closest friends in the kibbutz belonged to a family who had come here as youngsters just after Hitler's war. Once Ofer expressed his puzzlement about the whole business by saying to one of the girls: "What are you anyway? You're not really either a *sabra* or a Diaspora Jew." Apparently this living link with the danger of Jewish extinction really concerned him. He was very interested in this girl who'd been there and is today an organic part of our own community.

Our generation has been brought up on the need to be strong, to be ready and able to defend ourselves. This is something you can educate people towards for ten or twenty years. But what happens over a longer period? That's why the generation that's already been through two or three wars has this fatalism. Quite a lot of people have expressed a feeling of fatalism in our discussions.

Apparently that's our fate. There was someone who said, "I'd be quite ready for a war if I knew it was the last one. But I know I'm going to die for something that has no end to it." I'm convinced that that sort of feeling is going to be far stronger after this war than it ever was after previous wars. People have felt the pointlessness of this never-ending struggle.

Yehuda G.: There's a connection between an army which is representative of its people and the people themselves. One of the good things about the army is that in some respects it's on a level, or it's got a spirit, which isn't exactly the same as the spirit of the people as a whole. I think the army's the only place where the potential of the younger generation finds its really full expression.

Yet why should this happen in the army of all places? In an organization which in the final analysis educates one towards killing?

There are other things that bother me: what should I educate myself towards? What's my future here going to be? How do I see this country? What am I prepared to do? To do and to think?

Amram: You ask what we're to do: but the question is really what are we going to be?

WE TAUGHT OUR SONS TO GO TO THE DANGER-SPOTS

Discussion at Na'an. Interviewer: Giora Mossinson

A discussion between Yoske, one of the founders of
Kibbutz Na'an, and his son Kobi.

Giora: As a generation which fought many wars in its time,
which fathered a revolutionary way of life, how did you feel now
that all of a sudden you were no longer bearing the brunt of the war,
that you are no longer the ones who decide things?

Yoske: True, this was one war in which my generation as a
whole didn't take part, even though some of my contemporaries still
had a part to play as senior officers or at the policy-making level of
government. One of the hardest things for someone who's been a
fighter is to be passive, to have to sit back and wait for news. You
seem to be an inanimate object, without a say in anything.

But here I must say that the boys' participation gave us the feeling
that we too were taking part. The feeling that you're taking part in
the war through your sons is a very real one. It was as if I'd sent
some part of myself to the front. Really. It was a very strong sense
of participation.

We had a general meeting of the kibbutz. As zero hour drew close,
we were all uneasy, as fathers and mothers, as relatives, as wives and
brothers and sisters. At the same time, we had another feeling which
sometimes seemed to overshadow all else, and that was our pride in
the sons we had raised. More than in the Sinai Campaign, we sensed

that this was to be a momentous struggle. Then, Israel was not fighting alone. There wasn't this feeling that the State was face to face with destiny. In 1948, as well, there were moments when we thought we were losing. But we knew that even if we were defeated, what we had built up here would be established anew.

This time, the feeling of danger was stronger. After twenty years of existence, the fall of the State could be final. It could mean the end. This great experiment in Jewish history was in the balance. Someone like myself got up at the general meeting when you boys were all away, and tried to make the point that we must go to war, that we stood to lose for every day of delay. I remember as I left the dining-room hearing one woman say to another: "He's got two sons in the army. Why does he want a war so much?"

I really don't know, but I imagine that the people stationed in the front lines, waiting, functioning in the framework of the army, with someone to give them orders and regulate their day for them, didn't feel this as strongly as we did. In my letters to the boys, I tried to distil this feeling that our world was in the balance.

In the letters we got from Kobi and Ofer, they wrote that they didn't want war, that the general feeling was that there would be no war, but that if it came, they'd do a good job. I felt that it was their wish that there should be no war. At the same time, the kibbutz, to the extent that it appreciated the dangers or had access to information, was in favor of war. Despite the fact that they were parents, not direct participants, and that they knew that the price they would have to pay would be high.

After her son was killed, Hannah G. said to me: "After all, what do I want? What am I complaining about? What am I crying about? That's how we brought my Nimrod up. It's we who brought our sons up to lay down their lives. What do I expect? It's we who prepared him for the moment of truth; this was the moment, and we knew that it would have to be paid for."

We had a sense of pride in having raised a generation that we could depend on; in knowing that our boys would do what they had to do to the utter limit of their capability. That feeling was a deep consolation for the sense of non-participation, of bodily absence from the field of battle. I think that this war strengthened the bridge between the generations.

The generation that created the kibbutz had put all its hopes into the next generation. We, the fathers, gave everything in this war. More than ourselves. It's easier to give yourself. We had the feeling that we were hazarding our most precious possession — not only because these are our sons, but because this is the generation of our dreams, the generation that can give immortality to the enterprise which we began.

After the war I asked the boys: "Did you sense that we were with you? In fact we were right there in the midst of the slaughter, on the battlefield." Maybe one of the secret weapons that Nasser and the world are asking about is this close bond between the rear and front. You had the same kind of tie possible in Russia during the World War, or in England during the blitz. But in no book have I ever seen it expressed as strongly as what we felt. It encompassed every single Jew in the country, every single Jew.

Kobi: We were among the first to be called up. At the beginning, it didn't seem so serious. Just another alert. It was as if I was thinking on two levels, one of them seemingly subconscious. As long as I've lived, for as long as I've been able to think, nothing really extraordinary has ever happened to me. All the historic happenings, all the decisive events, either took place in books or films or else involved people who were there before me. I'd never faced a supreme test in my whole life. I'd only experienced the little things that go to make up life.

When we heard that Nasser was going to close the Straits, I told myself, and the rest of the boys, that war was inevitable. That's what my reason told me. But at the same time, I couldn't quite grasp it. Me and war? Am I going to have some influence? Even though I said all along, together with everyone else, that I hoped there would be no war, somewhere inside — and I say this in all frankness — I wanted it to happen.

I wanted it. I got the tank all ready, and like a pilot waiting for the bell, I waited.

It's an awful thing to say. But I waited. Now I tell myself that I was ready and waiting because in my subconscious I was pretty sure that there would be no war. In the years I'd been in the army, I'd been through dozens of alerts. They were already routine. I'm not married and have no family. Maybe that's another point of difference between me and the other fellows I was with. They were so dead set against a war that they convinced themselves there would be none. As for me, my reason clashed with my emotions.

Afterwards, when the order to move came, there was a sudden crisis. Suddenly the war was on! "What's going on here?" I asked myself. It was just like in books. I was off to war!

Suddenly I was aware that I no longer wanted a war. That upset my self-confidence. Suddenly I wanted to go home. Earlier, I'd had no thought at all for home. Suddenly I realized that the war had penetrated my feelings.

I became another person from the moment I realized that I was going into battle. I wanted to look at my watch, to see what the date was. Suddenly this was history. During the waiting period, you reached a point where you didn't care what day of the week it was, what time of day. It's something you don't even remember afterwards. Suddenly I realized that I was seeing history with my own eyes. All at once. We asked each other what day it was.

I had all along been at odds with the fellows who hadn't wanted war. Because of this, psychologically they hadn't wanted to get ready for battle. The more you adjust your weapons, the more you clean, the more you're getting ready for something that scares you. And we had fellows like that. Maybe it was a cross-section, right off the street, only concerned with their own petty affairs all the time. They wrote to their wives: "Send off the check, I forgot to arrange this and that." They didn't want a war. "Take the machine-gun in and clean it" – that frightened them.

Almost without realizing it we were in Sinai. I felt that Sinai was kilometers away. I knew the Negev well from maneuvers. That was routine, worn thin, even commonplace. You don't think about the frontier and beyond it, Sinai. It seems far away. All those names. Now I know exactly where Abu Agheila is, and Jebel Libne, and they exist for me. Then, they were still very unreal.

When you get the order to move, you suddenly feel enormous power. I would slip a shell into the breech, and be amazed at my own strength. I'd never felt like that before.

Giora: Tell me, Yoske, when the fighting was still going on, but after it was clear that we no longer had to fear for our national survival, did you feel any turning point? Did your apprehensions about our fate give way to a father's concern for his sons? Did you feel that there was some change either as far as you personally were concerned or as regards the other people in the kibbutz?

Yoske: Yes. There was a very clear turning point. The first day of the war concluded with that famous announcement, very late at night, of the destruction of four hundred planes and that our forces were already in El Arish. That was when the feeling of victory began to supplant all other feelings. People were in no position to count the cost yet, they didn't think about what the price was. People didn't feel that they were going to be affected directly. The will to live is so strong, both as regards a person himself and as regards his children, that you persuade yourself that "it can't happen to me." You distract yourself with that hope. The intoxicating feeling of victory swept everything before it. Everyone shouted out to the other what each separately had just heard over the radio: "What do you think about that?" — "And that?" — "They're already at such and such." — "We've taken so and so." Concentration on these emotions may have been a deliberate attempt to isolate in some distant corner of the mind the gnawing fear that you yourself might be the one to suffer.

This euphoria continued until the first postcard arrived. It's only natural that not all the postcards arrive on the same day, and that the ones that do don't come from everyone at once. Rumors spread immediately. "So-and-so sent a card." — "So-and-so sent a card." Some people received cards, others didn't. The kibbutz was divided between those who received their cards one day and those who got them the next. We got a card which Ofer sent on the second day of the war.

At the end of the six days, a great depression set in. People began to count the postcards, to check when they were written. And there were still families who hadn't received any at all. People who had got postcards were chary of meeting those who hadn't. I know that when we got a card, I didn't want to tell anyone, and I asked the post office not to mention it so as to preserve our solidarity with those who hadn't. It was hard to look at them, they hadn't got a card and you had. Everyone felt deeply for everyone else, much more than usual. From this point of view, Na'an really became one family. We rejoiced at every postcard which arrived as if it had come from our own son, as if a stone had been lifted from our own breast. Everyone wanted to be the first to bring the good news. And each time, there were fewer and fewer who had still received no word. A cloud of depression settled on the kibbutz in those days after the victory. Until we had the announcement about the dead. And even then, there were still two or three boys who hadn't been heard from. The parents walked around like ghosts. You couldn't talk to them. I was afraid to ask them if they'd heard anything or not. We would put our inquiries through a third person.

That week, between Tuesday and Saturday — news that they were still alive came on Monday — Ruhama said to me several times that they wouldn't come back. I had an irrational feeling, I can't explain it, that my sons weren't going to be killed. I don't know why, but I told Ruhama that I had some premonition that I couldn't explain that they would come back. My heart told me. There are things like that. My heart told me.

Possibly, to the extent that I can analyze myself, I think I felt this way because I had been one of those who'd said that we had to fight this war. I couldn't punish myself for thinking this way. I think this is the analysis. Others said that anything would be better, even concessions. I said that we had to fight, out loud, both in the general meetings at Na'an, and in the Central Committee of the kibbutz movement. I thought that this war would be our salvation for a long time to come. Maybe for all time. Possibly, because I held such an outspoken opinion on the issue, I couldn't allow myself to feel guilty. I had wanted the war, and my view could have been influential.

Giora: This reminds me of after the war, when we went to call on families of boys in our unit who were killed. In almost every case, the wives said: "We knew." They had also said so to other women friends during the fighting. Maybe that's the difference between a boy and a girl, maybe it's the verge of, I won't call it a breakdown, but some very sensitive state. Everywhere we went, they said they knew from the beginning, and they tried to prove it to us. And somehow that strengthened them, as if it hadn't come as a surprise. They knew what was coming and they talked about it.

Yoske: I think that if it had happened to me, it would have been harder to bear. I wasn't prepared for it. While I tried to imagine to myself what it would be like when they came to tell me, tried to visualize the hypothetical situation, it was only an intellectual exercise. Some irrational force within me said no. Ruhama was better prepared. Not only was she prepared, she even said she was ready. There was total identification in this war. And we had been to see Sheinke, for instance, Nathan's mother. When they told her, she said: "I knew it was coming. I knew we would pay the price." We sat with her one evening, and someone said that if we had known what the Egyptians had in Gaza, we would have attacked in greater strength and so on. She said: "Fine. There are all sorts of surprises in war. But we've got Gaza. It's not just empty talk. We've got Gaza." There was an extraordinary degree of identification with the overall aim. But in the rationale of war, there can be no victory without a price, and someone had to pay it.

There is a Jewish concept of acknowledgment of divine justice. There is something of this in war, the sense of partnership in a war like this somehow eases the pain. Just as Alterman said, only once in a thousand years does death have a meaning. Something like that does happen. And I think it made it easier for those who suffered. Most of the people here had had a chance to prepare themselves in advance. When they first announced the number of dead, we sensed that these were seven hundred individuals, seven hundred separate worlds. Each one a world of his own.

The way people felt after the victory was a truly human experience. I don't know how it can be expressed in art, in a symphony, a novel or in a poem. How, after the victory, the pain and the sorrow came. Sorrow for the soldiers and for our own sons alike. Especially for the soldiers, of course. The sadness descended on us in the midst of war, it was mixed up with the war all the time. I think it is one of the rarest feelings a man can have, this ambivalence: pride mingled with exaltation, the most exalted emotion at a time when our most cherished possession was in mortal danger. All this became a single feeling. You couldn't separate the emotions.

I don't know how these things will find expression. I think that people lived through moments of eternity. It's not merely a phrase. Minutes and hours that were an eternity. The only relief was not to be passive, to do something, carry out your duty.

Giora: You used the image of a sacrifice on the altar. If we read the biblical account of the sacrifice of Isaac, and try to imagine what Abraham felt, didn't you feel that somehow this too was a sacrifice, that the boys were being sacrificed to the God of their fathers? Intellectually, consciously, you know of course that your God is also the God of your sons. Didn't you ever have a moment of doubt?

Yoske: There is a Jewish destiny, and it is definitely something specifically Jewish. Even if he denies his faith, a Jew nevertheless has a rendezvous with his Jewish destiny. Even if you flee from that destiny, it pursues you. Earlier I told you what Hannah had to say. And we do knowingly bring our boys up to volunteer for combat units. We taught our sons to go to the danger-spots. I think that there were moments of identification during this war that can never be expressed in any form of words. From history, we know that this was what gave Zionism its impetus. People identified with the victims of a particular pogrom and so on. But this time it was the ultimate, the whole people identifying with the destiny of the nation to the point of being prepared to sacrifice everything. Even today there is an unspoken wish that the six days won't fade away. These are feelings from which great things come, that raise a man above the humdrum and give him spiritual sustenance for a lifetime. These are moments when a man is given a greater insight into Isaac's sacrifice. Kierkegaard asked what Abraham did that night. What did he think about? God didn't tell him to take Isaac out and sacrifice him right away. He was told to take him the next morning. He had a whole night to think. And Kierkegaard asks what he thought about during the night. It's a question that touches on the very meaning of human existence. The Bible says nothing about it. But we put the question to ourselves: what did Abraham think about that night? Did he accept the ways of God, or did he want to rebel against Him? Did he feel that it was he who had made God, or that God had made him? Did he inquire into the meaning of it all? For us, that night lasted six days. We thought: now we've sent our boys away and tomorrow we'll get the awful news.

It's bearable only in days of total identification like those. People can go out of their minds in six days if they have to spend the whole time wrestling with the thought that their son may be alive, or he may not. Only in times like these could people put up with the strain and come out of it strong and whole. They didn't break down. Because these were days like that, days of glory.

I had a long talk with Hannah. She said that she was looking for something, some way to perpetuate Nimrod's memory. To plant a tree at the spot where he was killed. Something connected with roots, with a tree, something rooted firmly in nature. That was what appealed to her. They were buried in a mass grave, a sort of cairn with only a heap of rocks separating one from the other, nothing more. You couldn't even stand there. If only that mound were a tree merging with the ripples on the Kinneret or a cloud in the sky — that would give the feeling that his death had some meaning.

What was it that sustained morale during the war, as the Bible says, "like a great wind blowing?" I gave the summing-up talk in the ideological seminar at Efal. Hannah G. took part. I said that the kibbutz movement mustn't concern itself only with the Nahal. The kibbutz has always stressed the security angle, every aspect of security. We have to give some thought to the armored corps as well. I have two sons serving in tanks, so I know something about armour. While I was speaking, Hannah was jotting something down. When I finished, she came over to me and said: "Take this and read it when you get home." "Why at home? I'll read it right here," I said. She replied: "It'll make you sad." And this is what she wrote:

> To Yoske, background music to your talk.
>
> "I know something about armor" said the father of two tank-corps men. He had never sat in the turret. He learnt about armor when their mother asked, asked from her heart, if they would both return. Both — or only one?
>
> "I know something about reconnaissance" said the mother of the scout. She was never on patrol, only went ahead of him in her heart, to save him from mines, from ambush. Day and night she travelled in her heart the dusty roads, the clefts and valleys. And still she could not save him.

"I know something about planes" said the pilot's son. Not that he had ever flown. Only his heart, proud and fearful, rose in prayer to the metal wings, that they keep his father safe. The heart knows, knows something about tears and pain, nights without sleep and days without rest.

"I know something about armor," said the father. . . .

She captured this sense of identification. We were with them, with a prayer in our hearts, and great pride as well. I want to ask Kobi how things looked to him during the war.

Did you ever have a moment when you could ask yourself what was going on at home? Had you heard that places along the Jordanian border were shelled? Did you ever suddenly wonder where your brother Ofer was? Did it occur to you that he might be in a tank near by, might be coming under the very same fire?

Kobi: A man always worries least about himself. He's there and sees what's going on. But you always feel that something might be happening to the one who isn't there, the one you have no way of knowing about. Especially when it's your brother. I wasn't afraid for Na'an, not for a moment. Maybe because I didn't have time. I wasn't at all concerned about the rear. But I was worried about Ofer. The company commander kept feeding us reports on how the company on our flank was making out so that we could co-ordinate our movements. Before we got to Bir Lahfan, he said that the other unit had fought well. I remember asking myself which unit it was. In my excitement, I used the tank's intercom to ask if the neighboring unit was E Company. My driver answered that he didn't know. Twenty minutes later I suddenly head him again over the intercom: "Now I understand why you were asking if that was E Company," he said. Ofer was in another column, not far from me. When I saw the bullets flying, I thought to myself that those bullets might be meant for him too.

Yoske: You spoke about attitudes to the Arabs. I grew up in Jerusalem. When I came to Palestine, I lived in an Arab house in an Arab neighborhood and played with Arab children. We bought milk and vegetables from the Arabs. For me, the Arabs were part of the scenery. Here at Na'an as well, we had contact with the Bedouin and with the Arabs living in the village of Na'ana. We did business with Arabs, and we fought with them. There were two sides. We always distinguished between the gangs and the others, between the *felaheen* and the Arabs who were closer to the Jews. And we had families who intermarried with the Arabs. The Arabs were simply part of our surroundings. Embedded deep in our upbringing was the certainty that we would live together with the Arabs, that our future was here with them.

The trouble was that they were in the majority. We believed that the State of Israel would arise only when we were the majority. During the Mandate, we did all we could to extend Jewish settlement. That was our big argument with the right-wing Zionists, and with the Irgun and the Stern group. We didn't want a state so long as the Arabs were in the majority. We wanted to go on, growing *dunam* by *dunam*, tree by tree, immigrant by immigrant. The Arabs were in the background of our lives, and we believed that it was our destiny as Zionists to live together with them. We hoped that we would come to some understanding. We were convinced that we could benefit the Arabs. Their standard of living rose during the time we were here. We had a feeling of right, not necessarily historic right, but natural right. There was no other place for us anywhere in the world. In the end we would come to some kind of *modus vivendi*. We believed that what we were doing wouldn't displace a single Arab. This was an important part of our creed. Nevertheless, we were a minority, a minority that sought to give the land a Jewish character, leave a Jewish mark on a country in which the Arabs were a majority. That was why, even in the youth movements, we thought it so important not to buy land which was worked by Arabs, so that not a single Arab was dispossessed. In 1948, the Arabs fled. It's very important for us to remember that we did them no wrong. We knew that our future had to be shared.

The generation that came after us doesn't have this background. Yet I have the impression that they feel no hate for the Arabs. I heard that even in battle there was no hatred. "*A la guerre comme à la guerre.*" But a minute before the war and a minute after, you have the feeling that the war wasn't based on hatred of foreigners or hatred of Arabs. Where does the younger generation get this?

Kobi: Our war wasn't the kind where you see your friends fall

all around you and then you begin to hate. Above all, we felt pity, because they were so miserable. Why did that tyrant send them again into that death-trap, Sinai? I always had the feeling that for him, it was only talk, only politics, a kind of chess where he makes a move here and people get killed there. Afterwards, all he has to do is deliver a speech to the nation and everything will be all right again. The more I saw of what happened to the Egyptians, the more I hated him, Nasser, the more I hated the régimes which were responsible for it all. I asked myself if he even knew or if he will ever know what happened there.

I met people who hated. Either it came on the spur of the moment or else they had something deep inside them from beforehand. There were also some who had no good reason, yet hated all the same. You see how a person is only what public opinion makes him. "Everyone says it's so": you know how it is. I always thought of home. What Dad would say. What Mum would say if she were there.

In what I did, in what the others did, I always carried with me the image of the gas chambers. They killed us, they annihilated us. It emphasized things for me. I think I'm especially sensitive to everything about the destruction of the Jews.

To bring out the good in people takes time, but to turn them into . . . that's easy.

I thought to myself: "It's a good thing it's not the other way round." What would have happened if it had been the other way? Their tanks could whip right through the Negev and get to. . . . I was sorry for them, but at the same time I imagined how every one of them would have behaved if it had been the other way round. They have no decency. You could tell from the way they suck up to you. If it had been the other way, they would have been wild beasts.

We had one fellow in our crew that I typed as a sadist the minute he reported for duty just before the war. He would tell how he liked to run over dogs when he drove a tractor, or how he liked to hang cats. And I curled up inside when I thought what he would be like in battle. There are sadists like that. In the tank, I kept talking to the crew all the time. Mostly for myself. And this fellow would pipe up: "It's only an Arab. It doesn't matter." And I'd tell him: "You see that one. He's got a wife waiting for him at home." That was my reaction. Gradually he began to see things differently. People convince themselves easily that Negroes are different from us. That's how he was about Arabs. I kept reminding him that Arabs are people too. It seemed to have an effect. Slowly I saw him change. In the end he would start arguing with people who thought just as he had in the beginning. This served to show me how important education can be. It's interesting how you meet people who impress you in some ways and you form an opinion about them on the spot. Later, under stress, you really get to know them. It's then that they show their true colours.

PART 5
AT HOME

THE WAR WAS RIGHT ON MY DOORSTEP

From a discussion in Tel Katzir. Interviewer: Muki Tsur

Tel Katzir is a young kibbutz, founded in 1950 by graduates of the Israeli scout movement. At the south-east tip of the Sea of Galilee, threatened for many years by Syrian guns in the hills above, it is still subject to attack from time to time by Jordanian artillery stationed to the south. It has a population of about a hundred.

Participants:
Barbara, thirty-three, was born in Germany, and brought to Israel by her parents as a child. After army service as a private in the Nachal she joined the kibbutz, where she works as an accountant. She is the mother of four children, one of whom was born in September 1967. *Zippora*, thirty-three, was born in Persia, and educated in a Youth Aliya group in Tel Katzir, of which she subsequently became a member. She is the mother of three children, and works in the babies' house. During the war she was in charge of the shelter where the babies lived. *Berela*, twenty-seven, was born in Tel Aviv, and joined Tel Katzir after service in Nachal. She is the mother of two children. During the war she was in charge of the kindergarten children's shelter. *Ruchka*, twenty-seven, was born in Tel Aviv, and joined Tel Katzir after service in Nachal. She is

211

the mother of two children. During the war she served as
radio operator in the headquarters bunker.

Barbara: As early as two weeks before the war there was a lot of
preparation in the kibbutz. In all the years I've been at Tel Katzir, I
know I never expected to have to spend more than twelve hours in
the shelter. I felt the same way in the weeks before the war. I was
one of the few who arrived in the shelter without having made any
preparation at all. Even after it was all over, I found it difficult to
grasp that we'd spent six days down there.

It's interesting how very quickly people can get used to things,
even the most horrible things. I talked it over with a friend from
Kibbutz Ein Gev and she said, "By Saturday, the fifth day of the
war, we'd even managed to create some feeling of the Sabbath spirit
in the shelter. We'd become more or less used to the fact that this
was where our whole life was at the moment. We even held our usual
Sabbath eve ceremony. Being down there made us feel obliged to
carry on normally."

Zippora: I was in the shelter with the babies. I kept thinking
about the worst that could happen; that maybe we'd have to
evacuate them to some other place. We didn't think it would finish
so well, and so quickly. The moment the war started I heard some
people saying how glad they were. I thought about it then, too, but I
didn't know whether to be happy or frightened. Those first
moments were among the worst and the best as far as I was
concerned.

Berela: I began to be very much aware of the war on the Friday
before, when the call-up notices started to arrive. Then you really
felt that something was going to happen. Two days later, it really
did. I was working in the dining room that morning, and we heard
the news over the radio in the kitchen. I didn't completely absorb
what was being said. We only heard the word "fighting." We didn't
wait to hear where or what, but just ran into the dining room to tell
everyone. The immediate reaction was one of joy mixed with fear.
Perhaps not exactly joy — but enthusiasm. Then we waited to be
told to go down to the shelters; and the order came soon enough.
The children were taken down immediately; the adults were a little

less serious about it all because it still didn't really seem to apply to us. Over the years we've had quite a number of "incidents" here. We've sat in the shelters, but never for longer than a few hours. The children used to think it quite an experience. But never before did it make such a strong impression on us as it did then. We sat down there and listened to the radio. We rejoiced over every victory, but it all seemed so far away from us. It was only when we came under heavy shelling that I really felt that the war was right on my doorstep. You might say, war didn't seem so pleasant at that moment. . . .

Ruchka: The worst part of it was when we left the shelters. The shelling, the noise — you get a bit frightened. But the worst of it all was when we came out and saw how much had been destroyed. When we got back to the shelters, and there was more shelling, the children said to me, "But they won't leave us anything at all," — they'd already seen the ruined houses. "They're good shots. When we come out of the shelter, after the war's over, there won't be any houses left at all." Even after the war, it hurt to walk around and look at it all. For us in Tel Katzir, the results of the shelling were the worst part of it — not the shelling itself.

Muki: Everybody had their own secret hopes about what would happen. Do you girls think that you felt differently from the men?

Berela: The girls are less communicative. The boys generally stand around and talk — amateur strategists. When a girl comes past, she contents herself with just listening to what they're saying. I think each of the girls thought about it, but they didn't talk much.

Muki: How did the children take the war? Do they still remember things?

Ruchka: One afternoon, there was a lull in the fighting and we took the children out of the shelters. The parents took them to have a wash and we spent a few hours behind the blast wall. We thought it was protecting us. After I'd washed Nir, Dudu asked me, "Mummy, tell me, have the Arabs got mouths? Have they got hands?" He'd pictured the Arab as some sort of imaginary monsters. When I told him that they were people just like us, I'm not sure he believed me. . . .

Barbara: I sometimes think we don't evaluate the children's reactions correctly. The teacher in Ein Gev told me that on the day school started again, she told the other children not to ask our youngsters about the war and the shelling. "Talk to them about other things," she said, "don't remind them of it." She thought our children would be coming to school in a state of shock. But no such thing. The children talked quite freely about the shelling and the destruction. They started talking about it proudly before anyone managed to say a word. They said what they had to say and then settled down to their lessons quite normally. Of course, afterwards there was all the business of collecting shrapnel and bullets, and all the others things that go with war. For us, for the adults, it was a pretty severe shock. For the children, it was different. They took it all very calmly.

Muki: Why were the adults so worried about the children's reactions?

Zippora: Coming out of the shelter after the shelling was a terrible moment. All that destruction — all the lawns covered with rubble — left you very depressed. It looked different when we finally came out of the shelters, when it was really all over. But that first impression was ghastly. Since we took it so badly, we thought the children would be hit even harder by it.

The burnt-out dining hall: the adults tried to take it lightly, to make a joke, saying, "Oh, lovely, now we'll be able to buy everything new. We'll have new furniture!" Then the kindergarten children asked their teacher, Zionele, "Why are they all so happy? It's been burnt down and it's ours!"

Ruchka: The children took thing as they came. It seems to me that it was the adults who took it to heart. The children were amazed at the adults' reactions. They had a very realistic approach to the war. They didn't show any signs of fear while they were in the shelters. On the contrary, they were calm all the time, even at night. But when I talked to them after the war, one little girl told me that before the war she was frightened that the war would be right here, in Tel Katzir. "But I saw that the war wasn't here — and we heard lots on the radio too — and I saw that the Syrians weren't coming here. So I wasn't frightened any more. And I'm not frightened now!" she said. The older children saw the conquest of the Syrian

Heights with their own eyes. That made a very deep impression on them. On the other hand, the toddlers were frightened by the noise of the aeroplanes — and they're still frightened. When they hear a plane they hold on to you. You don't see that with the bigger children.

Muki: What was it like in the shelters?

Zippora: In our case it was difficult, because it was the shelter where the babies were, crying twenty-four hours a day. But generally speaking, I think the atmosphere was similar to that all over the country: everybody was prepared to do whatever they could. People forgot their petty little quarrels.

Barbara: We were lucky that the fathers and the husbands were right here and not "somewhere in Israel." We saw them every day and that contributed to the calm atmosphere. You can't compare Tel Katzir to a settlement where no one was left at home but the women and the older people. All right, we went through a tough time, but apart from the shelling, I think the others suffered far more from the tension that we did.

Muki: You said that the children were afraid that the war would be right here in Tel Katzir. Didn't you have the same fear?

Zippora: There was one awful moment. It was the day they shelled us for seven hours on end. There were seven of us girls in the shelter, and only one man — and we were on the other side of the blast wall. It felt as if we were right outside the kibbutz. Altogether cut off. For two solid hours we couldn't get any telephone calls through. We waited to hear a sound. Suddenly I heard footsteps, the sound of a soldier's boots. "Who's there?" I shouted. No answer. "Who's there?" No answer. A few minutes earlier we'd been wondering what would happen if they invaded us. You hear these footsteps and in comes . . . at the last moment I saw it was Gideon. I really yelled at him. That was a terrible moment.

Muki: How did you feel after the victory, when you saw the soldiers climbing up the Syrian Heights?

Ruchka: We wept. We were so moved. The children were asleep. I went to wake them up so that they could see, too. I couldn't control myself. It was so marvellous to see the tanks moving up to the top. We couldn't hold ourselves back — even though we'd been told to stay in the shelters — we just stood out there and looked.

When it was all over, Dado* landed his helicopter here. You should have seen how everyone came rushing up to it: just to be there, to stand around him, not saying anything, just to see him, just to hear him say something. Someone lifted him up in the air — we just didn't know what to do. People stood there weeping.

Muki: And how did you feel when you went to Tawafik?

Berela: We said we hoped there wouldn't be another round!

Barbara: I said I'd be frightened if we ever gave the Heights back again.

Ruchka: Before, we used to think certain parts of Tel Katzir were more or less protected. People used to say it was better to live near the hill, because it was the safest place. But when we stood up there and saw how the kibbutz was spread out below in the palm of their hands. . . .

Muki: I suppose you toured around up there and saw just what was destroyed and what was still left standing. I'd like to ask what you felt when you saw the destroyed villages, the abandoned houses and so on. Did you think about yourselves, about them?

Berela: I found a satchel belonging to a child who must have been in the first grade at school. It was left behind in one of the houses. It didn't make me too happy. Although when I flipped through the pages of a textbook I saw a picture of a rifle with a bayonet pointing towards Israel. But all the same, it's not just the guilty who suffered. I didn't feel happy.

By the time the casualty list arrived — nobody was happy. During the war itself, there was some sort of enthusiasm. Afterwards, there was a general feeling of dejection. In the last week or two we've got over this a bit. But previously, the special feeling that supported us during the war had disappeared. Because of our losses and everything. We saw refugees. People going along with their donkeys carrying all sorts of bits and pieces. We thought more generally in terms of the whole of humanity. Wars are bad. Even when you win them.

*Commander of the Northern front.

MOTIK

The following portrait was found in the papers of *Yehuda
ben Ze'ev*, of Kibbutz Ein Hacarmel, who was killed in the
battle for Jerusalem.

Motik was not born to be wounded. He should never have been
injured. It is hard to connect the primitive energy that was Motik
with any form of restriction — to a bed, to a room. The plaster
seemed on him a gross error on the part of the doctors. These were
two separate worlds. He was a creature not yet complete, as yet
unformed — a sort of challenge to the accepted and the conventional. When he spoke it was like a voice from the first age of being,
from a primitive existence that knows no pretense, no accepted
custom. It was as though he used words differently from other men
— the very sound of the word, its tone and rhythm, told its meaning
and its connotations, as if you could grasp the content of his words
without understanding their logical meaning. And so we achieved an
almost unbelievable empathy with him: a few offhand words were
enough to arouse laughter and ridicule in us all. Almost without
knowing it we modelled our thinking on Motik's attitudes in every
word that passed between us. He created new ideas, new values,
which were accepted at once as if they had been hallowed by a
tradition of many years' standing. He, more than any other, knew
how to call things by their proper name. Nicknames which he
invented were accepted as if they expressed a person's very essence.
 Yona was the first to be killed in our company. With his death it

217

seemed as if some inner change came over Motik. We all felt despondent, dull-witted, as if we had just set foot on a long, winding, uphill path. We knew the facts of life in a combatant unit; but until we actually felt the sense of loss, until we were forced to feel the longing for a lost comrade whose memory was still fresh, it was no more than an abstract fact which scarcely affected us, as if it were not part of our world. And then we became conscious of it for the first time. It was a suitable moment for grave words about duty and responsibility. We were on the brink of that abnormal state of mind which dulls and darkens the senses: dull clay without self-reliance, without will, without God. We needed a saving word, a stone thrown into the stagnant waters of the soul to stir them to life; a spark, a hint that some other, more perfect world might yet be possible; a gleam of light with a radiance of its own, not a reflection from elsewhere. We needed a fresh link with the world before our bereavement, a world from which we had been cut off by the bonds of comradeship and common experience of death for the first time. But Yona was part of that world from first to last. It seemed that nobody would dare to desecrate his memory, to say a word which might detract from his image, already becoming almost hallowed. And at that moment Motik had the strength and the incredible honesty to tell a story about Yona's first leave: how he swaggered down the street in his fine new uniform, showing off to all the girls; how a woman of the streets attached herself to him; and how he fled from her for all he was worth. That was enough. It was obvious, broad satire, and it started the thaw. Another burst of humour from here and there, and the grim reality began to resolve itself into its thousand simple everyday components.

As the days went by, days full of action, the memory of our fallen comrades ceased to arouse in us that sense of shock and feeling of sanctity; so much so that we began to feel that they were still with us, that they had never left us at all. It was as if they took part in every one of the actions of those ever-active days. Their reactions to the events of the day remained part of the give-and-take of daily life within our circle. We told jokes about them, sang their favourite songs. Their death did not stop us from laughing at their weaknesses, even from exaggerating them. Sometimes it was hard, in our grief and sorrow, not to adopt the approach "*de mortuis nil nisi bonum.*" But we had to avoid it if we were to keep their memory fresh without being mortally wounded by their death. Only thus could we meet death face to face without perpetual trepidation at its existence.

In all this, Motik was the best friend of our fallen comrades. He had a sort of living bond with them. In the middle of an exhausting march he would turn to Yossi, who had been killed weeks before, and ask him to sing one of his marching-songs. On the last night of a gruelling exercise, he suddenly got up and began to imitate the weeping and wailing of Orik's family over his grave, as if the dead Orik himself were mocking his mourning relatives. The momentary shock we felt disappeared like chaff in the wind: it was impossible to resist such tremendous strength, which transcended the conventional notions of life and death.

Many of our men were wounded, in various actions and in training. We learnt how relative are the meanings which attach to different names in different circumstances. "Wounded" — at home an appellation which puts the bearer in the center of attention, of concern and care — lost this connotation in those days of continuous tension. "Wounded" came to mean "on leave" — short, long or indefinite. It was hard to connect an actual, living person with the frightful experience of being wounded, of having his body deformed. For us, Motik was the same gay, witty person with the same fertile imagination and ready smile even when he lay for many a long month with his leg in plaster and his ribs broken. And when we went to visit Giddy, whose stomach was shot to pieces so that he'd lost control of his digestive functions, one of us always asked how many of the holes were currently in use, and how far away we had to stand so that the juices wouldn't squirt over us. When we spoke to our wounded comrades as if they were fit and well, our relationship took full cognizance of the state they were in. They had to know all the latest slang, all the latest catch-phrases. They had to hear our estimates of the most recent recruits to the feminine admirers of the company — and, in return, to give their own view of the charms of the hospital personnel. After every action the wounded would get a detailed report and appreciation of the battle, as if they themselves had been fighting on another sector in the same operation. Just like the others just back from the action, they cursed this one's hesitation, that one's haste — and were, perhaps, more zealous than all the rest of us for the good name of the company.

Beneath all this there lay a deep layer of lack of confidence, of uncertainty. "One cannot look death or the sun in the face" says the old proverb. There was always the hesitation, the hidden fear. And the greatest danger for the man who lives with the mark of death on him is that he will lose his standards of everyday behavior. Life on the brink of death can be very exalted — or very debased. The hardest thing of all is to find the middle way, to live life as it comes. But that is what we had to do, and that is what we forced ourselves to do. This whole construction of everyday habits, which expressed itself in speech and in song, rested on a few "pillars of strength." Their very presence created a certain atmosphere. They must never be hurt, they were the mascots, the lucky charms of the company. And, indeed, we lived in the illusion that they would not be hurt. When insolent reality slapped our faces, and loudly proclaimed the truth, we turned our backs on it, left it alone and meaningless. The burden was redistributed, but our spiritual home still stood — on fewer pillars, but still whole. Within a few days it had found its new shape, new customs and new atmosphere. We had to have such a framework; and each time it was created anew.

Motik was more than such a "pillar of strength." If a single character can personify a spiritual entity, Motik was such a character. Not that he was an exemplary soldier. Above all, he personified indifference to reality, to difficulties, to the loss of one's comrades: no foolish dedication to shallow gaiety, but a clear, sometimes tragic perception of the state of affairs. When we first heard that he had been wounded, we assumed that a stray bullet had grazed him. When we heard of his wounds in detail, it hurt us deeply, cut us to the quick. And our visit to the hospital left behind it a terrible wound.

As events and actions pressed on, one after the other, we came to realize that Motik's indispensability was purely objective, that we could, must get over the shock. Men are not born to tasks like these, they adapt themselves to the task required of them. Some do it as if born to the situation, others learn their role. But there will always be someone to take their place. The very existence of a group implies a division of functions within it, and this division changes from time to time with the changes in the group it serves. So someone else took Motik's place. And he was treated, as were all our wounded, with the same level-headedness, the same rejection of the slightest emotion or melancholy which threatened to overwhelm them in their dealings with the outside world. Most amazing – he, too, adopted this style in his meeting with us. Sometimes one had the feeling that he adopted this tone just for the time we were with him. But he did it differently from before he was wounded: not as an expression of his inner world, springing ineluctably from within him, but as if he had thought and weighed up, decided – and forced himself to act in this way. And from that moment it was hard to laugh and jest with him simply and unselfconsciously. The laughter rang slightly false; sometimes we could not carry on laughing. And then there happened something for which there was no precedent, even in the case of the worst injuries, injuries which destroy the semblance of man. There came the storm which ends in rain, the emotion which brings forth tears, and which conquered, as it never had before, the insouciance even of the most impassive among us.

Yehuda Ben Ze'ev

HOME AGAIN

Business as usual. Tuesday — so there's a film. Monday — fish fingers or hake. At five in the afternoon, the kids come home. You drink cold Nescafé, you take back five slices of bread and a half a cup of milk to your room, and get up at quarter to five. The apricots are ripe, soon the apples will be, too. Yankele with a group of three others standing round the piano. Saturday night — snatches of gossip drift through the lighted windows, the murmur of conversation, whisperings on the lawn. Everything's in its place — at peace?

Life has gone back to normal. Army boots are back in the cupboard on the balcony, the khaki shirt's been ironed. We've come back. Everything is as it was. We were there — beyond the mountains of darkness, in the world of fear — and now, we have to forget. We have forgotten; later it will begin to haunt us. Sometimes in dreams, sometimes in an imperceptible shuddering, sometimes in a blank meaningless gaze, a remembrance of the past. The stories of the war are as foam on the water, just the outer shell of experiences that we will carry within us forever. We shall never be rid of them, we shall never be able to free ourselves of them. We'll be as we were, bad-tempered, good-hearted, superficial, serious. No, we haven't changed. Yet, how we have changed!

One cannot but smile ironically at the sight of the trenches criss-crossing the lawns. My dear Noam and Giora, how much anger and shouting, how many requests, notices, and quarrels were expended on keeping people off the grass, when one hour of war wrought more havoc than years of fence-jumpers taking short-cuts over the grass. . . .

222

I arrived home a few days after the fighting had stopped. I was still in a dreamlike state, to put it a trifle poetically. Victory and its sweet savor were still strong within me, I was happy and carefree. I was met with grave affection. The glances turned on me held no vestige of the jubilance of victory. Some gathered round me, and just wanted to look, to look into the eyes of one who had returned from that place of violence. Others looked at me jealously, because it was I and not one of their loved ones. But within their eyes a sort of sorrow was reflected, a pain which no one explained to me at that moment. Now I know how bitter and difficult is the life of these who wait back here at home, how much strength was demanded of these mothers and fathers, of those who stayed behind to bear the burden of passing on the news, of working, of waiting for letters, of waiting for regards from those at the front, for a voice, for an echo that would say we were alive and well. Today I know that the easiest thing of all in a country like ours is to go and do the actual fighting, and the cruelest thing of all is to listen to the din of battle from afar.

In the evening, as you go down to the dining hall, you can hear the strains of music, piano and violin, drifting from the music room. All is tranquil. From the children's houses you can hear the gentle tones of the kindergarten teachers reading bedtime stories. Along the paths leading to the dining hall, voices call out, "Good evening, keep me a place in the middle, opposite the door." A sea wind blows from the west, life goes on as usual. It's all over, lights shine out boldly, but we well remember, with an echo of fear, the heavy darkness which shrouded the entire valley only a few days ago.

Menachem Shelach (Kibbutz Mishmar Ha'emek)

PART 6
JERUSALEM

OUR HAPPINESS WAS COMPLETE

From a discussion in Hulda. Interviewer: Amos Oz

Shai: We went into Gaza on Tuesday. On Wednesday afternoon
we received orders to go to Rafiah for mopping-up operations. On
our way out of Gaza, in the bus, we listened to the radio. Suddenly
the announcer interrupted the broadcast and read an announcement
from the military spokesman: the Old City of Jerusalem was in our
hands. He repeated it, and afterwards they played "Jerusalem the
Golden." We were so overcome that the whole battalion began
singing the song. I remember that there in the buses people wept and
weren't ashamed of their tears although they were grown men. I'm
sure this will always be the highpoint of the war for me. One felt a
sense of unity in the singing. As we travelled along, all the people
from the settlements along the road came out on to the roadside and
waved at us. The buses stopped and we got out and fell into each
others' arms. There were great moments before this, too — there was
a feeling of elation earlier over all our victories — but in my opinion,
this was the high point of the war. We knew it would come. But
when it did happen, it symbolized the whole war for us. It was *the*
moment of the war for us.

Amos: Did people talk or pray?

Shai: They didn't talk. They sang "Jerusalem the Golden."
They weren't always in tune, there on the buses, but they sang it.

Amos: Shai, let me ask you a rather naïve question. Why
specifically Jerusalem? You say that you were very moved. I won't

227

ask about the others, OK, they were religious. But you aren't. What was so special about the Wall:

Shai: First of all it's not the Wall; it's the Old City. It didn't have a religious connotation — at least so it seems to me. Today, when I try to explain it to myself, I can't find an exact answer — but it seems to me that for us the Old City was a symbol of something unfinished. It's ours. The Old City should be ours. This is our capital. It symbolized what we strove for for nineteen years. Jerusalem was a symbol of something that had been taken from us, a symbol of some sort of defeat in the War of Independence. It's difficult for me to know exactly why. But it's clear that at that moment it didn't have a religious significance.

Amos: Shai, do you remember if you thought of your parents then? How they would be affected by all this? Or didn't it occur to you?

Shai: I don't think I thought about anything, there was just the feeling of being full of joy. We were all full of joy. At that moment I remember that we didn't think about those who'd died for Jerusalem. Our happiness was complete.

TONIGHT WE'RE MAKING HISTORY

From a discussion in Tirat Zvi. Interviewer: Amram Hayisra'eli

Micha: At the assembly point that night we learned what our objective was in Jerusalem.

Amram: What did you think about then?

Micha: I don't know. There wasn't much time for feeling anything at all. We certainly didn't have any grandiose sentiments. In any case, I'm not a very emotional person about this sort of business. But I do remember how this whole question of Jerusalem gripped us. We certainly saw it as something special. I can truthfully say I remember thinking that we were about to do something of real importance, of historical significance. That's how we put it to one another, "Tonight we're going into the Old City and it's. . . . "

Dani: Tonight we're making history. . . .

Micha: Yes. Without question, we felt we were doing something. Apart from the fact that the whole war was something of historic significance, Jerusalem was extra-special. That's how I felt about it.

Amram: And afterwards, while you were fighting?

Micha: I must admit that during the fighting there wasn't time for feelings of that sort.

Amram: So what did you think about?

Micha: Only about carrying out the mission to the very last detail. I spent every moment trying to do everything in the best possible way. My duties as an officer gave me plenty to do and there

229

wasn't time for anything else. I do remember that we managed to say prayers when we got to the Ambassador Hotel in the morning. It was about ten o'clock when I found a few minutes to pray and put on my *tefillin*. It felt so good to be in Jerusalem. There are passages in the Eighteen Benedictions. Verses like: "And may our eyes look upon Thy return to Zion ... " and so on. We said it a bit differently from the way we'd say it on a normal day, with more feeling, after the city was in our hands and later when we prayed at the Western Wall, in fact wherever we prayed in Jerusalem ... The afternoon prayer was the first one we said by the Wall and, of course, it was something very special for us.

Amram: Did any of the others in the company react differently to you?

Micha: Look, I don't want to destroy any legends, but it wasn't as earth-shaking as it looked from the evening papers that day. It's true that some people were very moved; that for some of them it was something special. Lots of the boys who hadn't had much to do with Judaism and weren't at all religious, said that this war had made them feel that the Jewish people really is something special. They appreciated the meaning of the verse: "Thou has chosen us." I heard a lot of people say that. But I also heard lots of them say that it didn't mean anything to them. To them it was merely the climax of a specific assignment, without any Jewish significance. Historical significance, yes; but not something specifically Jewish.

I remember that one of the things I thought about later on, something that really affected me, was the business of Giora, our company commander. He was killed right next to me, near the Wall. One evening, we'd had a big "do" in the amphitheater on Mount Scopus. We sang "Jerusalem of Iron," and there were some professional artists. It was all very impressive, the moment itself, the background, the place and all that — and that was when I thought about Giora. Why wasn't he here with us? It's what one generally thinks at these moments. I really was very moved then. But in the middle of the fighting — when it happened, I remember that my only thought was that now I had to carry on and continue to advance, without saying a word to any of the men. Just not tell any of them — only tell them when it's all over. Some of them were completely broken up by the news.

Dani: If you were to ask me what day the Old City was taken on, I wouldn't be able to tell you. We'd crossed the border without a single radio, so we didn't hear about it immediately. But when we did find out, there was a truly spontaneous reaction. Most of the men began dancing around, jumping on and off the vehicles, under them, over them, hugging one another. It was like being in exile and suddenly hearing that Jerusalem was ours. I had very mixed feelings about it. On the one hand, it didn't mean anything to me; on the other hand, it showed we'd given them a beating. I knew that one was supposed to feel pleased about it. But I wasn't specially happy about taking Port Tawafik. I wasn't even specially happy that Jerusalem had been taken in this fantastic way. I didn't feel particularly excited. . . . They asked me, "Is it true about the Wall?" And I said, "Okay, so what? We've taken Port Tawafik too!" I'll tell you something: holy or not, it left me cold.

Micha: Morning prayers at the Wall were very awe-inspiring. All the time I kept thinking that the Wall symbolized the Jewish people's yearning for unity, its deep roots in the country; that we represented a whole people, a whole history. It meant a lot to me. I can't say that I felt any deep spiritual link with the stones themselves. It isn't like that. People don't realize that Judaism doesn't attach any sanctity to places as such. For example, the Bible says about Moses' burial place, "And no one knew where he was buried." For the same reason, there's nothing holy about the Wall. But for us, the Wall's really — what I saw before me was the realization of our people's unity, of their longing, of the whole Jewish people. Not that particular place, but what it means to the whole Jewish people. . . .

THERE'S A POTTED PLANT

From a discussion in Mishmar Hasharon

Eitan: We advanced in jeeps through the streets of East Jerusalem. Afterwards, we occupied a flat and took up positions facing Mount Scopus. They started shelling us from the walls of the Old City and then went on to shell the Rockefeller Museum. I was amazed by their accuracy. One of our positions was in the Rockefeller tower, and the Israeli flag flew proudly about it. I sat and looked through the window: shells whistled round the flag all day. I was very moved when I saw that the flag remained untouched – shells, smoke, shrapnel, and the flag still flew! It inspired the boys who were with me: "Look how strongly the flag's flying . . . if it doesn't fall the Old City will be ours tonight" they said. This feeling was a terrific help to us in facing what happened that day.

Our position was on top of the wall surrounding the Old City and we'd occupied a Christian hospital adjoining it. When there was a few hours' lull in the fighting, we went to look for some place where we could wash off the blood, dust and soot. We went into a hotel. A lull in the fighting gives you a feeling of liberation from the tension. You go into a well cared-for house, surrounded by debris. There's a potted plant in front of you that's trying to grow up and you see that it's beginning to wilt. You pass it once, twice and then again, and you think: is this plant going to be destroyed like everything else around? It pulls you up short for a minute. Then whatever you've got in you – the result of education and your home

232

environment — shows itself. We found small cups and ran backwards and forwards watering the plant.

When we got back to our position near the hospital, we remembered the little kids there and collected toys for them. The head of the hospital, an American woman, was absolutely overjoyed. I was wearing filthy battle dress then, and a steel helmet. To my great surprise, a few weeks after the war, when I went back there on a visit with Tirza, the American woman recognized me. She talked to Tirza and told her how amazed she was to see such a loving and humane attitude on the part of soldiers who were still right in the thick of a war. She remembered exactly how we'd advanced along the walls and through the barricades until we reached the hospital. Today, when civilians come to visit the hospital by this devious route instead of by the main road, she knows that they were soldiers who fought here. And she's still moved by that humane gesture — bringing toys to children in the middle of war. She talked about it to Tirza.

LIKE A PSALM OF PRAISE

This letter, written to a young member of Kibbutz Mishmar Hasharon, is included as an example of a motif which is scarcely touched on in the discussions, but which forms part of the complex of emotions and associations surrounding the question of Jerusalem: the feelings of the deeply orthodox Jew.

Dear Ora,

My wife Etty gave me permission to read your letter which gave me great pleasure. I'm sorry that I've never met you personally and have had only a fleeting glimpse of you, but your letter expresses your feelings about social problems so well that I felt that I had to write to you. I don't want to take up your remarks about the dust that's collected around accepted principles, partly because I'd like to talk to you about this personally and partly because, despite everything, a whole generation of kibbutzniks and moshavniks has been brought up on these principles, and it's from these same people that the army — including my brigade — has drawn the great majority of its officers. I was lucky that I served with the paratroop brigade that liberated Jerusalem. I believe that the hand of God was in my participation in the battle for the liberation and reunion of Jerusalem. I see in it the hand of God, for ever since I reached maturity, and especially since I joined the army thirteen years ago, I've had a constant desire to take part in a war for the liberation of

Jerusalem. On the other hand, this contradicted my social and political belief in the need for a dialogue with the Arabs as a basis for peace. But my yearnings to fight for the liberation of Jerusalem were above and beyond my political ideas.

Fears, natural in the face of possible death, were replaced by a great pride. I felt jubilant, here I was about to fight — and perhaps to die — for Jerusalem. Do you know the significance of Jerusalem for a religious man who prays three times a day (in the Eighteen Benedictions): "And return speedily to Jerusalem, Thy city, in mercy, and dwell within it as Thou has spoken"? Of course, as you said in your letter, the Western Wall was never an archaeological site as far as I was concerned, not even a "holy place" as it's officially called. My education, my prayers and my longings transform Jerusalem in its entirety into an organic part of my very being, of my whole life.

Please understand, Ora, that it was against the background of these sentiments that I went to fight for the liberation of Jerusalem. I felt as if I had been granted the great privilege of acting as an agent of God, of Jewish history. Because of all the great tension and turmoil of the war, I didn't at first have the time to think about the experiences and feelings of the other soldiers. But the atmosphere was full of a sense of greatness and holiness. We were in the Rockefeller Museum, just before we took the Temple Mount, and I asked a fellow soldier, a man born in Kibbutz Sha'ar Ha'amakim, what he thought of it all. He answered with a verse from the Bible: "I was glad when they said unto me, let us go unto the house of the Lord. Our feet shall stand within Thy gates, O Jerusalem, Jerusalem is builded as a city that is compact together." He smiled as he spoke, perhaps because it's not "fitting" for a member of Hashomer Hatzair to talk this way. But I saw his eyes, and I knew that that was how he really felt.

When we broke into the Old City and I went up to the Temple Mount and later to the Western Wall, I looked searchingly at the officers and the other soldiers. I saw their tears, their wordless prayers, and I knew they felt as I did: a deep feeling for the Temple Mount where the Temple once stood, and a love for the Wall on whose stones so many generations have wept. I understood that it wasn't only I and my religious friends who sensed its greatness and sanctity; the others felt it too, no less deeply and strongly. It was easier for me to define my feelings, because I had my *tefillin* in my pack (perhaps King Solomon wore ones just like these when he built the Temple) and in my pocket there was the book of psalms written by David, the King of Jerusalem.

As I stood weeping by the Wall, there wept with me my father, my grandfather and my great-grandfather, all of them born in a Land of Israel where they needed Abdullah's permission to pray at the Wall. As I caressed its stones, I felt the warmth of those Jewish hearts which had warmed them with a warmth that will for ever endure.

I saw my friends, kibbutz-educated towards an attitude of scorn for traditional religious values, now overwhelmed by a feeling of holiness, and as elated and moved as I was. Then I saw the proof of what I had previously assumed, that there is in all of us, religious and non-religious alike, in the entire Jewish people, an intense quality of Jewishness that is neither destroyed by education nor blurred by foreign ideologies and values. The morning after the battle I said my morning prayers on the Temple Mount, and as the sun rose over liberated Jerusalem I lingered over the verse, "And may a new light dawn over Zion and may we speedily merit its radiance."

Forgive me, Ora, if I've digressed. But when people talk about the Six-Day War and especially about the liberation of Jerusalem, it all seems to me like a psalm of praise.

With regards,

Eliezer

PS. We've applied for permission to live in the Old City of Jerusalem; if it's granted, of course, you'll come and visit us there.

STRANGE CITY

I was born in Jerusalem and lived there throughout my childhood; when I was nine I lived through the days when Jerusalem was besieged and shelled. It was then that I first saw a dead man: a shell fired from the Arab Legion's gun batteries on Nebi Samuel hit a pious Jew and tore his stomach apart. I saw him lying in the street. He was a small man whose chin sprouted a meager beard. His face, as he lay there dead, was white and amazed. It was July, 1948. For many days afterwards I hated that man because he kept appearing in my dreams and frightening me. I knew that Jerusalem was surrounded by forces whose only desire was the city's death and mine, too.

Later I moved away from Jerusalem. I still loved her with a stubborn love as one might love a woman who holds aloof. Sometimes on my free days I would go to Jerusalem to pay court to her. Her alleyways knew me well though they affected not to.

I loved Jerusalem because she was journey's end, a city one arrived at but could never pass beyond; and also because she was never really a true part of the State of Israel; with the exception of a few roads Jerusalem has always held herself aloof, as if she had consciously chosen to turn her back on all the flat white commercial cities: Tel Aviv, Holon, Herzlia and Nethanya.

Jerusalem was different. She was the absolute negation of towns made up of cube-like blocks of flats, all painted white. She was different from the flat stretches of citrus groves, the gardens surrounded by hedges, the red roofs and irrigation pipes shining in

237

the sun. Even the blue of her summer skies was different. Not for her the dusty white heavens of the coastal plain and the Sharon valley. An enclosed city. Wintry. Even in the summer it was always a wintry city. Rusty iron railings. Grey stone, sometimes imperceptibly shading into pale blue, sometimes into a reddish hue. Tumbledown fences. Rocky hillsides. Walled courtyards, closed in as if in anger.

And its citizens: a silent people, bitter as if for ever overcoming some inner fear. Observant Jews. Ashkenazi Jews in their fur *streimels* and old Sephardim in their striped robes. Soft-stepping scholars wandering through the streets, as if at a loss. Dreamy-eyed girls. Blind beggars, dumb or cursing. Madmen abroad with the divine spark in their eyes.

For twenty years Jerusalem turned her stubborn back on the stream of modern life. A slow moving town in a country of feverish activity. An old, neglected mountainous suburb whose few flat stretches, crammed with buildings, burst at the seams with overflowing energy. The sad capital city of an exultant state. And the stranglehold.

There were mutilated streets descending to blocked alleys. Barricades of concrete and rusty barbed wire. A city which is all border. A city not of gold but of tin sheeting, bent and full of holes. A city surrounded at night by the sound of foreign bells, foreign odors, distant views. A ring of hostile villages surrounded the city on three sides: Sha'afat, Wadi Jos, Issawia, Silwan, Azaria, Tsur Bachr, Bet Tsafafa. It seemed as if they had only to clench their hand and Jerusalem would be crushed within their fist. On a winter night you could sense the evil intent that flowed from them toward the city.

There was fear too in Jerusalem. An inner fear that must never be expressed in words, never called by name. It grew, solidified and crystallized in the twisting alleyways and the desolate lanes.

The city fathers, the heads of government, the housing estates, the newly planted trees, the traffic lights, all tried to tempt Jerusalem into a union with the State of Israel; and she, with the exception of some few streets, refused that union. Twenty years. Jerusalem continued to preserve a faded obstinate Mandatory character. She remained sad.

Not within the State of Israel, but alongside it; Jerusalem as opposed to Israel.

I loved this town, because I was born there and because people who stand aloof tend to love towns which hold aloof.

This was a love which was received without mercy: Jerusalem was often the background for nightmares and dreams of terror. I no longer live in Jerusalem, but in my dreams I am hers and she does not relinquish her hold on me. I would see us both surrounded by enemies. The enemy in my dreams came not only from east, north and south, but completely surrounded us. I saw Jerusalem falling into the hands of her enemies. Destroyed, pillaged and burned, as in the stories of my childhood, as in the Bible, as in the tales of the destruction of the Temple. And I too, with no way of escape, with no place to hide, was trapped in the Jerusalem of my dreams.

Many were the stories I was told as a child of Jerusalem under siege. Jewish children always died in these stories. They died heroically, or were slaughtered, but the stories always ended with the town burning and the children dying. Sennaccherib, Titus, the Crusaders. Riots, terrorists. Military rule. The High Commissioner, searches, curfew. Abdullah, the desert king. The guns of the Arab Legion. The convoy to Mount Scopus. The convoy to the Etzion bloc. An incited rabble. Inflamed mobs. Blood-thirsty ruffians. Brutal armed irregulars. All forever aimed at me. I always belonged to the minority, to the besieged, to those whose fate was sealed, who lived a life hovering on the brink of disaster.

So this time too, the city will be attacked. We shall die there like that little pious Jew who lay in the street, his face pale and amazed, as if he had suffered some grave insult. And more.

After the siege was lifted, a border was drawn through the heart of the city. All my childhood was passed in dead-end alleyways, facing streets one was forbidden to enter. The scar of destruction, no-man's-land, mine fields, wasteland, ruined, blackened buildings. Twisted, despairing iron girders rising starkly out of the ruined houses. And ever opposite: the other Jerusalem. The city surrounding my city. Foreign sounds and smells emanated from it, pale lights flickered there by night, and the cry of the muezzin at dawn. Atlantis. The lost continent. A city which was forever the focus of one's most insubstantial visions. I had blurred memories dating from my earliest childhood, the memory of colorful alleyways in the Old City, the narrow arched street leading to the Wall, Mandatory Arab policemen, street-vendors' stalls, tamarind, a riot of color, an ever present sense of lurking danger.

From over there, from beyond the border, an angry threat has been directed at me throughout most of my life. I remember wandering down the streets of Musrara at dusk, to the edge of no-man's-land. A glimpse of Schneller Woods from afar. Forbidden views seen from the observation point at Abu Tor. The shattered square of Notre Dame. The towers of Bethlehem opposite the woods of Ramat Rachel. Desert hillsides falling away from the suburb of Talpiyot. The Dead Sea glittering in the distance like a mirage. Rocky valleys at dawn.

On Sunday, June 11, 1967, I went to see the Jerusalem that lay beyond the border. I came to places which with dreams and the years had become petrified symbols within my heart, and lo and behold – people lived here – houses, shops, stalls, signposts.

And I was thunderstruck, as if my whole inner world had collapsed. The dreams were a deception. The world of terrible tales became a mockery. The perpetual threat was nothing but a cruel twisted joke. Everything was burst asunder. Laid wide open. My Jerusalem, beloved and feared, was dead.

Now the town was different. Long-forgotten, neglected corners had come to life again. Bulldozers pushed new roads through heaps of rubble which I had imagined would be there for all eternity. Districts which had been utterly forgotten were filled with feverish activity. Hosts of pious Jews, soldiers in battledress, amazed tourists, smartly dressed women from Tel Aviv and Haifa, all streamed eastward. The tide flowed strongly to Jerusalem. The rest of the country poured into the open city. Everything within her orbit took an air of festivity. And I along with it.

These things cannot be expressed in words. Again I say that I loved Jerusalem in its entirety, but what does this mean? It is like a love affair, a contradictory, tortuous force: she is mine and yet strange to me, conquered but hostile, devoted yet inaccessible.

I could disregard all this. The skies are the same skies and the

Jerusalem stone is the same throughout. Sheikh Jarrah is almost like Katamon.

But the city is inhabited. People live within her streets, and they are strangers, I do not understand their language, they are there — in their homes — and I am the stranger who comes from without. Courteous people, courteous to the point of offense, as if they have reached the very peak of happiness in having merited the honor of selling me postcards or Jordanian stamps. Welcome, we are brothers, it is just for you alone that we have waited all these years, just so that we could embrace you. And their eyes hate me, wish me dead. The accursed stranger. It grieves me, but I cannot order my words in a rational way.

I was in East Jerusalem three days after the conquest of the city. I arrived there straight from El Arish, in Sinai, wearing uniform and carrying a sub-machine-gun. I was not born to sound the trumpet or liberate lands from foreign yokes. The lament of an enslaved people finds an echo in my ears, but I am deaf to the lament of "enslaved territory."

In my childhood dreams it was the Arabs who wore uniforms and carried machine-guns, Arabs who came to my street in Jerusalem to kill me. Twenty-two years ago, a slogan painted in red appeared on a courtyard wall not far from our house: "Judah fell in blood and fire; by blood and fire will Judah rise again." One of the underground had written these words at night in burning red. I don't know how to write about blood and fire. If I ever write anything about this war, it will be about pus, sweat and vomit and not about blood and fire. With all my soul, I desired to feel in Jerusalem as a man who has dispossessed his enemies and returned to the patrimony of his ancestors. The Bible came to life for me: the Prophets, the Kings, Temple Mount, Absolom's Pillar, the Mount of Olives. The Jerusalem of Abraham Mapu and Agnon. I wanted to be part of it all, I wanted to belong.

Were it not for the people. I saw enmity and rebelliousness, sycophancy, amazement, fear, insult and trickery. I passed through the streets of East Jerusalem like a man breaking into some forbidden place. Depression filled my soul.

City of my birth. City of my dreams. City of my ancestors' and my people's yearnings. And I was condemned to walk through its streets armed with a sub-machine-gun like one of the characters from my childhood nightmares. To be a stranger in a very strange city.

Amos Oz (Kibbutz Hulda)

JERUSALEM OF MY CHILDHOOD

The nocturne of Jerusalem which accompanied my childhood sounds again in my ears in these post-war days. Again I hear the whistle of the wind blown through the thousands of pine needles. Again I see the grey stone, the cramped alleyways which sought not breadth but only height, the narrow strip of sky high above, the heavy iron balconies, the bridges, the water tanks, the laundry blowing pennant-like in the backyards.

The days of the siege which filled my childhood come back again to me. Father helping us to fill sacks of earth to barricade the window-sill. Running off to school to see the Palmach soldiers; the sound of their evening sing-songs before they went out on duty. The onions which all the children planted in the gardens in an attempt to stave off the hunger of the siege. The refugees from the Old City who fled to the stone Arab houses of Katamon.

I remember a time when I cried: the tears I shed over the fall of the Etzion bloc. I couldn't grasp then how it could possibly have been taken by the Arabs. "But they're heroes," I wept in despair. So my father explained that knowing how to face defeat was part of the process of war. Many are the faces that flash before me now: the soft-drink vendor and his shiny steel barrel, the old lady who would bring a basket of strawberries or figs to the corner of the road and weigh them up with stone weights.

Yes, these days have brought back many a picture of the city, of the far-off days of explosions and tears and happiness, homesickness and many dormant question-marks. Sometimes I still hear my father's voice, in other words, but with the same tone, "In a war, my child, you have to know how to be victorious."

Muki Tsur (Kibbutz Ein Gev)

PART 7
FACING THE FUTURE

CARRYING ON—THAT'S OUR DEBT TO THEM

From a discussion in Ein Harod. Interviewer: Avraham Shapira

Since its foundation in 1921, Ein Harod has been a central point in the development of the kibbutz movement and the Jewish community. From its earliest days it aimed at a combination of industry and agriculture, as well as active participation in the defense effort and and political life of the country. In 1952 the kibbutz split into two parts on political grounds. Each part comprises a community of over 1,500. The speakers in this discussion come from both parts of Ein Harod.

Participants:
Zvi, married, with no children. Works in cotton. Warrant officer in the Naval Commando, one of the Israeli Army's crack units. *Gad*, unmarried, lieutenant in an armored unit. *Shmuel*, married, with one child, fought in a motorized patrol unit. *Ilan*, married, with three children. Works in the fruit orchard. Major, fought in the war as a company commander. *Avner.*

Zvi: My unit's a bit insulated, if you like. You don't see any blood, you don't see any firing. I thought right through the night. I had lots of time to think. The work needs maximum concentration all the time. Sometimes I seemed to get hit by a kind of

247

absent-mindedness, simply blinded by everything, and because I didn't know what the position was. One thought just kept banging away in my mind: I wasn't afraid of being killed, but that suddenly someone would come along and drag me out, I don't know how, and that I'd be taken prisoner. In my job this is probably the most likely thing that can happen. I thought about it, and it scared me. I thought about how I'd hold out against them during the first days of interrogation. I had it all worked out, just what pressure they'd put on me, whether I'd break under it. I had it taped, right down to the last detail. It paralyzed me completely. A lot of the time, I really didn't feel so good physically, and on top of it these quite paralyzing ideas were terribly distracting, and just when I was supposed to be concentrating like hell. And, every now and then, a depth-charge went off alongside of us. It shocks the hell out of you, your heart. . . .

Avraham: How does the war affect you now?

Shmuel: As far as I was concerned, when the war was over, it was over. I've begun my everyday life again. And that's that.

Gad: That's just not possible. You had friends and things. . . . Don't you ever think about them? Things happened to you, you were wounded. . . .

Shmuel: Of course I haven't completely forgotten. But it doesn't affect my daily life. I remember it when I see a film, but otherwise it doesn't affect me.

Gad: Impossible. Perhaps it would be more accurate to say that you don't *want* it to affect you. I don't want it to either, but I can't get out of it like that. I can't simply say that it's all over and that's that. . . .

Avner: Before the war I was prepared to accept all sorts of things, I had my own personal plans, my own way of thinking — and now, it's quite clear that for a lot of the youngsters I've met things have changed completely. There are lots more who're ready to go into the regular army, or start new settlements. I feel that there's a lot less tolerance towards all those types whose attitude is that the war's over, and who've just gone right back along their petty little paths with all their miserable little intrigues. I used to be pretty sco   bout what went on in the country, sort of standing on the s   now — it grips me.

Ilan: As I see it, a man who gets everything easily, without any special effort, feels differently from the man who has to pay for things. Up to now, and in the conditions we've lived under, this feeling of belonging to Israel — with all that it implies — has been a very theoretical thing. And yet when it came to it — you really felt this sense of belonging, this identification. The very act of going off to fight — the fact that you were ready for anything — gave it reality. Now you feel a stronger sense of belonging. And more than the feeling that you belong to it — it belongs to you. It's a feeling which forces you to give more of yourself. You feel that Israel is yours. You often hear it said in the kibbutz that the kibbutz belongs to us, all that it owns belongs to each and every one of us. But in actual fact the individual belongs to the group more than to himself. That's one of the things the war's done for us — given us a greater sense of belonging.

Avner: I won't claim that we were all ready to get killed — and yet in our half-track we all had the same feeling: if the boy on your left was killed, you felt you had to be somehow specially worthy of this terrible sacrifice. We've got to carry on doing what the others didn't manage to do. Carrying on — that's our debt to them.

WAR CHANGED MY SENSE OF PROPORTION

From a discussion in Gat. Interviewer: Shlomit Teub

Shlomit: How do you feel about the future? Has your perspective returned to normal?

Amnon: When the Sinai Campaign was over, my father came to see me in Dir el Balah. I was overjoyed. "Now there'll be peace," I told him, "it was all worthwhile." I was sure we'd dealt the Egyptians a crushing blow and that they'd have no alternative but to make peace. I said it on what seemed to be completely rational grounds, even if I'd also hoped for it so much. This time, I went through the same process. I firmly believed that after such a crippling blow, our neighbors would have to revise their thinking and recognize our existence, and perhaps the way to peace would be open. Today, I'm quite skeptical about it. There's no shadow of doubt in my mind but that there'll be another round.

Shlomit: People have said that the war pushed them into making all sorts of personal decisions and quickened the pace of things for them. . . .

Amnon: I had a youngster under me whose wife was about to divorce him. She took their child away — all sorts of trouble. Just before the war, he told me all about it, really let it all out. I tried to buck him up a bit. When things got very tense, when people started wo⸴⸴⸴ if they'd see their women-folk again or not, I said to him, ⸴⸴ 've got six hours. Go and see your wife." She'd taken ⸴⸴ staying with relatives. They patched it up. I don't know how long it'll last — but all that pre-war tension brought them together again.

Dan: War does something to us. Anyway as far as I'm concerned it changed my sense of proportion a great deal.

Some of the boys in my unit had been going out with the same girls for a long time. But they hadn't thought of getting married yet. After the war, they all said, "That's it. Now we're getting married." I think that what pushed people into taking drastic steps and doing things that formerly they thought could wait, is the desire to create a situation that'll stand in sharp contrast to war. They want something complete in their lives, something good, something that will give them personal security. It's true that people's order of preference changes. Little quarrels lose their importance. Other things suddenly become much more important and meaningful.

About a month after the war was over, I came back to work. It was very difficult. I couldn't concentrate on what I was doing. It's still a bit difficult — working to plan, keeping a sense of perspective. I used to do the technical side of it, and that's all. Apparently my mind's still back there. I had to go and clinch a deal; I knew that if I pushed them I could get a reduction in the price, but suddenly I couldn't be bothered to argue about it, it seemed so unimportant, so lacking in any proportion. "To hell with it, another few hundred pounds more or less." That's how I felt about things as far as work was concerned and as far as a great many other social problems were concerned, things I had to deal with as a member of the central committee of the kibbutz. Life goes on — it's awful — and you've changed so much. You can't accept that life goes on, you look at things differently. So you become a bit apathetic or cynical. Your perspective changes.

Amnon: I had to struggle with two contradictory feelings. On the one hand, I loathed talking about the war, telling people what I'd done and what I'd gone through. I don't know why. After the Sinai Campaign I spent two whole evenings talking to anyone who'd do me the favor of listening. But this time I couldn't. I talked about it once to Dan, once to someone else. They were both people I felt I owed it to. Dan and I had an agreement: he'd tell me, and I'd tell him. I loathed the whole war. I didn't want to have anything more to do with it.

Shlomit: Perhaps it's because you've become more mature since then?

Amnon: I don't know. But I felt a real aversion to talking about it. Do you understand? If I'd had nothing to talk about, I think I'd have talked for days on end. But I did have something to say — and I wouldn't talk. I hardly talked at all. But on the other hand, when I thought about the farm manager's office, of how people keep opening that door and coming in with all sorts of problems about the bulldozer and the painters — all sorts of little problems which had suddenly become so trivial — I couldn't imagine a worse nightmare than going back to just that same type of life which I'd actually fought for. I had to force myself to be very rational about it and say "Look here mister, it's for this petty little routine (excuse the expression) that you fought. For these little problems. So that the children's house gets repaired in time, so that the committee buys the radios, etc, etc."

IT'S AS IF YOU WERE LOOKING FOR SOMETHING

From a discussion in Mishmar Hanegev. Interviewer: David Alon

Asher: Suddenly we heard we were going on leave. Our first leave. I was near Ismailia and once again we travelled along the same road, the same sector. We were in a convoy and it took about three hours. We were travelling slowly again, smelling the same smells, seeing the same sights we'd seen during those past few weeks. I got on the plane and arrived in Lydda. We began walking, happy that we were home for our first leave after the war, after the horror. We went a little further on and saw cars in the street, greenery and flowers and a young girl in a starched dress, people in decent clothes — we just stood there and gazed at it all. It was then that I asked someone if it had been raining; you'd got so used to a certain drab scenery and color that when you saw a car painted in a decent color, nothing out of the ordinary, it seemed as if it must have been raining and that the car was shining because the rain had washed it clean. All the cars looked as if they were brand new. The transition had been too rapid. As if you'd stepped out of hell and suddenly set foot in an ordinary everyday place. During the first meal at the airport, the food wouldn't go down, I couldn't swallow it. It's as if everything seemed cheap and nasty to us. After we'd satisfied our hunger a bit, we couldn't even manage the main course. I went outside and breathed the fresh pure air and felt good.

In general, those first days were very difficult. We went along in the bus and looked right and left as if we were searching for corpses.

How is it that there aren't any corpses by the side of the road? How is it that all the vehicles are in one piece? We arrived in Ramle: the houses were undamaged, whole. We knew they hadn't been touched, but when we actually saw it, it was like discovering it anew. It's a very difficult feeling to express, very difficult to explain. When you get back home and you're a big hero, you've conquered, we've conquered, all that rejoicing – it all seems unnecessary.

Everything you'd ignored previously, all the corpses: you suddenly start thinking about them and you ask yourself, while everyone's rejoicing over this great victory, what it's all about. It cost us dear. And this time, when you say dear, you take the enemy's corpses into account as well as our own. I begged them not to ask me so many questions, not to think so much of me, to tone down all the rejoicing over the victory. The feeling I had was that this wasn't the moment for rejoicing, for victory, for celebrations; it was the moment for some sort of mourning.

There were certain things that took on a new meaning. Little things that perhaps we'd considered important previously seem completely unimportant today. I can't even give you an example of what I mean, but when I came back to the kibbutz and people told me about all sorts of small matters and petty squabbles, things that perhaps would have made my blood boil earlier on, because I used to get very het up about all sorts of inequalities and injustice, now all these things had lost their significance, as if they were side-issues. Forget it! It's not so important, what difference does it make! Our sense of proportion's changed. When you've seen life and death hanging in such a delicate balance then suddenly other things lose all significance. What sense do these squabbles make as compared to death? Compared to a mangled Egyptian soldier – it's nothing.

I was very restless when I came back. I wandered around from place to place, and couldn't sit still. I couldn't do any of the things I used to enjoy doing. When I came home, Koka immediately asked me if I'd like to hear a certain record that she knew I loved. "Do you want to hear the record?" she asked. "No, no." – "Do you want to listen to the radio?" – "No," I said, "no, I don't want to listen to any music, it's hard for me to listen to music." She asked again, "Do you want a book to read?" – "No, no." None of the things you used to find relaxing have any more meaning for you. It's as if you're looking for some invisible object. You don't know exactly what you're looking for and nothing they give you helps.

Immediately after the war, for example, I was obsessed with the need to find more and more material about the war. I saw that quite a few albums had already appeared in the shops. I looked through a few of them, but rejected one after the other. Not one album or even one picture reflected what I was looking for.

David: What were you looking for?

Asher: I don't know. I was looking for something that would reflect what I felt during the war, what I feel now after the war. It was as if I wanted to go on living with it all, as if it was hard to leave it all without anything to remember it by. But all those pictures meant absolutely nothing to me.

Today, I'm more or less back to normal, partly because I forced myself into it, and these sort of feelings don't get you anywhere. I forced myself back into my old reading habits, and to go back to the hospital. The first time I went back, I ran away almost immediately. It was as if nothing had happened there. And that's not so, it's not fair to say that. They worked very hard, looked after the wounded, did everything they could. But today they're engrossed in the same professional problems that occupied them two or three months ago, before I was called up. It was just as if I'd left the morning ward round, the doctors discussing some problem or other, and I'd come back to find the discussion going on where I'd left it. But it's not true, it's just that they've got back into their own routine, and it's difficult for us to follow suit.

Now in regard to values. I don't think values have changed. I haven't stopped believing in what I believed before. From this point of view, the war didn't alter me. Yet we did have to do things that were directly opposed to our natures. The very fact of killing, for me especially — since I'm professionally orientated in a completely opposite direction — even though we did have to do it, the very fact that we knew why we were doing it, the very necessity, made a difference.

David: I'll ask you something a little personal. Do you still feel the same way about your family? Children for example: do you still behave the same way towards them? Is your affection for your son any different?

Asher: Yes, it's increased. That's to say, when I returned I felt as if I'd rediscovered the kid, and I can't rid myself of that feeling even today. It was as if I'd lost him and then found him again. That's how I felt. Maybe this comes from the fear I had all through the war, especially at the beginning — before the war — that the civilian population was vulnerable, very vulnerable, and this meant my family too. When I saw how unconscious they'd been of their own danger, it was very moving, like finding them again. As far as my wife and family are concerned I feel stronger. There are lots of things we haven't got, but that's not important. I have the feeling that my wife, too, thinks along the same lines as I do. She, too, doesn't feel the need of material possessions as much as she did before; what once seemed absolutely essential has lost all its importance. So from this point of view I feel that I and my family are stronger than previously; that's to say — what matters to us now is what should always have mattered to us, the basic thing. Everything else is secondary. Now I not only acknowledge this intellectually, I also feel it.

David: Do you think it's fair to say that inside of you you're looking for an answer to death? When you spoke about looking for something invisible, you didn't say exactly what it was that made you so restless.

Asher: That's a difficult question. The question isn't difficult, but the answer is. Because I do think about the problem of death sometimes. Especially in the hospital, when you see a child or a young man die suddenly — that's when the question comes up most. During a war, too, when you know that in the main it's young people you'll be treating, then the question comes up again. This time it came up more sharply than ever. Perhaps you're right. Look, I have a feeling that I'm trying to push these problems away, I haven't gone into it very deeply but I think you've hit right on the point. It may be that the answer to this question means a lot: closeness to death doesn't make me say, "Get what you can while you can" nor act that way: rather the opposite. It makes me think that I should live in accordance with certain moral standards. That's what's important. All the rest, all the superfluities, not just the material ones, but even when it comes to behavior, as far as people and all sorts of other things are concerned, it's all superfluous, it doesn't give you anything. What counts is living a life built on moral principles. Maybe once I tried to deceive myself with all sorts of other things, but now I think I'm stronger and I won't try to do it again.

Let me tell you something else. That moment when the planes were attacking us was perhaps the only moment when I really had to make some sort of spiritual reckoning with myself. I tried to figure out if it had been worthwhile. Perhaps all of us here would be wiped out. Has it all been worthwhile? Wife, children and family? And I said to myself, "What a foolish question, of course it has." I'm telling you this because I thought about it then, not in the same way as I'm thinking about it now. Then it was a sort of inner truth.

A WASTE OF READINESS

From a discussion in Giv'at Hashlosha. Interviewer: Yariv Ben-Aharon

Yariv: Now that the war's over, don't you have the feeling that you're part of the generation that led the country to war and victory?

Yigal: I wouldn't say that as kibbutzniks we did it all on our own, but we certainly did have a quite special role in the whole business. But does that mean that we're also capable of leading the nation as far as other things are concerned? Or is that perhaps going to be our job as kibbutzniks? Are we going to become the country's war specialists?

Zvi: It seems to me that most of us feel some sort of frustration and disillusionment with the current situation. Even though the war was a short one, it was still the greatest experience we've been through. There was a feeling that lots of things would have to change as a result. As far as the kibbutz movement is concerned: there's the issue of land settlement, the new territories, the whole way of life in the kibbutz which gives you a feeling that it's become complacent. . . . There isn't the same sense of awakening that existed during the war. You go back to the realities of everyday life — financial and material problems — just the same as before the war. You thought that the problems would have changed; and you find that they haven't. And people's response hasn't changed. It seems to me that it begins at the top and goes right down. I don't believe it's going to change, either. On the national scale, it begins right at the top with the people who sit at the center of the government. And on kibbutz level — it's the same sort of people. It seems to me that it's the same people who've been looking after the same problems for the last umpteen years. The bulk of the front line troops was the younger generation, people of the Sinai Campaign generation and younger. It's not that this younger generation ought to take control; what I mean is how to grasp the problems so as to get things moving on the right lines. . . .

As I see it, all this is a result of the Government's attitude which is becoming more and more entrenched. It's as if they're saying: "There's someone looking after things; there's someone to see to things; you've finished your job now, go home again and get on with your own life." You can see the same thing at work on a party level — in all the negotiations going on between the various labor parties. . . .

Ehud: The need for a new outlook and for new young forces must first of all be expressed in the sphere of security. We have to try to find new or unconventional methods of achieving peace. That's the top priority. Now, as to the question of whether anything has changed. You said that there's a feeling now that this wasn't the last war; but in fact that's a feeling we've had ever since the War of Independence. The fact that we're surrounded by millions of hostile Arabs has been with us for the last twenty years and it's given Israeli society a certain character — in fact it's affected our behavior, and everything that happens here. It's also affected this generation. It doesn't seem to me that we've changed in this respect, since there still does exist a quite serious danger of a further war. It's not possible to feel that this generation is any different because it fought and won. Our generation sprang from Israeli society as that society existed down to the war. If the conditions of that society continue to resemble pre-war conditions, then in fact nothing has changed.

Hillel: After the war, and even in the thick of it, when we saw what enormous territory we had hold of, when we saw a unified Land of Israel, when we realized all the emotion it aroused, when we understood how immensely it increased our freedom of action, of creating something new, when we saw the tremendous unity of the entire Jewish people both here and abroad: that's when our hearts were really wide open to all sorts of things. But now, two and a bit months after the war, I think that the greater part of that readiness has been wasted. The goodwill, the open heartedness, the enthusiasm — it's all been wasted. With each day that passes, it dies a little bit more. There wasn't any sense of how things might be, no advance planning, no guidelines. Everybody relaxed, withdrew, licked his wounds, and that was the end of it all. Even when you first come back home from the army, you feel . . . at first you still felt some of that enthusiasm, then you got back into the old routine. And as far as we're all concerned, I think it's stopped affecting us. The enthusiasm and open-heartedness is all beginning to disappear at a fantastic pace. Every day is a really immense waste.

Ehud: Waste of what?

Hillel: A waste of readiness. Look, all that business of national solidarity, something as great as that, all that tremendous enthusiasm — it could be directed towards something constructive, something permanent, it could have been directed into channels that would have brought thousands here from abroad.

Ehud R.: It could be directed into ridding the country of all these messy inter-party scraps, we could have exploited the fact that you and I fought side by side with relief workers and unemployed men, and there'd be a juster post-war society because all the various social strata established new links during the war. When did we ever have a better opportunity for doing something like that? What's been done with all the readiness that existed then? Not a damn thing! It's not just a waste. It's far worse than that — it's a real crime.

Zvi: Before the war we tapped every possible source — every spring, every stream, every droplet almost — and it produced a veritable flood of goodwill. But instead of exploiting it all and undertaking some really big project, it was neglected. Everyone's gone back to his own affairs. All the little rivulets have returned to their old channels. I'm not a pessimistic type, but my personal feeling is that everything's reverted to the *status quo ante*, and it's because the people at the top have again started concerning themselves with the same old things at the same dreadfully slow pace, with the same old worn-out attitudes, just like it was before.

There did exist a tremendous readiness. There was an enormous enthusiasm. And it's all gone. So as far as my own personal feelings are concerned, everything's gone back to where it was, just as if nothing at all had happened. The war was a personal experience for me — and that's all there is to it — and as time passes, as the days go by, it gets forgotten; and that's it. . . .

Ehud: We're exaggerating the opportunities that existed. I don't think that all our concepts have undergone any fundamental change as a result of the war. People get inspired during a war. But can you really pin so much hope on that sort of inspiration? I think it's quite a dangerous thing to do because there's liable to be a big letdown afterwards, even if there's some sort of formal act of unity or something like that! Politically speaking, Israel's remained in pretty much the same situation as it was before and the internal friction is only a reflection of that state of affairs. If the situation itself doesn't change, then those things can't change either. Perhaps a few opportunities were missed here and there, but it's still pretty dangerous to put all the responsibility on this business of the war.

Zvi: Before the war there was a desire to change established forms both in the kibbutz movement and on a national scale. It was based on the fact that the political differences and frictions don't exist in our generation, mean nothing to our age group. And it's this will to change which should have been realized as a result of the war. Most of the conflicting concepts have been bridged over. It's mistaken to say, today, that the differences in the various kibbutz movements — judged in the light of their fundamental principles — are of any great weight. The way of life's the same and the things they have in common are far greater than the things that divide them. Yes, the war should have let us realize this desire for change, which should have been accompanied by a change of spirit — and that, too, didn't happen. The generation that wants this, that fought and won the war, just hasn't got the strength to change things. We should have exploited all that enthusiasm immediately after the war. If we'd really swung into it then, something new would have emerged. Maybe it wouldn't have been a long-term thing, but something would have changed. At the moment, I just don't see it happening or about to happen.

I FEEL THAT THE STATE OF HOSTILITY WILL CONTINUE

From a discussion in Hulda. Interviewer: Amos Oz

Amos: Would you be capable of going again as you went last time, or will you have changed?

Shai: It's very deep, this feeling that if we're asked to fight in a just cause, we'll go — just as we did before.

Amos: Don't you think that next time you'll be more worried, even more afraid? Perhaps there'll even be some element of unwillingness in the light of what you felt last time?

Shai: Unwillingness, yes. Now I know — from having seen it with my own eyes — what it's all about. I didn't know before. But what I must emphasize is the point I just made: if I know our cause is just, I'll go with exactly the same degree of readiness, the same ability to kill, the same ability to go into the attack — that's something I'm quite convinced of.

I don't think there's any enmity between us. Apart from the fact that they feel we've stolen their land and that we have imperialist tendencies and so on, I don't think there has to be enmity between us because we're two different nations. Maybe it's because I'm on the winning side and I don't have to overcome the feeling of having been defeated and shamed.

I certainly think it's possible to create a state for them. They've got to be given the chance to express what they want quite freely. That's to say, if we could announce today that we weren't going to give back the territory we've acquired, and if we could ask them whether they want to move on into the Arab states or to establish some sort of state here — a real state, with a parliament, with all the bases for a proper state with their own land — then I think they should be asked what they want.

Amos: And the choice should be theirs?

Shai: Yes. From the point of view of settlement and employment, I'm sure they could find a place in the other Arab countries. The question is whether being Palestinians they can also feel like Jordanians or Iraqis or Kuwaitis. If we're talking about the Arab nation, and if there is an Arab nation, then there's nothing to prevent them being good Iraqis and so on. But if they consider themselves Palestinians, then perhaps a Palestinian state should be created for them. In any case we can't let ourselves become the reason for their being nothing more than animals, forever herded together in refugee camps.

TO FIND OURSELVES

Part of a summing-up discussion held in Tel Aviv, after the material which forms this book had been collected and partially edited. The last discussion of *The Seventh Day*, and the first of a new series in a never-ending dialogue.

Participants:
Gad, thirty-two, married with two children, born and educated in Kibbutz Ayelet Hashachar. For many years he was in charge of the citrus grove, and a leading figure in the economic development of his kibbutz. He spent two years in Canada, working with a Jewish youth movement, and is now studying Jewish philosophy at Tel Aviv University.
Re'uven, twenty-six, born in Florence, spent the war years hiding, with his family, in various Italian monasteries. He arrived in Israel in 1949, and finished his schooling in Kibbutz Gal-Ed, of which he became a member in 1960. In the Six-Day War he served in a paratroop reconnaissance unit, and was wounded in the battle for Jerusalem. He has contributed a number of articles on cultural and educational problems to kibbutz journals. *Amram Hayisra'eli*, *Muki Tsur*, and *Avram (Avi) Shapira:* members of the Editorial Board.

Gad: This discussion is part of a search, part of the phenomenon of a generation seeking itself — our generation. It still

264

doesn't know what framework it wants to fit itself into, it still doesn't know what role is demanded of it. It's quite likely that we'll come out of this meeting, and out of a lot of other similar meetings, with the feeling that this isn't it — perhaps we won't even be able to explain just what it is that we haven't found — but it seems to me that this very "it" that it isn't will be the fact that we still haven't found ourselves. And I don't know if we will find ourselves so quickly or so easily. At the moment we're still under the influence of a very drastic episode in our lives, something which has, as it were, given us new standards. It gives us new opportunities to think things over, to take another look at ourselves.

First and foremost, we've got to try and overcome a sort of feeling — we don't talk about it much — I wouldn't exactly call it a feeling of inferiority, it's rather a sort of diffidence. After that, perhaps we can go further. This war seems worse than others in one particular respect: the course of the war and its results were so wonderful and yet, at the same time, the realities of the situation that followed it are no different from what they were before.

I think the words Avik used just now gave the most extreme expression to this view, when he said that there are people who say that in another nine or ten years there'll be another war, and so on and so on. A vicious circle. But perhaps there's even more to it than that. If I were to draw a graph of the whole process, I'd start with the period of economic restraint, when we were all affected by the general depression, the hesitant leadership — everyone in the country really felt that we were in a poor way. Then, suddenly, we were thrown into a situation quite unlike anything we'd ever been used to: a real physical threat to our very existence, and the people's moods went up and down, right up to the very minute. . . .

Amram: It had really never happened before?

Gad: I don't think you can say it was ever so extreme before. Perhaps there was something like it during the War of Independence, but I imagine that at least for us — the people in this discussion — there'd never before been such a feeling of tension as there was during the days before this war. And then, all of a sudden, everything's completely and utterly changed, and there was a period after the war when one felt that something must really have altered for good. Yet, just look where we are: it's already three months after the war and the labor parties are still negotiating their unification. The whole business leads you to a feeling of some sort of fatalism. You start asking yourself what your place is in all this. Then there are all the experiences you had during the war, and for the most part, they were very, very tough experiences indeed, whether they involved personal sacrifice or moral struggle. It all gets sucked into the maelstrom of your experience; and you start looking for your own place in this mess, and you ask yourself whether you've just got to reconcile yourself to it, or whether you really have some part to play, some mission to ensure that things really will change.

There are moments when I don't think anything can be done, when it all seems beyond us. I think that it would all be much easier if I were a religious person. But I'm not; even if I am to some extent a believer basically, my education doesn't give me what I need to answer all these questions. It's too rationalistic an education, let's say: or perhaps it's as if a certain sequence of events took place here, and it's difficult to rid oneself of the feeling that neither Marxist theses nor any other can really explain what happened. Things happened that I can't account for. We haven't got any control over things or events, we're just pawns in the game — and perhaps that intensifies the feeling of "What am I, who am I?" We talk about pacifist education, but I must say that this sometimes really mystifies me because the second generation of kibbutzniks have entrenched themselves in two areas in particular, and that's where they prove their worth: in the economic sphere (sometimes even to the point of anti-intellectualism) and in the military sphere. And how you can reconcile that fact with a pacifist education, I'm not at all certain.

Re'uven: The root of all this confusion lies in the glory of war, accompanied by the indisputable fact that war can't be a good thing and that nothing can be achieved by it. No one comes out of a war unscarred. I find it very difficult to accept the idea that it was through the war that we achieved great and wonderful things, things that no one dreamt of before.

Can you educate in the light of a war? Can you establish and build and develop a set of concepts, values and ideals in the light of a war, or in the shadow of a potential war? You can't build yourself on war. Whenever you hear the same theme, whenever you see the things that characterize every great war, you're faced by a contradiction that's very difficult to resolve.

Our generation was faced with a *fait accompli*. We came into the picture at the height of a social revolution, when all the great things had already been done. It's a pity that it had to be a war that made it possible; but this war gave us a chance to free ourselves of this feeling, to show ourselves doing something, creating something, getting somewhere in the same way as those who preceded us. If I were to be asked what symbolizes this war, then I wouldn't choose the great conquests. I'd choose something that appears to be much more modest, but is, perhaps, much greater than it seems at first sight. For me, what symbolizes this war is the paratrooper who stood facing the Western Wall and could find no outlet for his emotion other than tears. That same paratrooper wasn't just facing the Western Wall: he was also facing two thousand years of exile, the whole history of the Jewish people, and perhaps it was the first time that he was doing so in such a concrete manner. Perhaps there's some educational value in the whole thing: here we are standing in the places which have been sacred to our nation since its earliest history, here we are facing the whole of Jewish history. Not every generation has such an opportunity.

Avi: These last three wars have created a degree of faith in the fate of the people, and have strengthened the belief that its history will continue. It's obvious that if we're not going to be wiped out, then we're always going to have to fight for our existence: we have so many enemies, and perhaps that's understandable — because we're successful, and over clever people. As I see it, there's a lot of "the wicked prosper and the righteous suffer" about it all. I believe firmly in the future of this people. The stronger the blow its enemies suffer, the longer the interval between bouts. I think there'll be a longer space of time between this war and the next. That's my feeling.

Amram: In my opinion there's almost no point at all in discussing whether or not people were shaken up. Everyone experienced things differently. The question that occupies me more today is what we're going to do with the situation, how we're going to absorb it, what directions we're going to channel it into. The shake-up the war gave us has some very constructive aspects, just as it can also be something very destructive. I think we have to find a way of extracting the constructive forces from the negative ones. And that for me involves finding ourselves.

Muki: There are some people who claim that war — any war — is opposed to justice and that there exists an exact mechanism for recognizing the one who's in the right: he's the one who loses. As if this were the rule of justice — the opposite of "might is right." Over-simplification begins when one tries to explain everything according to this rule. It ignores the terrible memories of Jewish history and the challenge that that history puts to us. Sometimes it even stems from the desire for national suicide which is so deeply implanted in us just because we are the children of Jewish history and are perpetuating its negative aspects. And there are some people who claim that what we've wanted all these years is a return to our historical boundaries, to the Temple Mount. But it seems to me that if on June 4, 1967, Nasser had announced that his guns had all been sunk, and his tanks had gone up in flames (without any outside help), and if Hussein had, on June 4, tried to reach a real peace settlement with us, and if the Syrians had immediately identified with him on this — then I am convinced that, despite our wish to return to the land of our fathers, we would have preferred not to go to war. This doesn't mean to say that I don't think we wanted to return to Temple Mount or that we are foreigners in this land, because that isn't true. Our attitude to the country is complex, one of longing and attachment, starting with the dreams of our childhood and involving a deep desire to take root, a desire which is sometimes the expression of a fear of being torn away. This desire also embraces the people in the country, the people living here. Once Jewish sovereignty was gained, once it became clear that this was the home of the whole Jewish people, that it was their shelter, the home of their dreams, their creative spirit, then we were left with another great dream, one no less fantastic, perhaps, than the vision of the establishment of the State: that we should be able to take root not only on the mountains, in the soil, but also in the human scene — among the Arabs.

What we do is more important than what we dream, but there are dreams which can't be forgotten. One of our dreams was that we'd return to a unified Jerusalem, and it did finally come true even if it was after very many years and in a manner and at a moment which we had not envisaged.

Those who came back from the war preferred at first to remain silent. It was only their eyes that spoke: the fear of death was reflected there. Many of them prayed that these great days wouldn't be drowned in wordy speeches. A prayer was born in the hearts of many that we would emerge from the war as different people. Those who took life and were granted life must also know how to live that life. But there could be no real certainty that the country would really change.

Now that the war is over, life is quickly returning to the rhythm which characterized the period before the war. On the one hand many of those who took on heavy responsibilities during the fighting now feel that they have both the right and the duty to shoulder more responsibility for what's going on in the country; they fear that the brotherhood of arms, the feeling of mutual responsibility may fall prey to the political parties and other organs of the establishment, with all their old traditions. Yet on the other hand there's also a tendency towards relaxation, as a sort of compensation for the strain of war. I've heard thousands of people say: "There's been a war, now we're entitled to a holiday." There's always a danger that the whole country will want to "take a holiday," and victory is just the thing that encourages a feeling like this. The question is whether it's a historical necessity, or whether it's possible to rebel against it. How can we prevent things like this happening? How are we going to translate the things that crystallized out of those fateful hours into everyday language?

We need some sort of spiritual concourse, something different from the usual institutionalized forms of meeting. A genuine meeting of minds, frank and wide-ranging discussion on many intellectual levels. We must give some depth to life in order to open up new horizons before we reach the stage of decision. Such a discussion could save us from the vicious circle of courage in practical affairs combined with superficiality and timidity in spiritual matters. One can see the danger that empty iconoclasm and obstinate conservatism will between them prevent a genuine renaissance with its roots in reality.

An attempt of this nature must be made with a great deal of modesty, yet it must be ready for many spiritual adventures, it must be prepared to listen to many trends, to many temperaments. It must not pretend to be anything more than true spiritual dialogue. It must not advocate a program, it must avoid publicity, dogmatic pronouncements and identification with political decisions.

EPILOGUE

It was before the outbreak of the Six-Day War. The battalion was stationed in the Negev along the old border. It was terribly hot, and water was rationed, so we were all covered with dust and filthy dirty from the maneuvers. We were only waiting to be given a chance to lie down and doze off in our pup tents. I shared my tent with a reservist, a man older than most of us, who had nevertheless stood up well to the tough conditions. As evening fell he amazed me by pulling out of his rucksack two sheets, laundered and ironed. I couldn't help smiling as I watched him spread them out, but then he started speaking — quietly and sadly: "Everywhere I've been for years now I've taken these sheets with me — ever since the Second World War. I worked in a laundry then, washing sheets for German soldiers. There weren't any sheets in our ghetto . . . yet every day we washed sheets for them. I swore an oath then that if I got out of it all alive, I'd always sleep on a clean sheet." And so saying, he lay down between the sheets and fell alseep.

GLOSSARY

Achan: In the Book of Joshua (Chapter 7) Achan was executed because he had broken the law by keeping spoil captured in war.

Arabush: A derogatory term for "Arab."

Ashkenazi(m): Jew(s) originating from European or American communities, as distinct from Sephardi(m), originating from the Jewish communities of Asia and the Middle East.

Bar Mitzva: Jewish confirmation ceremony, celebrated at the age of thirteen by boys, and twelve by girls. In the kibbutzim the celebration and preparations for it are largely non-religious in character; in the towns its main feature is the "calling-up to the Torah," which symbolizes acceptance into the religious community.

Beit Ha'arava: A kibbutz at the northern tip of the Dead Sea, abandoned during the War of Liberation.

Dunam: 1,000 square meters (about ¼ acre).

Eighteen Benedictions: A group of prayers recited daily by pious Jews.

Etzion Bloc: A group of kibbutzim between Bethlehem and Hebron which were surrounded by the Arab Legion during the War of Liberation, and surrendered after a protracted struggle. They have been resettled since the Six-Day War.

Gevalt: (Yiddish). A cry of dismay or despair.

Golan Heights: Previously known as the Syrian Heights. The range of hills bordering the north-east of Israel from which the border settlements were constantly bombarded up to the Six-Day War, and which were conquered by the Israeli Army in the final stage of the war.

Hagana: Defense force of the Palestine Jewish community before the establishment of the State of Israel, which formed the nucleus of the Israeli Army.

Hannuka: The Feast of Lights, celebrated in mid-winter to mark the victory of the Maccabees over the Syrian-Greek conquerors of Palestine in the second century BC.

Harod's Well: The site of Gideon's camp on the eve of his victory over the Midianites. (Judges, Chapter 7.)

Hashomer Hatzair: Jewish youth movement, which originated in Europe about 1914, and whose graduates founded many kibbutzim which later united to form the Kibbutz Artzi kibbutz movement. The youth movement was influenced by the teachings of Martin Buber, particularly with regard to the importance of Arab-Jewish understanding, and also adopted a Marxist ideology.

Ichud Hakvutzot Vehakibbutzim: See kibbutz movements.

Irgun Zvai Leumi and Stern group: Dissident para-military organizations which carried on an active struggle against the British Mandatory Government up to 1948, in opposition to the policy of the Hagana.

"Jerusalem the Golden": Popular song about Jerusalem, old and new, which was universally felt to express the national mood during the Six-Day War. Different words to the same tune ("Jersusalem of Iron") were written by a soldier who took part in the battle for Jerusalem, and were sung during and after the war.

Ka-Chetnick: An Israeli novelist who writes about concentration camps.

Keffiah: Broad scarf used as head-dress by Arabs.

Kibbutz movements: The three major kibbutz movements differ today mainly in their political affiliations: the Kibbutz Artzi is connected with the Mapam Party, Ichud Hakvutzot Vehakibbutzim with Mapai and the Kibbutz Me'uchad with Achdut Avoda; though Mapai and Achdut Avoda combined in 1968 to form the united Israel Labor Party, the movements still retain their separate organization. *(The Seventh Day* was recorded at the time of the negotiations for the formation of the united party, and these negotiations are referred to in the discussions.)

Historically, the differences between the movements, and between the parties, have often seemed much more important than they are today. Most of the generation of *The Seventh Day* believe these differences to be no longer valid; but, at the time of writing, the organizational differences still exist.

Kinneret: Hebrew name for the Sea of Galilee.

Mandelbaum Gate: The crossing-point between Israeli and Jordanian Jerusalem until June 1967.

Mazal Tov: "Good luck": an expression of congratulation.

Melamed: Hebrew (and Yiddish) word, slightly derogatory, for a school-teacher.

Moshav: Small-holders' village, based on family holdings and co-operative purchasing and marketing arrangements.

Mukhtar: (Arabic). Headman of a village.

Nahal: A branch of the army consisting mostly of young kibbutz members.

Negev: Literally "the South," the desert southern half of Israel.

Palmach: Crack units of the Hagana, largely based on the kibbutzim.

Pitta: Arab bread.

Sabra: A local cactus-plant, whose fruit — prickly on the outside, but sweet inside — is said to symbolize the character of the local-born Israeli. The word is now commonly used to mean anybody born in Israel.

Sephardi(m): See Ashkenazi(m).

Shalom: Literally "Peace." Hebrew greeting: hello or goodbye.

Streimal: Fur hat worn by ultra-orthodox Jews.

Tefillin: Phylacteries, small boxes containing portions from the Bible and strapped on the arm and forehead by orthodox Jews during morning prayers.

Torah: Scroll of the Law, from which passages from the Bible are read during prayers.

UNRWA: United Nations Relief and Works Administration. UN agency administering the refugee camps in Gaza and on the West Bank.

Volunteers: After the Six-Day War, hundreds of European and American volunteers came to Israel to replace civilians who had been mobilized. The volunteers helped keep the economy operating.

Wadi Kelt: A scenic wilderness ravine between Jerusalem and Jericho.

Yeshiva: Institute of higher religious studies.

Youth Aliya: Organization for care and education of immigrant and underprivileged youth, which sends many groups to work and study in the kibbutzim.

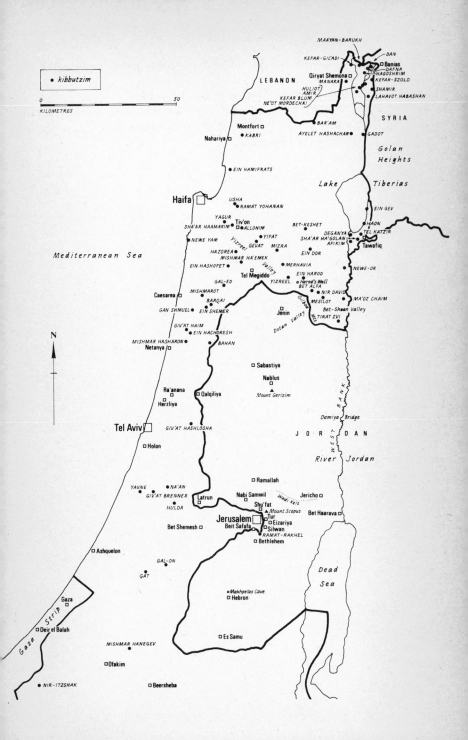

MAAYAN-BARUKH

KEFAR-GIL'ADI

DAN

Banias

DAFNA

HAGOSHRIM

Qiryat Shemona

KEFAR-SZOLD

MANARA

HULIOT

AMIR

SHAMIR

LEBANON

KEFAR BLUM

LAHAVOT HABASHAN

NE'OT MORDECHAI

SYRIA

Montfort

BAR'AM

Nahariya

KABRI

AYELET HASHACHAR

GADOT

Golan

Heights

EIN HAMIFRATS

Lake   Tiberias

Haifa

USHA

RAMAT YOHANAN

EIN GEV

YAGUR   Tiv'on

HAON

SHA'AR HAAMAKIM   ALLONIM

BET-KESHET

TEL KATZIR

NEWE YAM

YIFAT

DEGANYA

SHA'AR HA'GOLAN

Mediterranean Sea

HAZOREA   GEVAT   MIZRA

AFIKIM

Tawafiq

MISHMAR HA'EMEK

EIN DOR

EIN HASHOFET

MERHAVIA

NEWE-OR

GAL-ED   Tel Megiddo

EIN HAROD

Caesarea   MISHMAROT

YIZREEL

Harod's Well

BET ALFA

BARQAI

NIR DAVID

MA'OZ CHAIM

GAN SHMUEL   EIN SHEMER

MESILOT

Jenin

Bet-Shean Valley

GIV'AT HAIM

TIRAT ZVI

EIN HACHORESH

Dotan Valley

MISHMAR HASHARON   BAHAN

Netanya

Sabastiya

Nablus

Ra'anana

Mount Gerizim

Qalqiliya

Herzliya

J O R D A N

Tel Aviv   GIV'AT HASHLOSHA

W E S T   B A N K

Holon

Damiya Bridge

River Jordan

Ramallah

YAVNE   NA'AN

GIV'AT BRENNER   Nabi Samwil   Jericho

HULDA   Latrun

Bet Haarava

Shu'fat

Mount Scopus

Jerusalem   Tur

Bet Shemesh   Beit Safafa   Eizariya

Silwan

RAMAT-RAKHEL

Bethlehem

Ashquelon

Dead

GAL-ON

Sea

GAT

Gaza

Makhpelas Cave

Deir el Balah   Hebron

Es Samu

MISHMAR HANEGEV

Ofakim

NIR-ITZHAK   Beersheba

N

Mediterranean Sea

kibbutzim

0   50

KILOMETRES

ST. MARY'S COLLEGE OF MARYLAND
ST. MARY'S CITY, MARYLAND

C54134